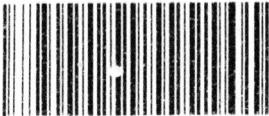

AGRIBUSINESS AND COMMODITY RISK

AGRIBUSINESS AND COMMODITY RISK

Strategies and Management

RISK
BOOKS

Published by Risk Books, a division of Incisive RWG Ltd.

Haymarket House
28–29 Haymarket
London SW1Y 4RX
Tel: +44 (0)20 7484 9700
Fax: +44 (0)20 7484 9758
E-mail: books@riskwaters.com
Sites: www.riskbooks.com
www.riskwaters.com

Every effort has been made to secure the permission of individual copyright
holders for inclusion.

© Incisive RWG Ltd 2003

ISBN 1 904339 10 7

British Library Cataloguing in Publication Data
A catalogue record for this book is available from the British Library

Managing Editor: Sarah Jenkins
Assistant Editor: Tamsin Kennedy
Editorial Assistant: Steve Fairman

Typeset by Mizpah Publishing Services, Chennai, India

Printed and bound in Spain by Espacegrafic, Pamplona Navarra.

CONTENTS

LIST OF PANELS

AGRIBUSINESS AND COMMODITY RISK
Throughout this book special panels introduce key themes and offer illustrative examples

AUTHORS

Rodolfo Barros is president of TFX Services, Inc., a Daimler Chrysler Services company; as well as managing director of the trade finance group of Daimler Chrysler Capital Services. In these capacities, he plays a key role in the identification, assessment, and management of investment/lending strategies and processes. Prior to this, he was the regional head of trade and commodity finance for Latin America at ABN AMRO. During his 14 years experience at ABN AMRO, he worked in various capacities (marketing, sales, and operational and risk management) and locations (Europe, Latin America and the United States). Rodolfo holds an MBA with a concentration in IT from the Rotterdam School of Management. He earned his BA in economics and political sciences from University of Pennsylvania.

Pierre Bascou is deputy-head of the unit in charge of quantitative analyses, forecasts, statistics and studies at the Directorate General for Agriculture of the European Commission. His current work includes the preparation of medium-term market forecasts for the major agricultural commodities, and of impact assessment of changes in the agricultural policy and trade

policy of the European Union in the field of agriculture. He has previously worked as a consultant at CEAS Consultants (Wye) before joining the statistical office of the European Commission. His main research areas concern modelling of the farm sector for economic and policy analysis, farm income and risk management tools (notably futures markets). After graduating from Toulouse (*Ingénieur*) and Wye College, Pierre earned a PhD from the University of London.

Rolf W. Boehnke is currently the managing director of the Common Fund for Commodities (CFC), a multilateral financial institution. Whilst in this position he has strengthened the commodity development project, streamlined operations and reduced costs. Previously, he worked as secretary general of the International Lead and Zinc Study Group (ILZSG) and has also held roles within the embassy of the Federal Republic of Germany (1984) and the Federal Ministry of Economics (1983–1984). His publications include *Competition and the Size of Firm* and *Diversified Enterprises*. Rolf holds an MA in economics from Free University Berlin, Germany, an MPA in economics and politics from

Harvard University, and a PhD in economics from Free University Berlin.

Erin Bryla is a consultant with the Commodity Risk Management group at the World Bank. Within this role her work has focused on expanding the access of developing country producers and organisations to risk management instruments. This work has also included the design of training materials for producer's organisations, NGO's, and rural finance institutions on risk management instruments and their applications. Erin has received a BA with honours in International Relations and an MA in Sociology, both from Stanford University.

Bernard W. Dan is the president and chief executive officer (CEO) of the Chicago Board of Trade (CBOT). He joined the CBOT in July 2001 and, prior to his appointments as president and CEO, served as executive vice president to, and was responsible for, the CBOT's open auction and screen-based business units, as well as the exchange's product development and marketing initiatives. Previously, he has been president and CEO of Cargill Investor Services and has also held positions within the company as an administrative manager in London, responsible for all operational activities, and as a director in Singapore. Prior to joining Cargill, Bernard worked at the National Futures Association from 1983 to 1985. He actively serves within the futures industry both on exchange committees and industry user groups. Bernard holds a Bachelor of Science degree in accounting from St. John's University, Collegeville, Minnesota.

Daniel Day-Robinson specialises in project management in the international commodities and finance sector. Through his companies (Day Robinson International Consulting Ltd and Day Robinson International Ltd) he has directly managed large-scale international aid projects, including an undertaking for the UN Chartered Common Fund for Commodities. Dan has also been responsible for numerous direct contracts for both the British government and the European Commission. His consultancy is connected with risk management, inventory finance and collateral management. He provides expert witness services and advice to corporations and banks in relation to commodity trading strategies. Previously, he has worked for the Thomson Corporation and for Cargill. His publications include *Commodity Risk Management in Developing Countries (2000)*, co-authored with Lamon Rutten. He has also written numerous articles for trade press and journals internationally. Dan holds a degree in geography and economics from the University of London.

Alastair Dickie is a crop marketing director at Home Grown Cereals Authority (HGCA). This department is responsible for the provision of market information, and for the promotion of the consumption of British cereals at home and abroad through two marketing groups, Market Development (formerly BCP British Cereal Products) and British Cereal Exports (BCE). Alastair has spent the last 25 years as a trader in the world's commodity markets. His experience includes trading in grains, soyabeans & meals, all vegetable oils (including managing softseed crushing plants), sugar, and metals (ferrous & non-ferrous). He is also experienced in international foreign exchange and interest rate futures. Working for Louis Dreyfus from 1977 to 1988, he was MD of Louis Dreyfus Trading Ltd from 1986 to 1988. Alastair holds a BSc (Agric) from Glasgow University and a dip FBA from the University of London.

Ineke Duijvestijn is head of the international markets division of the sustainable economic development department of the Netherlands Ministry of Foreign Affairs. The division's responsibilities include the formulation of trade and development positions for the EU and WTO, food aid/security issues and agricultural commodities. Prior to the current position, she was a senior policy advisor at the rural development unit of the West Africa division in the same ministry. Her main research interests are market liberalisation and the need for new public and private institutions in developing countries, as well as the global market liberalisation and the need for "behind the border" measures in developing countries. Ineke holds an MA in human geography (with majors in human geography in developing countries and development economics) from the Free University of Amsterdam.

Geert Embrechts is head of the portfolio management desk of the structured trade and commodity finance group of Rabobank International. He is responsible for allocating bank and country limits, distributing risk to third parties, and effectively calculating risk/return both on a transactional and a portfolio level. Geert is actively involved in the BIS II project within Rabobank and has done extensive research on the consequences of BIS II for the University of Amsterdam. Previously, Geert headed the country risk department of Rabobank. Geert has published in various international and leading Dutch journals on banking, macroeconomics and country risk on BIS II, and has presented his findings to the Basle Committee. Geert holds a master's degree in economics and international law from the University of Maastricht and a PhD in finance from the University of Amsterdam.

Henny Gerner is a policy advisor at the environment and rural development unit of DG Development of the European Commission. His main responsibility is assisting in formulating a coherent EU-policy on agricultural commodities. Previously, he worked at the Netherlands Ministry of Foreign Affairs, where he was in charge of agricultural commodities. From 1987 to 1998 he held various positions including international advisor on modernisation of the Ministry of Agriculture in Guatemala, manager of the West Africa policy & market development programme of IFDC-Africa (Togo) and economist in Cabo Verde. His main area of interest is in improving private and public market services in developing countries. He has published technical articles and books on earlier work overseas. He holds an MSc in agricultural economics (which includes majors in development economics and finance & cooperatives) from Wageningen University.

Ulrich Hess is an economist at the commodity risk management group in the agricultural and rural development department of the World Bank. He advises private and public sector clients in India, Morocco, Ukraine and other countries on weather and price risk management. Previously, he worked for the agribusiness department of the International Finance Corporation (IFC), where he started IFC's work on weather risk management in Morocco and Mexico, and initiated IFCs investment in a global weather risk facility with a global re-insurer. As a young professional, Ulrich has been working in management and development consulting, on enterprise development, fisheries, and environmental services, in Italy, Germany, France and Denmark. Ulrich holds master's degrees in economics from Bocconi University, and political science from the Freie Universität Berlin, and also studied at Institut d'Etudes Politiques de Paris and Yale Law School.

Tom James is a director in the global project and structured finance group of Credit Agricole Indosuez bank. He has over 14 years experience in commodity derivatives, specialising in the field of energy and commodities. During his career he has been involved in, futures/OTC derivatives trading and broking, risk management advisory and training, market analysis, trading advisory, project management, and structured finance. He regularly acts as a risk management consultant to firms in Asia, the Middle East and merging European markets, and has assisted many companies in taking their first steps in the use of derivatives for risk management and trading purposes. Tom also holds derivatives licenses with the Securities and Futures Authority in the UK. Tom is currently working towards a PhD in financial commodity markets.

Arie Oskam is Professor of agricultural economics and rural policy, Wageningen University (WU) and fellow of the Netherlands Network of Economics. He was scientific director of the Mansholt Graduate School of Social Sciences (1998-2003) – a graduate school of circa 100 (senior) researchers and circa 135 PhD students. He functioned as editor of the *European Review of Agricultural Economics* (1988-1993) and coordinated the EU Concerted Action "Policy measures to control environmental impacts from agriculture" (1993-1998). His research is oriented on agricultural economics, agricultural policy, environmental economics in relation to agriculture and rural areas, and rural policy analysis. He has edited or authored 10 books and published circa 30 articles in refereed journals.

Jagdish Parihar is the managing director of Olam International and is currently heading their global cotton business. In addition, he is the head of audit function and is part of the risk committee and policy team. Previously, he has worked in Singapore as vice president in-charge of the cotton operations. The main focus in Singapore was to develop the markets in Russia, China and the USA, which was successfully achieved. Prior to that, he worked in London, where he has been involved in developing the growth plans of Olam International across 9 commodities and 30 countries. Jagdish takes a personal interest in the area of risk control and has been teaching risk management at various international forums. Jagdish holds a degree in management from Birla Institute of Technology & Science, Pilani (management programme under MIT ford foundation programme).

Joost M.E. Pennings is currently a faculty excellence Professor at the University of Illinois at Urbana-Champaign, department of agricultural and consumer economics, and the AST Distinguished Professor at the Wageningen University in The Netherlands. His research has been published in a wide range of academic journals including, among others, *American Journal of Agricultural Economics, International Journal of Research in Marketing, Journal of Banking & Finance, Journal of Business, Journal of Economic Psychology, Journal of International Money & Finance* and *Management Science*. Joost received his PhD in marketing and finance *summa cum laude* from the Wageningen University in 1998.

Benedict Roth is a risk manager at West LB. He

branched into agribusiness after training in banking in the traditional financial markets: treasury, fixed income, emerging markets, equities and equity derivatives. In addition to his interests in credit risk and commodities he has published and presented on market risk, on banking regulation and on operational risk.

Keith Schap is the senior marketing writer in the business development department of the Chicago Board of Trade (CBOT) where his primary task is researching and writing trading strategy white papers. Previously a senior editor with *Futures* magazine, where he specialised in risk management and market outlook topics, Schap has contributed over 300 articles to magazines and journals including *Futures, Treasury, and Risk Management*, and *Derivative Strategies*. Author of several books, his most recent, with co-author Paul Kasriel, is 7 *Indicators that Move Markets* (McGraw-Hill, 2003). Keith earned a PhD from Indiana University.

Nigel Scott is an executive director in capital markets at Rabobank International, London. He is global head of the commodity price risk management (CPRM) unit. CPRM trades soft commodity price swaps & options with the bank's clients to hedge their risk. Nigel also heads up the OECD structured commodity finance team. He has worked for Rabobank since 2000. Previously, Nigel has worked for Cargill as a senior structurer on the financial markets platform, where he started a number of swaps markets in cotton. He also developed and traded

cocoa and fertilizer swaps. Nigel has acted as an arbitrator, as a member of the Liverpool Cotton Association (LCA) for the last 9 years, and regularly serves on technical appeal committees. Nigel has a BSc (Hons) in microbiology from Imperial College, London.

Bruce Tozer is global managing director in the structured trade and commodity finance group for Rabobank International. His role covers trade and structured finance, asset backed commodity finance and soft commodity derivatives. Bruce has previously held a variety of roles in Rabobank, involving providing products for the food and agribusiness clients of the bank. His current research interests focus on the impact of Basle II banking regulation proposals on commodity finance, and developing product solutions to anticipated changes. He is a member of the World Bank's international task force on commodity price risk management for emerging market commodity producer organisations. He sits on a number of consultative committees reviewing sustainability issues in respect of commodity production. Bruce holds an MBA from IMD, Lausanne, an MSc in international food/agribusiness marketing from ESSEC, Paris, and a BSc in agricultural economics from the University of Newcastle upon Tyne.

Panos Varangis is currently a lead economist at the World Bank's agriculture and rural development department. In his current position, he is leading the commodity risk management group (CRMG)

that looks into issues related to commodity price and weather risk management. He joined from the development research group, where he was involved in research areas related to commodity markets, and in particular risk management and finance, weather index insurance, and commodity market liberalization. Prior to that, he was with the commodities policy and analysis unit. Panos has worked extensively in the areas of agricultural policies, risk management, and commodity marketing and trade finance systems. He has initiated a project to examine the application of weather risk management products to agriculture in developing countries. Panos holds a MA degree in Economics from Georgetown University and a PhD degree in economics from Columbia University, New York.

Cliff White joined Queensland Cotton in 1991 and is responsible for buying and selling of the company's Australian, US and most recently Brazilian cotton. He has worked for 27 years in the raw cotton market and has extensive experience in Asia. He lived and worked in Hong Kong in 1986 and 1987 and has also worked in Dar Es Salaam in Tanzania, Mersin in Turkey and Memphis in the United States. Cliff is currently active in a variety of institutions, for example, he is an associate director of the Liverpool Cotton Association, a director and past chairman of the Australian Cotton Shippers Association and a registered representative of the Sydney Futures Exchange. Cliff is a graduate of Australian Institute of Company Directors (GAICD).

INTRODUCTION

The Unique Characteristics of Agricultural Production and its Influence on Market Perception and Government Policy

Bruce Tozer*

Rabobank International

Agricultural production is the most broadly and geographically practised economic activity known to man. Indeed, the development of settled farming techniques some 12,000 years ago was the crucial step that allowed human society to evolve from that of the nomadic hunter-gatherer to the economic trade- and city-based civilisation that dominates the world today. Despite its long history and the development of incredible technology to better manage the physical risks of primary commodity production and crop storage, agriculture remains dependent on a number of unique production characteristics that make it an economic activity subject to high levels of risk and uncertainty. These in turn shape the way that commodity markets behave and the evolution of government policy to agricultural specific issues.

What are commodities?

A commodity, in economic terms, is defined as a portion of wealth that is demanded because it has the power to satisfy human needs and wants. Commodities are homogeneous products, limited in supply, and therefore have value in exchange, which defines their "utility". Commodities in the classical sense of the term are natural substances, which can be owned and transformed by processing, quantified and classified by their quality. They have value in exchange and this is determined by the relative supply-and-demand conditions for a specific commodity or by their relative value if they are substitutes. Commodities broadly fall into three categories: soft commodities (agriculturally produced), metals and energy.

The unique characteristics of agricultural commodity production

Farming is the general term given to the agricultural production of soft commodities. Unlike the production of energy and metal commodities, which is executed using

* The author wishes to acknowledge the input of Paul Braks, Joyce Cacho, Andy Duff, Thon Huijser and Henk Rijkse.

THE UNIQUE
CHARACTERISTICS OF
AGRICULTURAL
PRODUCTION AND ITS
INFLUENCE ON
MARKET PERCEPTION
AND GOVERNMENT
POLICY

mining extraction processes of identified reserves, that of soft commodities is achieved by manipulating biological processes and resources such as land and water supply combined with labour and technological inputs. It is the biological nature of agricultural production – linked to the fact that many of the basic soft commodities produced in agriculture are essential in the form of food and fibres to sustain mankind – that makes them unique.

Let us look at a number of key parameters that have significant influence on agricultural production and soft commodities.

THE DISCONTINUOUS SEASONAL NATURE OF PRODUCTION

Soft commodities are generally grown in an annual production cycle. The ability to plan an output on an annual basis has important implications for production and overall supply, because it creates a situation whereby production is discontinuous in nature and cannot respond rapidly to extreme increases or decreases in prices between crop years. Once the decision to plant a given acreage of a crop has been taken and executed, the farmer has every incentive to try to maximise the output (yield) to his planted crop acreage. Only in extreme cases where prices decrease rapidly between planting and harvesting would a producer decide that it is an economically rational decision not to harvest the output or to destroy it.

The seasonal nature of agriculture means that the supply side of commodity production is "sticky" as production decisions can be made effectively only annually. Some commodities, such as cocoa, coffee and palm oil, are perennial tree crops. It takes several years and significant capital investment to bring them into full production, which further increases supply inelasticity, as the switching costs between crops is much higher given the long production cycle.

WEATHER RISK AND SYSTEMIC CROP FAILURE

Weather is consistently the key parameter determining the yield and quality of soft commodities. Weather, in the form of either too much or too little rainfall and temperature, has profound effects on output. Weather can also have dramatic effects on demand. Too little rain, and crop growth is inhibited during the growth phase; too much rain can also cause crop failure or destroy crop quality at harvesting. An extreme weather case is drought, and this still afflicts many arid parts of the world, such as India, Ethiopia and Australia, on a regular basis. Drought causes systemic crop failure, the ultimate tragic consequence being famine. Another economic impact of drought is the reluctance of banks and other suppliers of farm credit to advance crop loans to farmers in drought-prone environments because no crop means no revenue, and therefore credit default. Even in a highly sophisticated production environment such as Australia, where irrigation is widely used along with modern machinery, drought-resistant crop varieties and the full array of modern pesticides and fertilisers, the impact of drought can be devastating. The Australian drought of 2002 caused wheat production to plummet from 20 million tonnes in 2001 to 9 million tonnes. Drought also has an impact on animal production. Scarcity of grains to feed animals results in sharply reduced head count through forced slaughter and a sharp drop in livestock prices. Too much moisture during the main growing season can lead to high incidence of fungal disease and inhibit grain fill.

Temperature variation also has significant effects on crop production. Late frosts can decimate the Brazilian coffee crop or orange juice production in Florida. Severe frosts in Russia, Ukraine and Northern Europe can cause "winter kill" of autumn-sown crops and loss of production.

The number of ways that weather can impact agriculture and the risk it creates for producers are too numerous to list. Weather is the dominant risk factor on the supply side and, given the appropriate market conditions, a source of significant innovation in financial risk management. It is little wonder that the weather shapes not only the production of crops but also the stoic and risk-aware nature of farmers. There is a

XV

THE UNIQUE
CHARACTERISTICS OF
AGRICULTURAL
PRODUCTION AND ITS
INFLUENCE ON
MARKET PERCEPTION
AND GOVERNMENT
POLICY

famous ditty that well reflects this called "The Farmer" whose first verse is:

> *The farmer will never be happy again;*
> *He carries his heart in his boots;*
> *For either the rain is destroying his grains*
> *Or the drought is destroying his roots.*

GEOGRAPHIC AND SOIL CONSTRAINTS AND COMPARATIVE ADVANTAGE

Generally, different crops grow better in some geographies and soils than others, which gives rise to specific production constraints. While soft commodities, such as wheat and maize, have a very wide growing distribution in both the northern and southern hemispheres, others, such as cocoa, coffee and oil palm, can be grown successfully only in tropical climates. In the case of cocoa, the concentration risk, from a geographical perspective, is probably the greatest of any commodity, with 80% of production coming from three major producing countries (Ivory Coast, Ghana and Nigeria). This also creates significant associated country event risk for end consumers of cocoa, where supplies can be interrupted because of political instability.

Underlying the geographic and climatic parameters is the suitability of soil for growing specific crops. Natural comparative advantage should favour crops being grown predominantly in the right climates on suitable soils with trade taking place as appropriate to optimise resource allocation in global production.

CROP AND ANIMAL DISEASES

Crops and animal production are subject to a wide range of diseases and pests of varying degrees of severity. The ability to contain the economic impact of disease (yield reduction or loss of quality) by husbandry techniques varies both by case and in time. Disease and pest resistance evolve, creating new production problems. In extreme cases it can cause the almost total breakdown of commodity production in a specific geography. For example, cocoa production in Brazil was decimated as a result of "witch's broom". Animal diseases can be devastating in their impact and the response to eradicating them. Simply think BSE, foot-and-mouth, swine vesicular disease and avian flu for examples of the devastating impact of disease on animal production.

ENVIRONMENTAL RISK

Agricultural production involves the extensive use of the planet's cultivable landmass and water resources for irrigation, it therefore has a high impact on the environment. The use of inappropriate technologies or cultivating crops in the wrong location can lead to environmental degradation. Although this is not factored into market pricing of soft commodities, it is increasingly a significant concern of producers, consumers, NGOs and policy makers. Government policy often increases environmental damage, because it encourages production in locations unsuitable to a given crop.

COMMODITY DETERIORATION

Unlike metal and oil commodities, soft commodities are organic and subject to physical deterioration in store. This has implications for their quality and value over time and their cost of storage and for financiers of commodities, as it is an additional risk factor in valuing collateral.

Market perception of soft-commodity risk

As can be seen, the production of soft commodities is an activity fraught with risk beyond the control of the producer. Two major impacts of this on agricultural commodity markets is that price formation is often subject to high degrees of volatility within a crop year and subject to lags on the supply side, since production decisions can be adjusted only annually. This gives rise to commodity cycles and "cobwebs", such as the "pig cycle", where high market prices lead to large increases in production, followed by

THE UNIQUE
CHARACTERISTICS OF
AGRICULTURAL
PRODUCTION AND ITS
INFLUENCE ON
MARKET PERCEPTION
AND GOVERNMENT
POLICY

oversupply in the next crop year and low prices. This in turn reduces supply in the following production cycle as individual producers then switch production, which leads to higher prices and the start of a new cycle. Markets, where governments do not intervene, have to factor into price formation all the inherent uncertainties that exist in production of commodities as well as the demand characteristics that influence prices.

Historically, markets for the physical exchange of soft commodities developed in line with the evolution of exchange and trade in commodities. Primitive markets for physical trade existed in pre-Roman times. They took place on a regular basis at a set time and location and created the rudimentary rules for the exchange and pricing of commodities and the maintenance of market order. Specialist commodities markets developed out of the spectacular growth in trade flows and industrial innovation, such as cotton ginning, that occurred in the 18th century and rapidly expanded the demand for basic commodities.

The development of commodity derivatives

Commodity markets developed in the main trading and consuming centres for specific commodities. Forward sales contracts and futures contracts and the market exchange mechanisms underlying them evolved at the established physical auction markets. The main driver for the development of these contracts was to hedge the risks that occur in trade due to short-term price fluctuation, and thereby to ensure a more continuous supply of commodities. These forward sales and futures contracts for commodities were, in essence, the first derivatives markets, where spot markets for cash transactions in the physical commodity are complemented by forward trading in the underlying asset. This development also allowed for the introduction of speculators to participate in price formation and increased the liquidity available to markets.

The effectiveness of these markets to assist producers and consumers in managing price risks can be measured by the widespread development of commodity markets and exchanges across many commodities (hard and soft) and geographies (London, Liverpool, New York, Chicago, Japan, Singapore, India and so on) during the 19th and early 20th centuries. For this period, commodities markets were key instruments available for producers, traders and consumers to hedge their price risk, as on the whole OECD governments took a back seat in price support and formation. Exchanges proliferated because of the localised nature of physical price formation and associated basis risk.

However, in the past 50 years, OECD governments have become increasingly active in supporting agricultural production and commodity prices directly through price support mechanisms. In some commodities this has led to a reduced need for market-based mechanisms to manage price risks and as a result commodity exchanges have withered and died in some locations. When trading of a commodity contract becomes "thin" and illiquid, the attractiveness for speculators and hedgers in that market declines sharply.

Dramatic growth in financial derivatives

Since the early 1980s there has been a massive increase in the use of financial derivatives for equities, bonds and credit. The driver for this was greater volatility in interest rates and currencies, the globalisation of financial markets and investors, and the development of cost-effective technology (personal computers) for pricing and distributing risk. The assets underlying financial derivatives do not suffer from the same problems associated with the physical delivery of commodities. The absolute scale and liquidity of financial markets, has driven massive volume and growth in their utilisation, as banks, financial institutions and corporates have become more adept at quantifying and hedging their financial risks. By comparison, soft-commodity derivatives have become relatively less important and their market perception has suffered.

In the last two years, however, commodities have attracted renewed interest and significance, and, while this has been focused mainly on energy and metals, soft commodities, too, are benefiting from the upswing in alternative investment asset classes. This trend is also being reinforced by a growing shift in government policy with respect to agricultural production, as governments progressively seek to withdraw from agricultural price support. The need for commodity derivatives for producers and users to hedge their risks is growing again.

Market structure in production

Agricultural production is highly fragmented in nature, with many small firms making individual decisions as to future production and allocation of resources based on current and future expectations in price for their output. No individual supplier can influence ultimate market price, although on the demand side purchasing of certain commodities is concentrated into the hands of a few processors. Agricultural cooperatives are a producer strategy that responds to the industry structure, but they have rarely been commercially successful in improving market bargaining power. In theory markets and market mechanisms are essential to inform suppliers in their production decisions. In practice, in OECD countries, government intervention has as great an impact on production decisions as market prices.

Government policy and agriculture

Governments have interfered in agricultural commodities markets to a greater or lesser degree since biblical times, because, along with the inherent risk in production on the supply side, basic demand is inelastic. Failure to meet this basic demand leads to famine, which is often associated with political upheaval and regime change. The need to keep the population and, in the case of war, army fed is a political necessity. It is no coincidence that Lenin said, "Grain is the currency of currencies" or Napoleon is quoted saying "An army marches on its stomach".

A HISTORICAL PERSPECTIVE

One of the earliest recorded instances of government intervention in commodity supply management is that of Joseph and the Egyptians in the Book of Genesis. Everyone knows that Joseph interpreted the pharaoh's dream to foretell seven years of plenty to be followed by seven years of famine. The policy response was to use the years of good harvests to reserve strategic surplus stocks to be distributed during the time of famine that followed. What is rarely mentioned is that in successfully implementing this strategy the Egyptian regime was ruthless in extracting maximum political advantage. Initially the strategic grain stocks were sold to desperate consumers (domestic and foreign). When they ran out of money, their cattle were confiscated, next their land and finally they were enslaved. This elegantly makes the point as to why managing food supply has always been a key function of national governance.

MALTHUSIAN FEAR

Another persistent reason for government intervention in food production and supply is Malthusian and neo-Malthusian thinking. Robert Malthus first argued, in 1798, that food production grows arithmetically but population growth is geometric and the inevitable consequence will be repetitive and drastic famine. This argument has been revived on numerous occasions and has had a significant impact on policy formulation. During the economic and commodity crisis of the 1970s, neo-Malthusian thinking was to the fore. Again, deficits in world grain production in the mid-1990s triggered forecasts of persistent future shortages as a result of population growth, environmental degradation, water shortages and Asia's insatiable growth in demand for grain and animal protein as disposable income increased. To date, where market forces are allowed to play out, his forecasts have remained unfulfilled.

WAR AND TRADE HAVE LONG BEEN KEY POLICY DRIVERS

The Corn Laws in Britain were imposed to protect domestic food supply during the Napoleonic Wars and support farm income. They were repealed, after years of lobbying,

THE UNIQUE
CHARACTERISTICS OF
AGRICULTURAL
PRODUCTION AND ITS
INFLUENCE ON
MARKET PERCEPTION
AND GOVERNMENT
POLICY

in 1846. The main argument for repeal was the need to expand trade and encourage imports of cheap grain from the newly opened colonies in exchange for manufactured goods. Cheap food was essential to feed an increasingly urban, industrialised population. Equity was also an argument, in that the Corn Laws were a regressive tax on the consumer that benefited landowners and the corn merchants but did little to improve farm incomes. Ultimately, the decision to repeal them was enabled by the potato famine in Ireland on humanitarian grounds. Sir Robert Peel successfully argued that the Corn Laws were an impediment to importing American corn, as a relief measure, in 1845. The impacts of the repeal were far-reaching in that opening the UK market to wheat imports created the incentives for trade to follow the most efficient production of grain in the world, to the development of vast territories, extensive low-cost production techniques, new trade routes and trading empires. All of which encouraged the development and extensive use of commodity exchanges. Incidentally, Peel lost the next election, underlying the commonly held view that is easier to grant subsidies to lobby groups than it is to take them away, and explains the reluctance of elected politicians to do so. *Plus ça change*.

POST-WW2 GOVERNMENT POLICY
During the last 60 years, direct government intervention in market price support mechanisms has been and remains the dominant feature of agricultural policy in most OECD countries. The two most visible blocks where this has been overtly the case are in the European Union via the Common Agricultural Policy (CAP) and in the US via the Farm Bill in its various forms.

The CAP
At its outset the CAP was designed with the aim not only to underpin farm incomes in the EU, but also to foster food security and political stability in postwar Europe. It is worth noting that, in mainland Europe, tens of thousands of civilians died of starvation during the last year of the war and the chaotic conditions of the peace that ensued. Clearly, this plus the Korean War – during which acute commodity shortages persisted – had a profound influence on the initial formation of the CAP. The major concern of policy makers up until the end of the 1970s was not about how to manage and dispose of surpluses but to secure food supplies at reasonable costs to consumers while providing suitable income support for a consolidating farming industry. A variety of commodity price support mechanisms and import protection tariffs were utilised in order to create the price incentives for farmers to produce the main staple commodities consumed and to lock out lower-cost imports.

Over the last twenty years the problem for policy makers with respect to the CAP has been how to manage and dispose of subsidised surpluses onto world markets, while finding the political will to reform the CAP towards a more market-based set of mechanisms. The pressure for reform is now driven by trade concerns (WTO) and the market-distorting effects of export subsidies, the expansion of the EU and the unacceptable budgetary cost of applying the CAP to CEE countries.

The US Farm Bill
The common reference to a group of laws, policies and legislation, the US Farm Bill links aspects of agricultural production, labour, trade and foreign policy, food distribution and rural community development. The original Farm Bill, enacted in 1949, was established to protect farmers and stabilise rural economies by incorporating the principle of flexible price support, and changed the rural–urban income-parity formula. Although the various policy tools have been employed over time – from production support to supply control to market price transparency and production support – the objective of the Farm Bill is effectively unchanged.

Increasing commodity prices in the early 1990s, and the associated market-driven opportunity for increasing farmer income, led to garnering of sufficient political support to pass the 1996 Farm Bill, or the "Freedom to Farm" Act. In the "first-time-ever" scenario, guaranteed government programme triggers were set at levels that seemed to ensure that farmers' planting decisions would be based on consumer demand and market prices, rather than on government programmes. The dramatic shift in farmer–consumer linkage, away from the government, presented the opportunity for changes in the financing products demanded by food value chain participants – from retailers through to farmers. For example, commodity price risk management tools were increasingly demanded because price volatility was a "new constant" in the market in the form of crop insurance schemes with embedded optionality. Subsequently, their provision and use by the private sector diminished as price support and subsidised crop insurance schemes were reintroduced. The political support for "freedom to farm" quickly eroded as agricultural prices declined and, in short order, the US Congress started a pattern of annual "Emergency Spending" that soon dominated farmer income. As debate began on a new Farm Bill in 2001, with the 2002 Congressional elections on the horizon, political support for "freedom to farm" evaporated and returned to a sharp focus on the government, providing for stable farmer incomes. An additional catalyst for stepping back from supporting a market-linked relationship with farmers was the then pending global trade negotiations, where agriculture is instrumental to "success". The "positioning" for WTO negotiations has been a factor in policy decisions in several OECD countries.

Other significant agricultural policy impacts and developments

The Cairns Group of producers have pursued market-based and free-trade policies because they are recognised low-cost producers of commodities and economies without sufficient non-agricultural economic power to be able to afford the luxury of subsidising their primary producers. Along with emerging market producers of soft commodities, the Cairns Group stand to gain the most from the successful conclusion of WTO trade negotiations. Among their number are commodity giants such as Brazil, Australia and Argentina. Unsurprisingly, in these countries producers are among the most sophisticated in the world with respect to risk management, both in hedging commodity price and currency risk. Where the government does not step in, the market will – and does.

One of the great "ignored" agricultural policy impacts of the last 60 years was that of the collectivisation policies pursued in the FSU, CEE and China. These have been even more damaging to production, economic efficiency and the environment than the worst effects of the CAP. At times they have been outright catastrophic, as in the 1958–61 Chinese famine, which, it is estimated, killed in excess of 50 million people. Divorcing production from market price signals and centralising production and distribution decisions in the hands of politicised bureaucrats has a frightful track record.

Market-oriented reforms in China over the last 20 years have had a positive impact on production. Chinese domestic markets remain protected, although WTO membership will be a force for change on this front. In the FSU and CEE, following their break-up and ensuing economic reforms in the early 1990s, grain production initially decreased significantly. However, in the last two years significant exports of wheat have taken place from Russia, Ukraine and Kazakhstan. While production levels remain volatile, and Ukraine will import grain this year, it is a sobering experience for Canadian producers to have Russian feed wheat landed at market-competitive prices on its Eastern seaboard.

Impact of market-driven agricultural policy

Clearly, the impact of a gradual but persistent reform of agricultural policy, driven by a combination of political reform, trade negotiations (WTO) and economic policicis to foster growth, is leading to an increase in commodity price risk and volatility for both producers and consumers of soft commodities. While the pace of change may be glacial, the trend is consistent, as borne out by the slowly declining price subsidy equivalence

THE UNIQUE
CHARACTERISTICS OF
AGRICULTURAL
PRODUCTION AND ITS
INFLUENCE ON
MARKET PERCEPTION
AND GOVERNMENT
POLICY

figures published in recent OECD reports. Commodity production is slowly moving in the direction of least cost-comparative advantage underpinned with a more liberalised trade regime. It should be recognised up front that a "free-trade" regime in agricultural production is unlikely because governments simply will not let this happen for strategic and political reasons. However, policy support is gradually becoming less "market-distorting". Nonetheless, the changes already visible in production, trade flows and related economic activity indicate a stepwise change in global activity that has possibly not been seen since the repeal of the Corn Laws in 1846. New commodity-trading and -processing giants are appearing rapidly in countries such as Brazil, Russia, Ukraine, Indonesia, China and India, and a host of lesser-producing countries. In the EU and the US, labour, capital investment and education are being withdrawn from agriculture and redirected to other parts of the economy.

What does this mean for soft commodity risk management?

These macro changes are creating an upswing in interest and the use of risk management tools that address risk throughout the food-supply chain from farmer to food manufacturer. This interest is unevenly distributed and is focused most on those markets where government support is low or reducing or on players who have always been exposed to risk in their business, such as the international trade houses. It is my experience, that major listed food corporations have to date been surprisingly unsophisticated in respect of understanding and managing the commodity-based risk in their business, while at the same time being advanced users of interest rate and currency risk tools. There are few companies that have an integrated view of commodity risk management with a risk committee to oversee and implement their strategy. For those that do, the goals are clear: to lock in product gross margins, reduce the volatility of the EBIT and report smoother earnings.

At the farmer end of the chain, interest is growing in yield and revenue hedges that combine insurance and derivative elements in their delivery. Nor is this interest restricted to more developed countries. The World Bank has run a task force on delivering commodity price risk management tools to emerging-market producers. The first transactions have been concluded and the benefits include security of finance at lower cost because local banks feel comfortable lending when a floor price has been sold to the producer cooperative. Profitability delivering these products remains challenging but the demand and potential benefits for producers is demonstrated. Commodity exchanges are working or in development in São Paulo, Dalian and Mumbai and are considered in many other "unexpected" markets. Commodities being counter cyclical to equities has lead to increased investment activity in commodity derivatives by hedge funds.

On the product supply side, major trade houses, banks and insurance companies are increasingly interested in delivering product to the agribusiness commodity risk market. The challenge has been and remains how to do so? Complex derivatives and the legal documentation that are associated with them are alien to many players in the supply chain. Understanding client needs and designing risk management products that meet their needs in contract forms that users understand and for which the pricing is transparent is the key to success. Importing complex financial engineering technology from the capital markets world has not been a success, apart from in the field of energy derivatives. In the banking industry, commodity finance stands to be significantly impacted by the proposed Basel II regulations. In all probability this will lead to an increase in asset-backed commodity finance with the underlying asset being hedged. This, too, will be a driver for the increased use of commodity risk management techniques.

Objectives of this book

This book reviews the latest thinking in respect of many aspects of agri-commodity risk management, with contributions coming from a distinguished panel of users, product suppliers, academics and development bankers.

The first seven chapters focus on defining and understanding risk, hedging behaviour and motivation and characterising the market players. The last seven chapters generally cover more specific aspects of commodity risk management and finance.

The appendices tackle in a novel way some of the burning issues of the day touched upon in this Introduction.

The title is designed to be a general reference manual for those interested in commodity risk management. It is not exhaustive but covers those issues deemed to be most important in this area at the time of writing. The use of GMOs, de-commoditisation, sustainability, supply chain transparency and structural inefficiencies, demand shifts, climate change and water shortage could all have a profound impact on soft commodities and markets. They merit consideration for those interested in soft commodities but are not addressed in this book.

BIBLIOGRAPHY

Genesis 41.

Hobhouse, Henry, *Seeds of Change Sixth Edition.* (Pan McMillan).

Morgan, D., *Merchants of Grain,* (Weidenfeld & Nicholson).

OECD, 2003, Agricultural Policies in OECD Countries, Monitoring and Evaluation 2003.

OECD Agricultural Outlook, 2003–2008, OECD.

Review of Agricultural Policy and Trade, 2003, Rabobank Group, Food and Agribusiness Research and Economic Research Department.

Ritson, C., *Agricultural Economics: Principles and Policy* (Crosby Lockwood Staples).

Roche, J., *Commodity Linked Derivatives* (IFR Books).

Stratton, J. M., *Agricultural Records: A.D. 220-1977,* (John Baker).

THE UNIQUE CHARACTERISTICS OF AGRICULTURAL PRODUCTION AND ITS INFLUENCE ON MARKET PERCEPTION AND GOVERNMENT POLICY

RISK

1

Risk and Uncertainty in Agricultural Markets

Jagdish Parihar

Olam International Limited

What are risk and uncertainty?

Risk can be defined as "potential loss of equity capital". Risk has two components: uncertainty and exposure. If both are not present, then there is no risk. For risk to materialise, there should be exposure to the uncertainty.

Let us say that, if the flights are delayed on account of pilots' strike and you have not made plans to travel during the strike period, then, though there is an uncertainty, your exposure to it is nonexistent and hence you have no risk. The "uncertainty" in business cannot be eliminated. However, what can be controlled is your exposure to it – by identifying the elements of uncertainty, quantifying them and setting appropriate exposure limits.

The elements of uncertainty in agriculture business can be affected by fundamental and technical reasons. Fundamental reasons could be weather, crop inputs, agronomic practices, demand pull for the finished product, global supply trends, release of buffer stocks. Technical reasons could be behaviour of speculators, support and resistance levels on prices, market aberrations/squeezes.

Risk control process

A balanced evaluation of uncertainty factors affecting the exposure of the participant in the agricultural supply chain is imperative for effective risk management. The risk control process should try to ensure that risk exposures emanating from the conduct of business participation do not lead to financial distress and that shareholders obtain a fair return on the equity/risk capital that they have invested.

This process involves a constant trade-off between controlling risk and taking risk in an attempt to enhance return. Risk management has therefore to be part of larger financial optimisation process and is an essential survival as well as growth-enabling skill.

How much risk should one take?

In business, what you can afford to lose is your equity capital and not the borrowed funds. Hence the risk capital is a function of a company's equity capital. The risk capital further depends on the risk appetite of the shareholder of the company. Figure 1 shows the risk capital allocation process that a company can adopt.

Broad risk categories

The broad risk categories facing an agribusiness can be defined as under.

❏ Outright price risk: This is risk of loss due to adverse changes in the value of positions (spot and forward).
❏ Basis risk: This is particularly for futures-traded products. The risk mainly arises from imperfect correlation between futures and physical price.

1. Process for risk capital allocation

Determine risk capital/risk appetite
↓
Allocate risk across various risk categories
(Price/credit/counter-party)
↓
Set exposure limits for each risk category
↓
Set risk factors based on historical volatility
↓
Capture weekly/monthly risk exposures
↓
Assuming risk factor/market rates calculate VaR
on actual exposures
↓
Assign notional risk charge on the VaR
↓
Calculate risk adjusted returns
↓
Assessment of risk adjusted return

Adjust risk appetite

2. Trading risk control system

Activity	Risk exposure	Control system
Physical procurement	Outright price risk created	Volume, value and tenor limits Front office raises deal tickets
Sell futures	Outright price risk closed Basis risk exposure created	Basis limits Volume/value/tenor
Sell physicals on differential	Counterparty risk exposure begins	Counterparty ratings Volume, value and tenor limits
Fixing physicals	Basis risk closed Counterparty risk continues	Counterparty ratings Trading limits
Buy back futures	Basis risk closed Counterparty risk continues	Settlement by back office Middle office tracks exposures
Shipment of goods	Counterparty risk continues	Middle office tracks exposures
Deliver docs to customers	Counterparty risk closed Credit risk begins	Credit exposure limits set Ageing analysis & tracking
Collecting payment	Credit risk closed All trading risks closed	VaR model for risk measurement Reporting risk capital charge

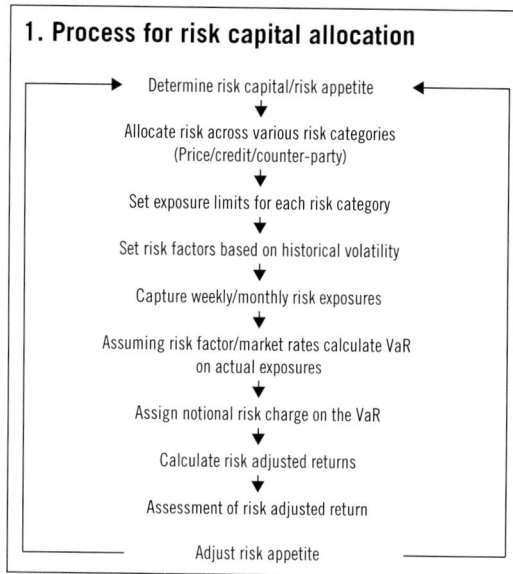

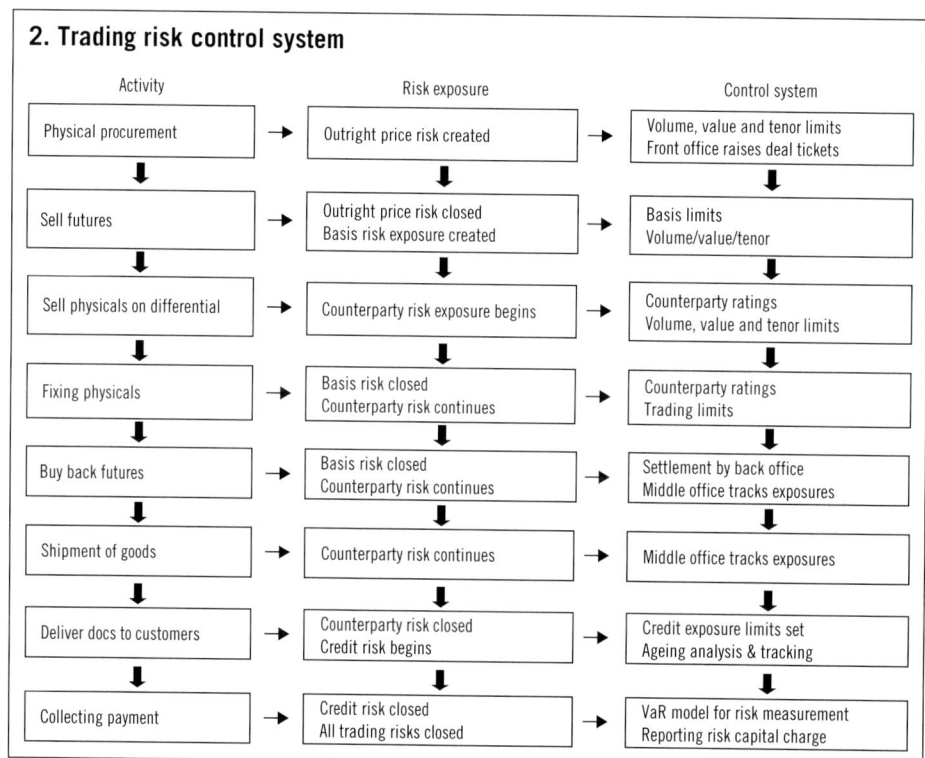

❑ Currency risk: This is risk of loss due to exposure to exchange-rate movements where there is mismatch in the currency used to buy and sell a physical position.
❑ Regulatory risk: Changes in political/regulatory context could quickly alter the business landscape of a region in which the business operates. This includes the risk of sovereign events in a country where a firm may have assets "locked" in or ongoing operations.

Global political risk cover is provided by some insurers and can be taken to de-risk the business from various sovereign events such as coup, war, confiscation, nationalisation, deprivation (including selective discrimination), forced divestiture and forced abandonment. Figures 2 and 3 give the key risks and controls involved of various trading and operational risks for an agribusiness.

3. Operational risk control system

Activity	Risk exposure	Control system
Physical procurement	Quality risk	Primary sourcing infrastructure Implementing field ops manual
Primary storage upcountry	Storage (stock) risk	Stock throughput insurance All-perils cover
Inland transit of stock	Stock transit risk	Stock transit insurance Stock throughput cover
Processing/grading	Quality risk Outturn risk	Implementation of processing manual systems
Consolidating/making stocks export ready	Storage risk	Origin sourcing infrastructure Stock throughput insurance
Shipment of goods	Marine transit risk	Open marine transit insurance
Hedging Sale/trade conclusion	Authorisation risk Monitoring risk	Middle office daily deal capture Broker trade reconciliations Broker limits
Deliver docs to customer	Documentation risk	Implement order processing system

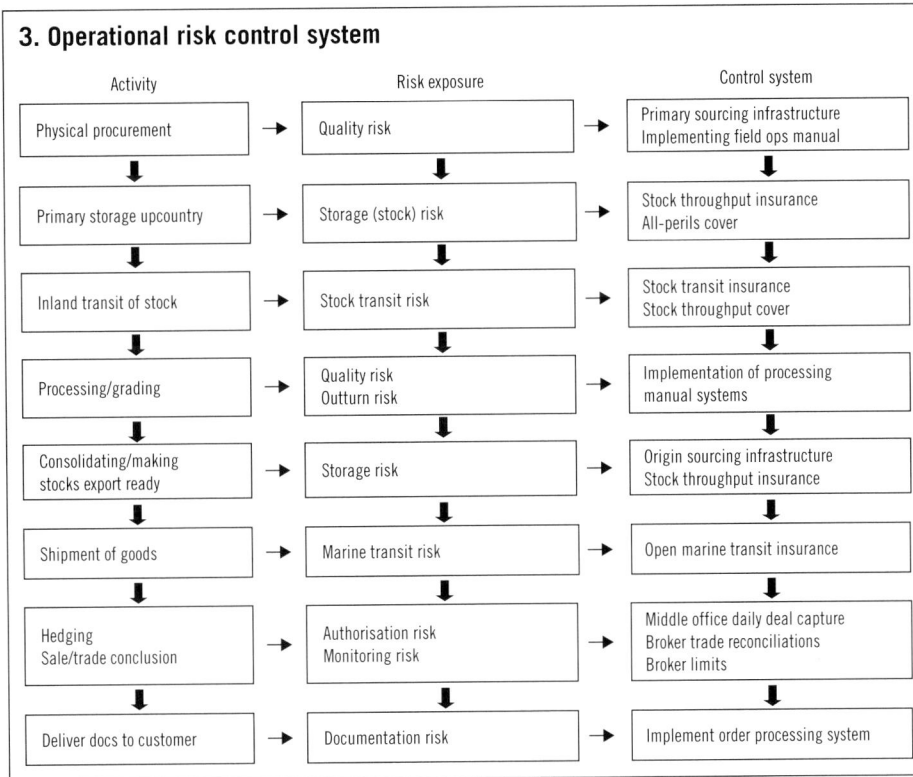

Factors contributing to risk level

The key factors that contribute to the risk level in agriculture markets are to be found under the following headings.

FINANCIAL VARIABLES

The currency and interest-rate fluctuation can have significant impact on pricing for commodities. We have recently seen the US$ lose ground almost 15% over the last year. In countries such as French West Africa this has impacted commodity price returns, as base earnings are in CFA.

Also, in some nations, there is hardly any forward market for currency and it is almost impossible to lock in a forward price based on a farmer sales for purchase.

POLITICAL AND ECONOMIC EVENTS

The government plays an important regulatory role in determining export/import quotas and minimum floor pricing. Governments can impose embargoes on commodity movements. For example, India has banned at times the import of Pakistan cotton. Similarly, a number of buyers in China could not secure import quotas for contractual commitments made.

CONCENTRATION RISK

During the Asian crisis, a number of commodity merchants had significant sales exposure to Indonesia/Thailand. There was steep devaluation during the crisis and the situation was further compounded by the drop in commodity prices, leading to an extreme loss situation. A prudent risk strategy will be to avoid concentration of exposure of business to a particular market origin or period.

LIQUIDITY RISK

Agricultural producers are at times faced with liquidity risk on commodities. This happen when it is difficult to sell at a reasonable price. It is imperative that the size of position be built, taking in to account realistic liquidity considerations.

CREDIT RISK

The grower receives credit from bank and buyers for inputs such as fertiliser and seed. The buying agents also advance monies at the start of crop season. All such advances, if not sufficiently collateralised, could lead to credit risk. It is imperative that estimates about crop size be carried out methodically. It is also necessary that the grower's track record be maintained and used as an input on deciding individual grower advancing limits. Spreading of advance across a large number of growers can reduce credit risk.

Risk control system

The "soul" of the system should be a "risk culture". This implies a strong respect for risk and respect for capital. It also induces the participants to consider all possible market scenarios and trade in a methodical and disciplined manner. The body of such a system should be a set of periodic "reports" that should provide the following information:

❑ Position exposure – what, how much, at what rate, for what maturity/tenor, long or short.
❑ Risk exposure – given normal/abnormal market volatility, how much money can be lost.
❑ At the macro/strategic level, the assessment of portfolio and component risk exposures should be used as a key input in a risk-return framework. This is a useful input for performance measurement and capital (equity) allocation.

Linking risk to return

To round up the process, it is essential to take Risks to Return and use the "Risk Adjusted Returns" for performance measurement of businesses as well as people.

RISK-ADJUSTED FINANCIAL PERFORMANCE MEASURES

In agribusiness portfolio, there could be varying risk levels across products/regions. While normalising the component level returns it is essential to take into account the returns achieved with respect to the risks. Business with high levels of risks should be expected to deliver commensurate higher return or they should reduce their risk exposures.

Conclusion

It is very important to have a clear policy on identification of risks, measurement of risks, exposure limits and risk return parameters. Risk management uses science but ultimately depends on judgment, and therefore alertness of key personnel is important.

2

Understanding Volatility and its Implications on Price Expectations

Alastair Dickie

Home Grown Cereals Authority

Introduction

The key to using derivatives is to accept the inherent nature of price volatility. This chapter presents an analysis of market volatility in the major segments of the agricultural industry.

Natural variation

The essence of uncertainty in the agricultural market is the natural variation in supply that is inherent in biological processes. Even with improved genetic stock and husbandry practices, it is impossible to predict the yield and production of crops and most livestock accurately enough to stabilise markets.

Figure 1, showing world wheat production and consumption over the last 40 years, illustrates this. The trend lines are broadly similar because, in the long-term, the world consumes what it produces. However, year on year, the variation in production is much greater than that of consumption. Consumption is driven largely by population, income and purchasing trends. Production responds to this, following price, so planted area is largely a function of the market. But the ultimate yield of wheat from that area is influenced much more by the weather than it is by husbandry. This effect varies around the world with some parts, such as Australia, prone to huge potential swings of up to 50% in yield, and others, such as Western Europe, where the variation is normally less than 10%. This effect is true for all annual planted crops. Plantation crops give the impression of greater stability since the planted area cannot be changed quickly. However, the

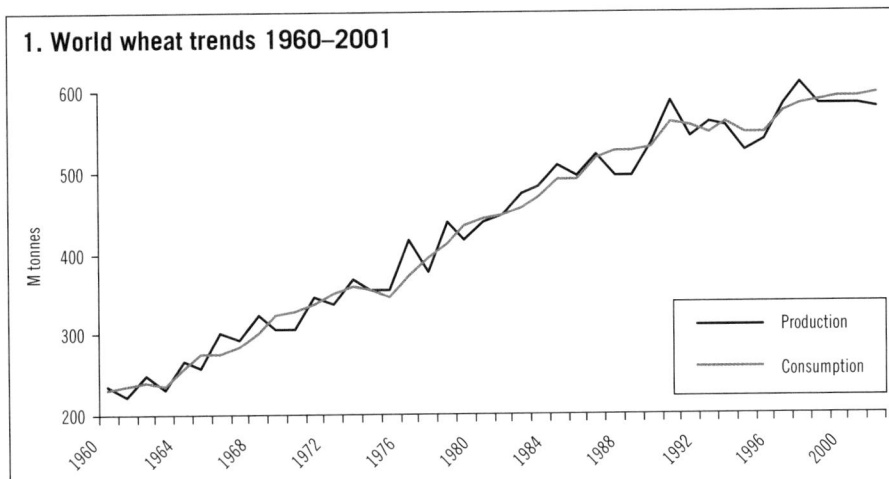

1. World wheat trends 1960–2001

weather effect is still pronounced and the very fact of a time lag on production makes the crop slow to respond to market needs, and this actually increases the potential for volatility.

Livestock production should be more predictable since the cycle is frequently less than one year, and supply response can be more easily adjusted. However, beef prospects are usually linked to the dairy market, as the outlet for male calves. So the supply of beef is linked to the profitability of dairy (good milk prices permit bull-calf "dumping"). The very short production period for pigs and poultry creates a different problem. In these cases the market frequently follows a classical cycle of "boom and bust". Rising prices stimulate new supplies and more expensive production as higher yields are "bought". This then leads to oversupply followed by depressed prices. Loss-making businesses then reduce their production and the cycle starts again. Pig markets are famous for this (see Figure 2) and, more recently, the stability of the poultry market has started to break down as demand levels slow and production expands. A "poultry cycle" now becomes feasible.

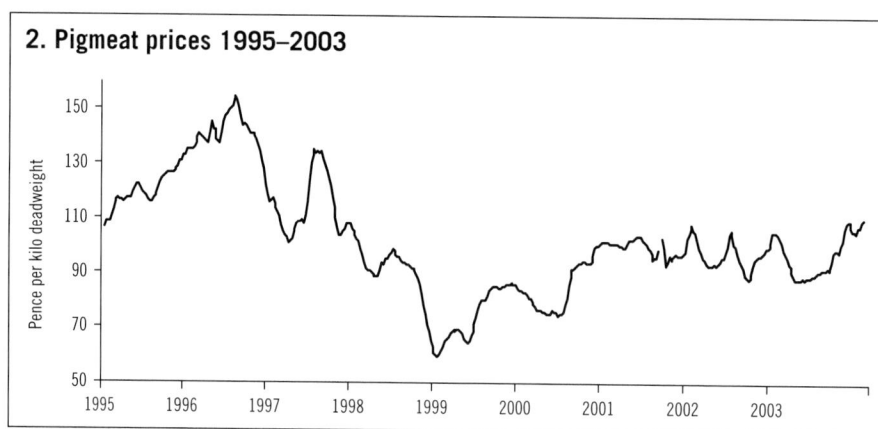

2. Pigmeat prices 1995–2003

Returning to the example of the cereal market, the balance sheet analysis permits an assessment of market equilibrium/or lack of it.

Table 1 shows the balance sheets for UK wheat for 2001/2 and 2002/3. In the first example the crop was poor because of bad weather during planting. In the second there was a reversion to more normal conditions. Prices were much higher during the first period since the market was able to trade at "import parity" for much of the year (see Table 2). (Import parity means that the UK market is priced to encourage imports since local supplies are insufficient.) During 2002/3 we can see that the "export parity"

Table 1. UK wheat balance sheets for 2001/2 and 2002/3

('000 tonnes)	2001/2	2002/3
Openning stocks	2,382	1,968
Production	11,570	16,053
Imports	1,490	1,050
Exports	578	3,979
Total availability	**14,864**	**15,092**
Human and industrial	6,382	6,348
Animal feed	6,158	6,531
Seed and other	356	380
Total domestic consumption	**12,896**	**13,259**
Closing stocks	1,968	1,833

Table 2. Import/export parities based on French wheat			
per tonne	Import parity	Export parity	
French export price	€112	UK export price	€112
Currency €1	£0.70		
Freight	£4.0		
Port costs	£2.0	Port costs	£2.0
Inland freight	£2.0	Inland freight	£4.0
DD price	£86.4		
Inland freight	£3.5		
UK ex farm price	£82.9	UK ex farm price	£72.4

was the driver (this is where UK prices are geared to encourage exports in competition with France and other exporters). In an international market, it is a myth to suggest that inhibiting production will improve farm incomes. Unless other land uses are obvious, a reducing crop cannot be expected to raise prices (and thus farm incomes) sufficiently to compensate for loss of sales. This is one reason why the EU set-aside policy has been discredited: it is too expensive for what it does.

It is also a myth to believe that institutional intervention and stock management can stabilise markets. The idea of creating buffer stocks is usually initiated by producers and the support price is generally set too high and ignores improvements in production efficiency over time so that the existence of the support price actually encourages supply. This creates a stock build-up followed by a cost crisis. In each case where this has been tried it has failed or ended up costing too much. Examples: Tin Council, International Coffee Agreement, US loan stocks, EU intervention stocks. Even OPEC, the most famous cartel, having caused the original price spike in 1973, has brought forward an expansion of supply that would not otherwise have come forward so that oil prices are permanently under pressure except at times of political crisis.

Other sources of volatility

If the basis of volatility is in the natural variation in agricultural supply, prices can be influenced by other, more market-oriented, factors. Around the world, the direct costs of production vary and this impacts on producers' reactions to price moves. In industrial commodities (metals, vegetable oils), the higher-cost producers are the first to cut back at low prices. Technical developments also affect production costs and create comparative advantage. For example, aluminium production was developed in the Middle East to use "free supplies" of natural gas from the oil wells. Within agriculture, with the EU and the USA subsidising agriculture, it is the unsubsidised South American and Australian producers that vary their production most in response to world price moves. The arrival of the Former Soviet Union (FSU) as a competitive exporter is now creating a new force in world grain trading that will alter the balance of power. All these factors contribute to price volatility.

Processed commodities such as soya bean, sun or rape oil and the associated meals suffer from the "joint product" nature of their process. Oil cannot be produced without meal and vice versa. This causes price variation in the market if supplies come forward that are not needed because of demand for the joint product, or the market is starved of material because the crush process is unprofitable because the stocks of the joint product are becoming a burden. So an analyst of the oil market must also be expert in the meal and feed trade to avoid surprises. This argument also applies to starch/corn gluten feed and even wheat flour/bran at times.

These factors all provide a longer-term effect on price moves but the day-to-day variation is caused by variables within an annual balance sheet. Short-term, the balance sheet is constructed not by absolute numbers but by attitudes and needs of the market participants. In theory, the balance sheet can be constructed daily, weekly or monthly. The supply "selling rates" are provided by farmer attitudes to price, cash flow and stocks, the demand side by the consumer's and processor's view of sales and stocks. So here the market psychology becomes important and no amount of analysis can guarantee a prediction.

The market lives on a daily diet of news of events. Some of these may be predictable but with an effect on the market difficult to assess. Others may be surprises, either difficult or easy to assess. So this creates uncertainty in the price moves. The commercialisation of the market is carried out competitively by many different players and the needs, wants and objectives of all of these are varying and their assessments of the market are also different. No two balance-sheet or trade-flow assessments are the same.

Trade flows are triggered by the interaction of relative price moves against costs. A national, annual balance sheet may provide grain for exports; but a lack of farmer selling may, for a period, deprive the market of supplies so that the price is obliged to rise to a level where export markets can be met from another origin or even to bring in supplies to the UK from another origin. In 2001/2, UK production of wheat was poor, as a result of atrocious planting conditions (see Table 1). The size of the crop, at 12.9 million tonnes, in fact allowed for some export but farmers were encouraged to believe that the UK processors would pay higher prices to compensate them for their low production. Post-harvest prices rose to a level that prevented exports and even reached a level that caused millers to buy imported goods, not because the quality in the UK was not appropriate but because farmers would not sell it at a competitive price. Later in the year, the market had to fall sharply to provide outlets for the total export tonnages available. The switch from import parity to export parity (Table 2) is worth around £8–12 per tonne, depending upon how far inland imports penetrate. This price swing is a significant proportion of the value of UK wheat, currently trading around £70 per tonne, and actions such as this illustrate how volatility occurs.

Most countries are now moving to free-trade systems so that the local markets are exposed to world markets. This provides less security and results in international events having a greater impact on local markets. It also imposes currency volatility on commodity markets. Virtually all world trade is denominated in US dollars, so there is a high sensitivity in markets to their currencies' rate against the dollar. In the UK, with sterling floating within a still regulated EU market, the influential rate has been with the euro. As the EU liberalises and decouples aid from farming, this link can be expected to move to the dollar. In the event that sterling joins the euro, the markets will still be influenced, as the French, Spanish, Germans etc are, by the rate of the euro against the dollar. Currency rates in a free market affect local prices, and this is a factor that agriculture in the EU has to get used to after years of "monetary compensation" schemes and import protection, which reduced the effects of currency on price.

Figures 3–5 illustrate this. A comparison between UK wheat and French wheat suggests that the price correlation is limited. Recent rallies in the UK during 2003 are greater than those in France (Figure 3). Comparing the UK wheat price against the euro explains much of this with the weakness of sterling lifting UK wheat prices as the forex makes UK exports more competitive (Figure 4). However, the latest rally in the pound is not reflected in weakness in the wheat price. And the answer to this phenomenon is found in Figure 5, where the price of UK wheat, expressed in euros tracks the rising price of French wheat as supply concerns cause buyers to lift the price to secure their needs. The UK, as a major competitor to France, benefits from this, despite the strength of the pound. Since the French market rallies more than the pound, the net effect is for the UK wheat price to rise in sterling terms, despite the stronger pound!

This is a very good illustration of how markets interact and reflect the underlying economics. The effect of currency is important, even key, but markets have to take account of all factors and this is expressed in the volatility of the price.

3. UK wheat vs French wheat in sterling and euros

Nov 2003 wheat futures
LIFFE vs MATIF

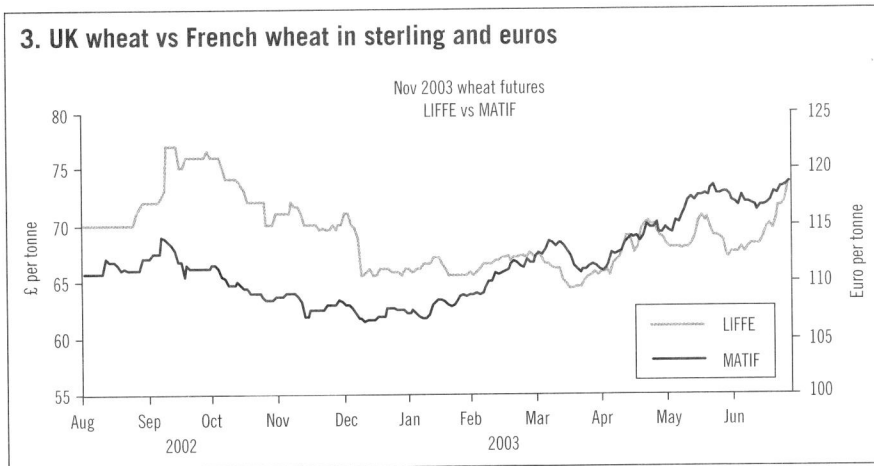

4. UK wheat vs sterling/euro

LIFFE Nov 2003 vs euro/£ spot rate

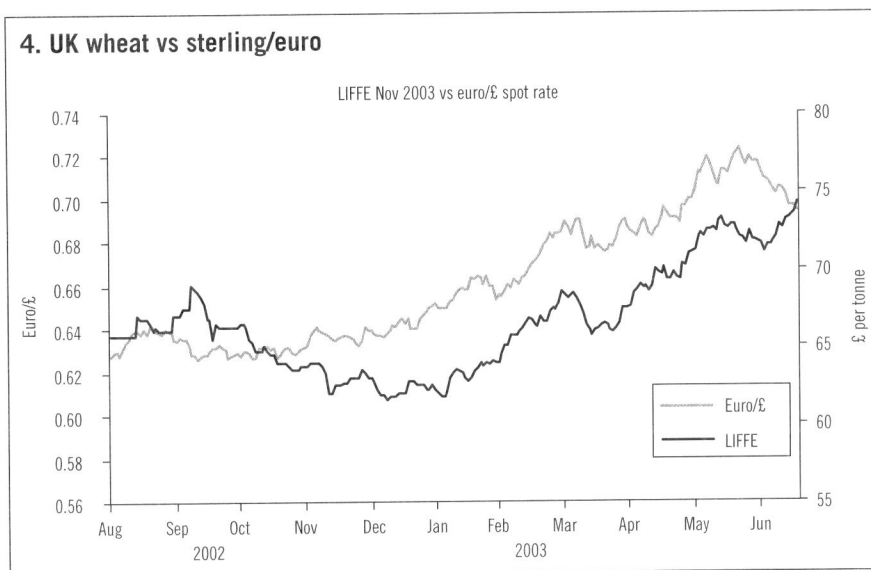

5. UK wheat vs French wheat in euros

LIFFE vs MATIF—in euro

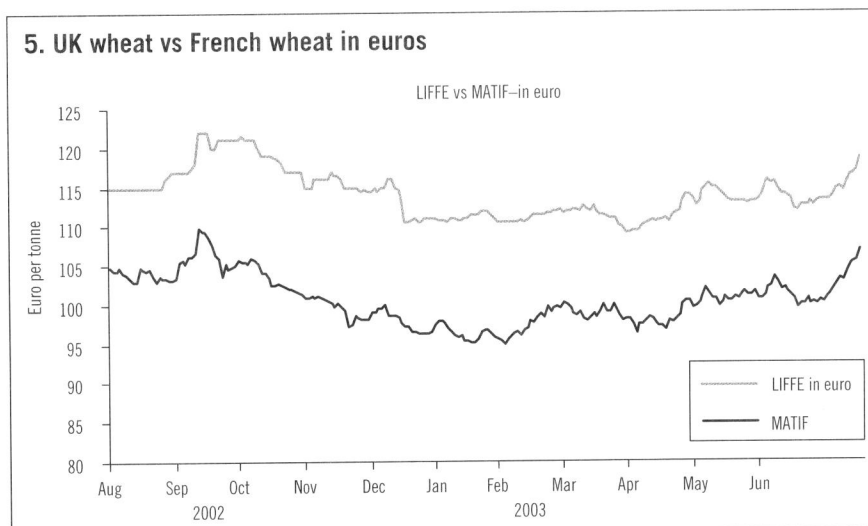

The strong relationship between UK wheat prices and the Euro since 1995 is shown in Figure 6. Although the correlation is, of course, not one to one, it is strong. This kind of linkage makes a perfect scenario for the use of price options to protect businesses.

As far as the UK is concerned, this relationship is not limited to grain. The prices for pig meat, milk and poultry show significant linkage to the sterling–euro rate since 1996.

6. Wheat prices 1995–2002

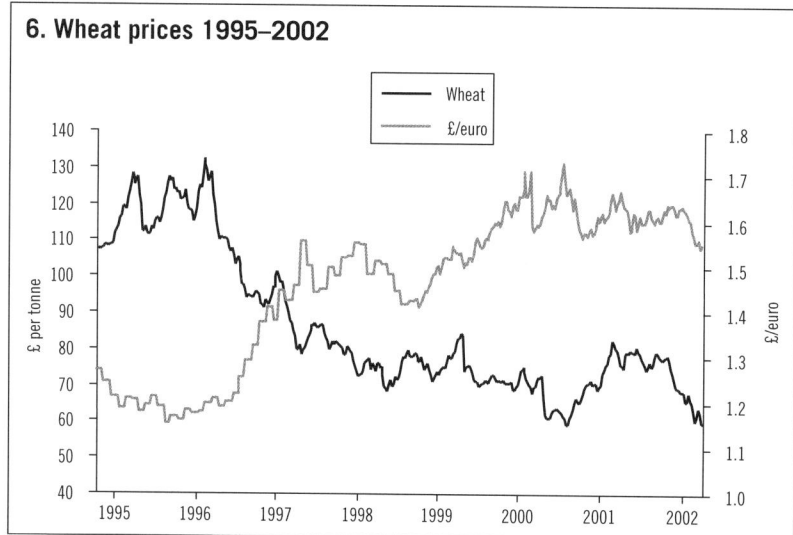

7. Pigmeat prices 1995–2003

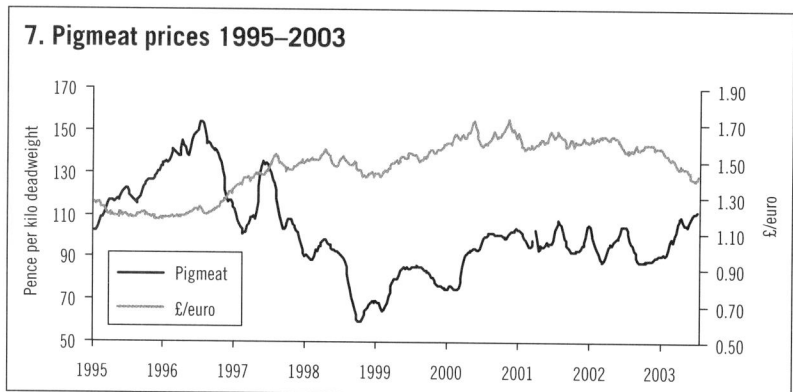

8. Milk prices 1995–2003

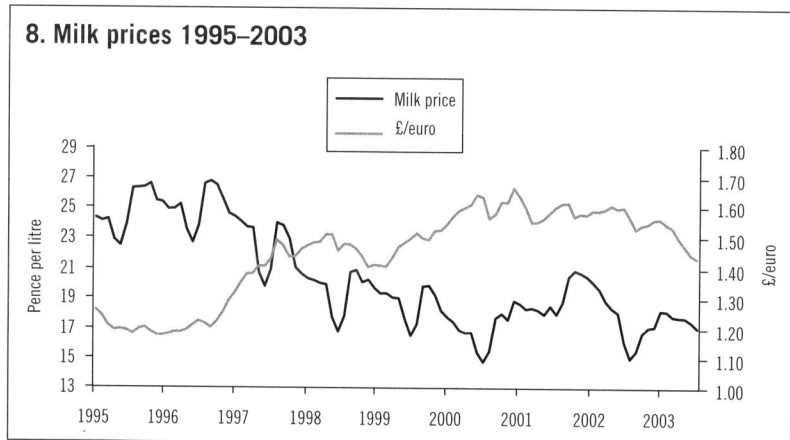

Again, the relationships are not fixed but there is a strong enough link to explain that much of the depression caused in British agriculture over the last seven years was caused by currency depressing prices: pigmeat comes in from Denmark and Holland, milk processors have to compete with French yoghurt and imported cheeses, and the poultry market is always complaining about imports of chicken from Thailand and Brazil. With the EU mechanisms ruling many markets, these product prices are affected by the sterling–euro rate; or, in the case of direct non-EU imports, by the sterling–dollar rate. In any event, currency is part and parcel of domestic price formation and volatility. This cannot be altered, regulated or predicted by those in the industry. Nor is it likely to be taken up by government as a political requirement. Those in commerce, therefore, have to look for other ways to protect their businesses.

9. Poultrymeat prices 1995–2003

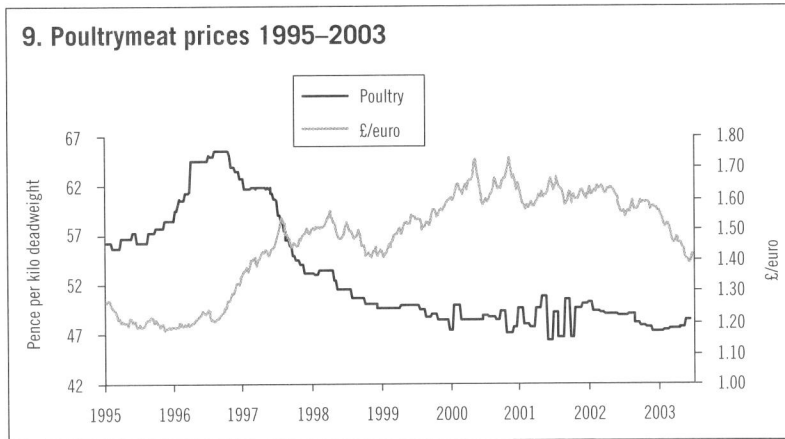

This currency effect is, of course, not limited to the UK. All agricultural countries that are involved in free trading experience price movements relating to currency shifts. This can be seen by examining the recent strength of agriculture in New Zealand and Australia. Their currencies experienced massive devaluations against the US dollar over the period 1996 to 2001 (Figure 10). During this period, when New Zealand agriculture was hailed as the "miracle economy" and held up as an example of farming and free trade, the currency devalued over 70%. In Australia the devaluation was 55%. Of course, farming prospered. Both of these countries need to export agricultural goods, and, as the US dollar rose, so the prices received in local currency rose. Costs were local and so profits were good. Now that the dollar has dropped back and these currencies have rallied between 25 and 50% against it, we shall see how prosperous they are over the next few years. Note also from Figure 10 that, at the same time, sterling rose about 20% against the euro, depressing UK agricultural prices. This is not farming: it is currency volatility.

10. UK, NZ and Australian Forex 1996–2003

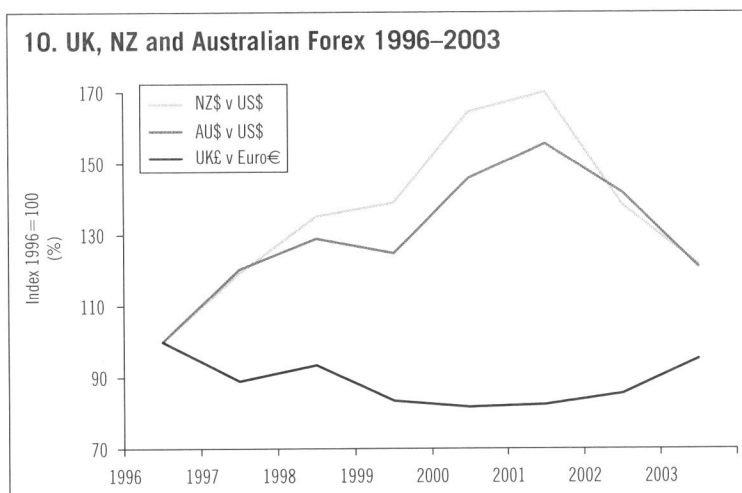

So, if we can see that there are coherent reasons that explain why agricultural markets have permanent volatility, how can businesses be protected? Marketing and procurement policies can assist security of sales and purchases, but only a pricing plan with pricing insurance based on derivatives can protect those involved in the markets.

But of course history and a lack of technical expertise argue against the use of "derivatives" for a basic industry such as farming. Farmers feel comfortable that prices can move in mysterious ways, and fully accept that these are heavily influenced by currency. But they feel uncomfortable taking what many regard as "speculative" positions in currency options as a means of achieving compensation – although it was all right when the government took the responsibility for this via agri-monetary compensation. The fact is that the EU government might be persuaded to assist in the development of a self-help currency insurance policy, but they are very unlikely to revert to full currency compensation. The arrival of the 10 new member states would make such a system unworkable anyway. So industry leaders must take the initiative to assist the derivatives or insurance industry to offer competitively priced schemes that offer farmers – and not just cereal farmers – the possibility of protecting themselves from a resurgence in strength on the part of sterling.

The impact of volatility

The food industry is serviced by different speciality activities: farmer-producers; shippers, traders and distributors; processors; retailers; consumers. And each has a problem with volatility.

Farmer-producers, being at the start of the chain, bear the brunt of the negative aspects of volatility. Their whole revenue stream and part of their cost base are linked to commodity prices. Problems further down the chain are often passed back to the farm. Traditionally, government provided support for farm prices that usually included stabilisation and protection from currency. In the modern world, however, food supplies are more secure and the political will to protect domestic supplies has faded, and, increasingly, markets are being deregulated and liberalised. This leaves farmers exposed to all the variations and uncertainties previously discussed, and they are probably the least equipped to cope with this. In addition, since they tend to be producing the raw material for food products rather than a finished added-value item, they have little cushion in their trading margins to protect their profit. The essential requirement for the farmer is to work to a budget and have a marketing/pricing plan that can be followed.

The main areas of volatility affecting the farmer are:

❑ yield;
❑ fuel, power and energy costs;
❑ output prices;
❑ interest rates;
❑ input prices; and
❑ currency.

The *traders, shippers and distributors* are generally the most professional risk managers in the chain. This is because their trading margins are very small in relation to their turnover and as a result they can suffer disproportionate losses under adverse market moves. The essential requirement for the traders is daily position reporting so that all sales and purchases can be hedged as required.

The main areas of volatility affecting the trader are:

❑ grain/commodity prices;
❑ fertiliser/feed prices;
❑ fuel and haulage rates;
❑ interest rates;
❑ spot v forward prices; and
❑ currency.

Agricultural processors have an intrinsic added value in their business from the conversion of raw materials into saleable outputs. They can be seriously affected by volatility and therefore need to follow some of the disciplines of the trader so that exposure to the market is monitored and controlled. Some processes, such as crushing, sugar production and flour milling, are basic, requiring expertise in both raw material and output commodity markets. Others, such as baking, refining, brewing and breakfast cereals, use commodity inputs to create marketable products. This reduces an amount of volatility, since the product prices are more predictable and are likely to be determined at least partially under the control of the processor.

The main areas of volatility affecting the processor are:

❑ extract/yield of raw material;
❑ raw material prices;
❑ power and energy prices;
❑ fuel and haulage rates;
❑ costs of packaging;
❑ interest rates;
❑ output prices;
❑ industry capacity; and
❑ currency.

In general, *retailers* believe that they can avoid most of the impact of volatility on their business. For basic goods such as flour and vegetable oil, volatility will interfere; higher-added-value items will be less affected. In general, however, they can either pass price increases on to the consumer or they can minimise any increases asked for by suppliers via their negotiating power. Currency volatility means that they are obliged to maintain contacts with many different suppliers in order to optimise their procurement plans across boundaries.

The main areas of volatility affecting the retailer are:

❑ purchase prices of basic goods;
❑ fuel and haulage rates;
❑ power and energy prices;
❑ interest rates; and
❑ currency.

Consumers are least exposed to volatility. The modern shopper buys less than before in the way of basic foods (potatoes, raw vegetables) and more in the way of prepared foods. These have added-value prices and therefore usually absorb much of the volatility. The market also presents to the consumer a derived "cheapest solution" from efficient sourcing. In the end, of course, the consumer pays, but this is more a result of consumer purchasing trends and food marketing techniques than the result of basic volatility. This also means that volatility affects the poorest consumer in society the most.

The main areas of volatility affecting the consumer are:

❑ prices of basic foods;
❑ energy and fuel costs;
❑ interest rates; and
❑ currency.

So each link in the chain has problems with volatility, some more than others, and it is the farmer who has most to lose from ignoring these problems. Left to the market, all the problems of the chain will end at the farm gate. Farmers should therefore focus on their need for protection and work to achieving it.

It is worth noting that, although some problem areas (transport, fuel etc) are common to several sectors, the major factor that affects all parts of the food chain is currency. Currency affects certain areas directly (e.g. foreign receivables) but in other areas (particularly local prices) it has an important influence that can have a material effect on business profitability There should therefore be demand for instruments that address this issue as the food industry around the world wakes up to the potentially negative effects of currency volatility. Correct use of derivatives will create protection against bad news while permitting businesses to keep a large part of windfall gains.

The value of derivatives and the reason that they are used extensively worldwide is that sensible businesspeople realise that it is much easier to determine the needs of their businesses than to determine price moves, and that, rather than waste time wrongly predicting prices, they should direct their energy at running their businesses and trading defensively in the markets. Those that do not do this usually lose money, sometimes enough to destroy their companies. Often, in innocence of the reasons for the loss, they will express the view, "It could not have been predicted!" This sort of business management is equivalent to a weekend sailor crossing the Bay of Biscay in March or a rambler in a T-shirt reaching the heights of Ben Nevis in May.

Exploiting volatility

Most businesses involved in agriculture see the volatility of the market as a negative force. And indeed it adds an element of danger to the operating environment that must not be ignored. However, the required exposure to the market, properly applied and run as a part of the business, can permit significant opportunities to be taken for the profit of the business. Most businesses do not do this. They approach the market either aggressively or passively, instead of defensively. And they manage their exposure to the market passively or defensively instead of aggressively. Buying is done by buyers; selling is done by the sales-force; forex is controlled by the finance department (although very few financiers understand forex!). If a business must be exposed to volatility, the management should incorporate this fact into their planning and budgeting and, by segregating it into an "activity" within the business, managing all volatility as one profit centre reporting directly to the chief executive as a main board function.

Volatility is harnessed by the trade in options and, without getting an advanced qualification in the "Greeks", most businesses should be capable of getting involved with these. This then permits them to exploit time value: minimising the costs of protection in the market against the needs of the business. Well-managed businesses should consider integrating options purchases within their purchase or sales budgets so that covering the market risk to the business opens opportunities to profit from the inherent volatility of the market. By being budget-driven, with a cost allowance for insurance, repeated options purchase as the market moves in favour of the business can reinvest profits to the benefit of the business. This can also generate windfall gains, which the unwary can experience today only by speculating in the market.

Scenario analysis – managing exposure to volatility

By managing their exposure to volatility, all the links in the chain can improve the quality of their business.

Farmers can:

❏ budget for low-yield and cost-price insurance for high yields;
❏ plan their use of fuel, power and energy costs and negotiate maximum prices;
❏ take price insurance for their output prices;
❏ ask for capped or fixed interest rates;
❏ negotiate maximum prices for their inputs;
❏ carry rolling currency options as part of their overhead.

Traders can:

❏ rigorously monitor the exposure to grain and commodity prices;
❏ take price or currency insurance against the stocks of fertiliser or animal feed;
❏ create "default insurance" via derivatives when necessary;
❏ negotiate price insurance on fuel purchases and negotiate long-term haulage rates;
❏ ask for capped or fixed interest rates;
❏ arbitrage markets between spot and forward prices as part of their storage operations;
❏ exercise precise monitors of currency exposure and use options where appropriate.

Processors can:

❏ budget cautiously for expected rate of extract or yield from raw materials;
❏ include a budgeted allowance for price insurance for raw-material purchases;

❑ negotiate fixed or capped power and energy prices based on usage rates;

❑ ask for capped or fixed interest rates;

❑ negotiate price insurance on fuel purchases and negotiate long-term haulage rates;

❑ break down the components in the costs of packaging so that price insurance can be established;

❑ establish minimum but not entirely fixed levels for output prices;

❑ react to industry capacity changes by following comparative advantage;

❑ maintain a permanent protection in currency options for critical parts of the business.

Retailers can:

❑ negotiate long-term fixed prices (or maximum prices) for basic goods;

❑ negotiate price insurance on fuel purchases and negotiate long-term haulage rates;

❑ negotiate fixed or capped power and energy prices based on usage rates;

❑ ask for capped or fixed interest rates;

❑ maintain a permanent protection in currency options for critical parts of the business.

Consumers are least interested in formal derivative solutions to their problems. "Shopping around" usually provides the best deal. However, they can still use derivatives for mortgage-rate protection and they could consider investments in currency options to protect the sterling value of foreign purchases or pensions.

Conclusion

Decision making in a volatile environment requires business planning. Specialisation and trade have long been the main source of increasing prosperity in the world. Technology has permitted the development of detailed monitors of markets and market exposure. Businesses have to respond to this with innovation in the way that they innovate more conventional processes in the manufacturing, product design and distribution areas.

Business planning has tended to use predicted price expectations as a means of assessing projects. Any such price assumptions are deeply flawed. Rather more important is the understanding of the underlying causal forces – links with currency etc, so that hedging structures using derivatives can be used to protect current and future business plans.

The point is that traditional ways of business management predate the existence of options and other modern derivatives. Modern businesses need modern tools. Derivatives are available, the best businesses are using them sensibly and they are the only way both to protect against and to exploit the natural volatility of the agricultural and food industry operating environment in order to optimise revenue streams and cost profiles.

RISK MANAGEMENT TOOLS AND INSTRUMENTS: THE PRODUCTS

3

Agricultural Futures and Options

Keith Schap and Bernard W. Dan

Chicago Board of Trade*

During a question-and-answer session at the end of a seminar, a banker asked a grain-elevator merchandiser exactly how important futures were to the grain people – the banker's tone implying he saw no point to futures and options. The merchandiser said, "Sir, in our business, if we didn't have futures, we'd have to invent them."

What the merchandiser went on to explain are the fundamental facts of life in the grain trade that ultimately caused futures, and later options, to be invented. Grain and oilseed producers can raise one crop a year, yet demand is constant. In the absence of futures markets, this leads to a classic lose–lose situation.

This occurs because, in the first weeks after harvest, the new supply gluts the market, and a market in glut is a market with low prices – ruinously low for the farmers. Yet, nine or 10 months later, the grain bins are likely to be close to empty. This drives prices higher – ruinously higher for such grain users as millers or livestock feeders.

These wild boom–bust swings serve the interests of neither producers nor end users. At one point, towards the middle of the 19th century, post-harvest prices were so low that a large group of farmers who were seeking wheat buyers in Chicago dumped their wheat in the river in protest. If they couldn't make a living from this wheat, neither would they let the millers.

Cooler heads realised that they had to find a way to regulate the flow of grain to market so this annual crop would last through the year and so prices would be such that both sides could meet their business goals. This led to the use of forward contracts – hardly a new financial tool. Now a farmer could transact a series of forward contracts that set quantities and prices in advance. Forward contracts can work and remain a staple of the grain trade. The chief drawback of a forward contract is that it is inflexible. Only the original parties can alter the terms or unwind the contract mid-term.

Often this is not an issue, and forwards can work well. This inflexibility becomes an issue when the needs of one party change before the delivery date. The grain buyer might decide that he doesn't need as much wheat as he originally thought and just not honour the contract. Performance failures on these contracts became frequent enough that grain-market participants realised they needed another kind of tool – in effect, a fungible forward contract. This implies a need for standardisation of contracts, and that's essentially what a futures contract is – a standardised, fungible contract for delivery at a specified future date.

Any futures contract defines, and so standardises, these elements: the commodity or index that provides the basis for the contract, the contract size, the form of price

* The information in this chapter is taken from sources believed to be reliable. However, it is intended for purposes of information and education only and is not guaranteed by the author or the Chicago Board of Trade as to accuracy, completeness or any trading result, and does not constitute trading advice or constitute a solicitation of the purchase or sale of any futures or options. The Rules and Regulations of the Chicago Board of Trade should be consulted as the authoritative source on all current contract specifications and regulations.

quotation and the method of settlement. Given that the contract defines these elements, they are not open to negotiation. The only factor that is open to negotiation is the price.

These contract specifications make it perfectly clear what the obligations of the buyer and seller are and what kind of performance is expected of each. The specifications of any good futures contract give rise to a curious fact: "Ironically, a well-functioning futures contract will represent an imperfect transaction for both parties, being general enough to apply to a broad range of buyers and sellers" (Petzel, 1989, p. 6).

To illustrate…

A small-scale and completely informal example will illustrate how futures can help market users smooth the peaks and valleys of the annual cycle in, say, wheat prices.

Suppose a wheat user buys 20,000 bushels a week, which is equivalent to four Chicago Board of Trade (CBOT) wheat contracts or 16 contracts a month. In anticipation of these purchases, and sometime prior to the month in question, this wheat user can buy 16 contracts of CBOT wheat futures. As he buys physical wheat, he will sell futures back to the market.

At the beginning of Week 1, he will buy 20,000 bushels of actual wheat at the market price and sell four futures contracts to offset his earlier purchase. At the beginning of Week 2, he will buy another 20,000 bushels and sell (offset) four more futures contracts. Suppose that during this two-week period wheat prices have gone up 5 cents a week. The futures price will have gone up as well. This means that, although this wheat user will have to pay the higher market price for his wheat, he will make 5 cents a bushel on his futures the first week and 10 cents a bushel the second week. His effective wheat price will be the same as the price at the time he originally bought the 16 futures contracts. The futures will have taken away the price increases – in effect.

So far, all of this could have been accomplished with a forward contract. However, futures offer additional advantages.

Perhaps this wheat user's firm has altered corporate strategy or perhaps it is feeling the effects of a slowing economy. Whatever the case, it might decide upon a 25% production cutback. With forward contracts, the original wheat supplier would expect to deliver – and be paid – on the full 20,000 bushels regardless. Changing the terms of the contract would be likely to be both difficult and expensive.

For a futures user, this situation causes no problems. The wheat user will simply offset the two extra contracts. When Week 3 rolls around, he will go to market for only 15,000 bushels of wheat and sell three of his remaining futures contracts.

Granted, prices don't only rise. When they fall, the advantage gained in the price of the physical wheat will be offset by a loss on the futures, but the effective price will be the same as it was when the price of the physical wheat rose. In this way, the use of futures can help to smooth the cyclicality inherent in these markets. More important, the use of futures can help firms achieve their business goals by helping them protect their operating margins.

Along with the flexibility that standardised futures give market users, they generate volumes of crucial information about the underlying markets and obviate concerns about credit risk. This is one of the advantages of a centralised marketplace.

Exchanges facility price discovery

Futures exchanges exist to provide a centralised marketplace where market users can discover the prices of commodities for future delivery and where risk-averse people can shift commodity price risk to others willing to bear it.

Consider all there is to know about wheat on a given day. The complete set of this knowledge is vast – too much for any one person to master. It must include existing supplies, acres planted, worldwide crop yields, normal rates of consumption in all the countries of the world and a variety of other supply-and-demand factors. In addition to these statistics, which are publicly available from government and other official surveys, wheat producers, millers and users need to know about a variety of weather factors, political issues and economic factors that can affect supply–demand patterns. These are more speculative – more matters of opinion than of counting. And this list is only suggestive of the scope of the task.

Obviously, no person can possess more than a small subset of this information. Yet all of these factors enter into the price of the commodity. One of the primary functions of a futures exchange is to provide a central meeting place – whether on a trading floor or on an electronic trading platform – where large numbers of people, each acting on his or her subset of that knowledge, can make bids and offers. This auction process results in the market clearing price of the moment. This is not a fiat price. Nobody sets it. Rather, this price is discovered in this free-flowing interplay among all the market participants.

Exchange clearing enhances financial integrity

Perhaps the most important development in the exchange-traded derivatives field, other than the original invention of futures contracts, is the development of a clearing system. Consider that no CBOT customer has suffered loss from counterparty default since the institution of the clearing system in the mid-1920s. Given the flow of news concerning the accounting difficulties and other problems that many users of over-the-counter derivatives markets have had during the last decade, this is a remarkable claim.

On the surface, the keys to the success of the exchange clearing system would seem to be that the futures clearing houses interpose themselves between counterparties (becoming seller to every buyer and buyer to every seller) and that they require daily margins and daily mark to market. A deeper probe shows that the clearing-house system also focuses on financial reporting.

In practice, each clearing member firm of an exchange is responsible for reporting the aggregate net positions of all of its customers to the clearing house. The clearing house also has the right to investigate the financial statements of the clearing members and, if need be, of their customers.

All of this creates an invaluable information asset for low cost relative to the cost to every market user of having to monitor all of its counterparties as in the over-the-counter market. In this way, the exchange clearing system reduces the incidence of nonperformance and the extent of the resulting damage by internalising the cost of contract nonperformance in the rare cases that do occur. This generates important economic advantages for users of exchange-traded derivatives. The key, it is worth emphasising, is this centralisation of information.

The specifying of futures contracts

The contract specifications provide focus for the price discovery and hedging activities of an exchange, so it is worth considering how a futures contract comes into being and how the exchange staff determine what they deem the appropriate set of specifications for a contract on a given commodity.

To begin with, the underlying market must be large enough to support a futures contract. This has at least three aspects: volume of production, market value (production times price) and the length of the marketing chain. Table 1 provides data that allow the comparison of US corn, soybean, wheat, sorghum and rice markets in these regards.

Table 1. A sample of US crop sizes and values			
Crop	2002 US production (bushels/rice cwt)	2002 US production (short tons)	Market value (US$)
Corn	9,010,000,000	252,280,000	21,624,000,000
Soybeans	2,730,000,000	81,900,000	16,762,200,000
Wheat	1,616,000,000	48,480,000	5,155,040,000
Grain sorghum	370,000,000	10,360,000	1,646,500,000
Rice	211,000,000	10,550,000	1,270,220,000

The first two columns of the table compare 2002 US production of corn, soybeans, wheat, grain sorghum and rice in bushels (but hundredweights for rice) and short tons. The third column lists the dollar value of each crop. This is based on the price per bushel (or hundredweight) times the bushel (or hundredweight) production figure.

Using corn as a basis for comparison, the table shows the US soybean crop to be roughly one-third the size of the corn crop, but the dollar value of soybeans is more than three-quarters the value of the corn crop. The US wheat crop (all varieties lumped together) is about one-fifth the size of the corn crop while the sorghum and rice crops are about 1/25 the size of corn. The dollar values of these three crops are larger fractions of the corn value but far from as much larger as is the value of soybeans.

Market critics from time to time complain about the fact that futures volume exceeds production. Looking only at US production of these crops, we see that 2002 corn futures volume is 10 times that of 2002 US corn production. Soybean futures volume is almost 25 times production for the same period. This is taken by these people to be clear evidence of speculative excess.

However, this overlooks several important factors. Corn, wheat and soybeans have extensive marketing chains. A bushel of any of these crops passes through as many as six or seven middlemen on the way from grower to end user. All of these people have price risk exposure, which they can use futures to hedge. Think, too, about what happens when any one of these people sends an order to the trading floor or screen. One of the exchange immediacy providers will take the other side. Subsequently, this person may decide this is too much risk and trade part of his or her position to other exchange locals. This will continue until all concerned have risk exposures they can live with. Far from being a sign of what has, in another connection, been called "irrational exuberance", this volume of trade signals an economic sector seeking a laudable measure of economic stability and strength.

Soybeans differ from the other contracts in that merchants and processors use the CBOT contract to protect against the risk exposures inherent in the South American crop, which has recently grown larger than the US crop. It is conceivable that factoring in South American production would result in a ratio of futures bushels to actual bushels that is close to that for corn.

Sorghum is included to contrast with rice. US production and dollar value of these two crops are similar, but there is a rice futures contract while there is not a sorghum contract. This is true because sorghum prices move in a pattern similar to corn prices so that corn futures are a reasonable cross-hedge. Rice stands alone among the grains. It has no relatives even as close as corn to sorghum. As a result, rice futures maintain a place in the market where sorghum does not.

Economies undergo structural change, and futures markets must change to reflect the new realities of the marketplace. Sometimes the change can be a contract revision. Other times the change requires a new contract.

Two recent contract revisions involved the CBOT corn and soybean contracts in one case, and the rough rice contract in another. As the grain distribution process decentralised, Chicago became less relevant as a delivery point. After careful study, the corn and soybean contracts were revised to allow delivery at a variety of locations along the Illinois river. Another contract revision involved the rough rice contract. Here the quality standard of the futures contract was recently changed to reflect quality improvements in the underlying market.

A change in the soybean market has motivated consideration of a new South American soybean contract. The impetus for this comes from the fact that the combined Brazilian and Argentine soybean crops exceeded the US crop in 2002 and promise to grow larger in the future. While South American brokers, processors and merchants have been using the US contract for many years, the basis risk can be worrisome – the more so as the increasing size of the crop increases the size of the risk. As a result, market participants have begun to ask for the new contract, and market size and value seem to justify its development.

Having observed this structural change and heard the reasons why market users favour a new contract, exchange staff began a series of conferrals with a variety of present and potential market users – including trade associations, large processors and merchants, futures trading firms and local traders.

These conversations led to the formulation of a contract specification. In designing the contract, the staff must consider a series of trade-offs involving contract size, pricing convention, minimum price increment (tick size), settlement procedure, and delivery locations and requirements. For example, the commercial users will probably prefer a large contract to minimise transaction costs. Local traders typically prefer a smaller contract that will keep their risk exposure within tolerable limits. US contracts are denominated in bushels, but local convention almost anywhere else mandates that this contract use metric tonnes. Again, a very small tick size allows commercials to make very fine risk adjustments, but local traders can't profit enough to motivate their participation if the tick is too small. All of these matters require a balancing act on the part of the contract designers.

With this particular soybean contract, another important feature is a partnership with one or more of the South American exchanges. This will facilitate participation in both hemispheres while still allowing users of the new contract to participate in the liquidity pool of the US contract through spreading between the two contracts.

Once all the balances are struck, exchange staff can go back to the market participants to ask if they can live with these provisions. If the consensus is that they can, the exchange goes ahead with the contract launch.

Futures contract failures

Anyone familiar with futures markets realises that, even after this careful research and extensive consultation, the odds are heavily against any new contract trading enough to be considered successful. Contracts succeed or fail for reasons that often remain shrouded in mystery. Once in a while, a contract failure is fairly easy to understand. Take sorghum. This plant is somewhat similar to corn, but the crop has its own fundamentals.

As a result of the differences in fundamentals, the use of corn futures to hedge sorghum introduces basis risk – the risk that the two markets will respond differently to a given market stimulus. Yet sorghum failed twice. The Kansas City Board of Trade launched a contract in the early 1920s. The Chicago Mercantile Exchange launched a contract in the early 1970s. Apparently, market users considered the trade-off between basis risk and liquidity, decided they could manage the basis risk and opted for the greater liquidity of the corn contract.

Another futures contract failure that may be possible to understand is the short-lived DAP (diammonium phosphate) contract that the CBOT launched in 1991. This is a widely used fertiliser. Factors that suggested such a futures contract might succeed included the fact that fertiliser prices can vary considerably. Because fertiliser is a major cost in crop production, it would seem that both the end user and the producer would have hedgible interests. Further, almost every country elevator is a fertiliser dealer. These people are comfortable with grain futures and could be expected to embrace the new contract.

In fact, not many people in any of these groups embraced DAP futures. The DAP producers never seemed to have fully understood what futures are good for. Their frequent requests for expansion of the number of delivery points suggest that they regarded the contract as a delivery tool rather than as a risk management tool.

Another factor that may have played a role is that the marketing chain for DAP is far shorter than that for commodities such as corn or soybeans. In the case of DAP, the product goes from manufacturer fairly directly to dealer-applicator. In a case like this, hedging seems less necessary.

At times, a flawed contract specification will doom a contract. Frozen turkeys began trading in October 1945, but the contract allowed processors to deliver their lowest-quality meat. Futures holders quickly decided this wasn't a good thing and declined to use the contract. Even rarer cases involve contracts being legislated out of existence. Both onions and potatoes have been targets of legislative displeasure.

While the stories surrounding the failure of contracts like onions and potatoes make for entertaining reading, the sorghum and DAP situations are probably more instructive. Market users place high value on a contract's liquidity. They need to be able to get into and out of positions quickly. Because of this, any contract that doesn't build liquidity is unlikely to enjoy success. The Commodity Futures Trading Commission (CFTC) lists all of the contracts that have ever been approved for trading on US exchanges in its annual reports. This list runs to many pages. The list of agricultural contracts that trade enough to be called successful – worldwide – would probably fit on one page.

The information function of futures markets

Along with the official economic justification for futures markets that involves the combination of hedging utility and price discovery, futures markets also generate incredible amounts of information that can provide helpful insight to people who are alert to it – and that simply wouldn't be available had these markets not been invented.

Consider the price spreads, for example. Any quotation service, or any of the news media that cover these markets, reports not just one price for soybeans or wheat but an array of prices. For example, on a late May day in 2003, the price arrays for different delivery months and associated spreads were those of Tables 2 and 3.

Table 2. Signalling a shortage in soybeans

Contract month	Price (cents/bushel)	Spread (cents/bushel)
July	623.00	
August	620.75	−2.25
September	587.00	−33.75
November	556.75	−30.25

These price spreads tell an important story about the storage situation. In April and May of 2003, analysts were noting that export sales of soybeans were running well higher than normal and were creating a shortage of domestic supply. The sharply inverted (read negative – some markets refer to "backwardated" markets, whereas the grain trade refers to inverted markets) August–September and September–November soybean spreads signal an immediate need for soybeans. The market was willing to pay 66.25 cents per bushel more for July delivery than November. Inverted spreads like these penalise storage and motivate the movement of grain.

Table 3 illustrates a carry market in US wheat (some markets replace the term "carry" with "contango"). The term "carry" refers to the cost of storing a commodity and incorporates the costs of insurance and financing as well as the actual cost of storage. These positive spreads indicate a willingness on the part of the market to pay at least partially for storage – a signal that wheat supply is plentiful relative to demand and the market feels no urgent need for a flow of supply.

Table 3. Wheat is plentiful

Contract month	CBOT Wheat		KCBT Wheat	
	Price (cents/bushel)	Spread (cents/bushel)	Price (cents/bushel)	Spread (cents/bushel)
July	319.00		326.25	
September	324.75	5.75	329.00	2.75
December	334.75	10.00	338.00	9.00
March	340.50	5.75	342.00	4.00

An interesting feature of the spreads in these two exhibits is that the inverted spreads are much wider than the carry spreads. Carry spreads are limited to the cost of full carry. Whatever the cost of storage, insurance, shrinkage and interest for the specified number of months, that is the widest carry spreads can be. No such limit governs inverted spreads. They can be however wide the market needs them to be to start grain moving.

In addition to the store–don't store signals, the spreads can guide hedging strategy. Suppose that, in October, a corn merchant (who typically sells futures to protect his inventory against falling prices) is thinking about hedging May sales. Looking at a carry market that is paying 80% of full carry, the wisest strategy might be to place this hedge in the May contract. The worst that can happen is that the market will rise to the level of full carry. This is a relatively small risk.

However, looking at an inverted market, the wisest strategy is to place the hedge in the December contract and roll it forward into the March contract and then into the May contract. That is, having originally sold December contracts, the hedger can buy these back in late November and sell the same number of March contracts, with a high probability of buying low and selling high. In late February, this hedger can buy back the March and sell May. To roll forward this way is the safest way to operate in an inverted market.

The basis moves grain

The basis, which is simply the cash-futures difference, is an especially important price relationship. A commonplace of the grain trade is that basis moves grain. If soybeans are 575 a bushel at one location and July soybean futures are 597, the soybean basis for that location is −22 a bushel, or 22 cents under the July futures.

Depending on the location, the basis can be characteristically positive or negative. For example, to lure grain downriver to the Gulf of Mexico terminals, merchants have to bid up the cash price. Thus, the Gulf basis tends to be strongly positive (primarily to pay the cost of transporting grain from the Midwest production areas to the Gulf). Basis analysts also talk about a strengthening or a weakening basis. Suppose the basis moves from 26.50 to 21.75 in one location while in another it moves from −10 to −14.75 during the same period. In both cases, this illustrates a weakening basis and, like the positive spreads, signals a market that wants grain in storage. Conversely, suppose the basis moves from 21.75 to 31.25 in the former location while it moves from −22 to −12.50 in the other. In both cases, this illustrates a strengthening basis that signals a shortage of grain, or at least the need to move grain.

This illustration of strengthening and weakening should demonstrate that absolute basis level is less important than the way the basis changes with the passage of time. Another grain-trade commonplace is that price has no history, but the basis does. Indeed, the basis follows strikingly regular patterns year after year. When it does break the pattern, that is often an early warning that something important, good or bad, is about to happen or is already in its first stages.

Hedging and trading strategies

End users of grains and oilseeds tend to be long-hedgers. That is, they characteristically buy futures to protect against rising cash-market prices. Consider the case of a corn processor who buys 100,000 bushels a week. At US$2.04 a bushel, a one-week supply will cost US$204,000. Suppose the price bounces to US$2.12 the next week. This US$8,000 difference could mean the difference between making or losing money.

To protect against such a loss, long-hedgers can buy futures against future purchases in the cash market. The futures price will rise more or less in concert with the cash price. Each time the processor buys 100,000 bushels of actual corn, he can sell the equivalent number of futures contracts (100,000 bushels = 20 contracts). If prices have risen, the futures gain should largely offset the cash-market increase. Table 4 shows how such a hedge should perform during a two-month period.

Table 4. A long hedge in corn protects the margin

Date	Cash	Futures	Basis	Cash (100,000)	Futures (100,000)	Futures result	Effective price
03/03/03	204	229	−25				
10/03/03	211	237	−26	211,000	237,000	8,000	203,000
17/03/03	207	230	−23	207,000	230,000	1,000	206,000
24/03/03	205	229	−24	205,000	229,000	0	205,000
31/03/03	214	237	−23	214,000	237,000	8,000	206,000
07/04/03	218	243	−25	218,000	243,000	14,000	204,000
14/04/03	215	239	−24	215,000	239,000	10,000	205,000
21/04/03	213	238	−25	213,000	238,000	9,000	204,000
28/04/03	205	231	−26	205,000	231,000	2,000	203,000
			Average Price	211,000 US$2.11/bu		Average Effective	204,500 US$2.045/bu

Here, the cash, futures and basis values in the first three columns are in cents per bushel. The last four columns denote dollar values for 100,000 bushel units. Notice that the cash price at this processor's location hovers close to 25 cents a bushel under the futures price throughout this period, and this hedge lowers the average price per bushel 6.5 cents. Where the average cash price for these two months is US$2.11 a bushel, the average effective price is US$2.04½ a bushel. For this two-month period, this amounts to a US$52,000 saving on a total purchase of 800,000 bushels.

While this relatively flat basis is typical for much of North Central Illinois during March, April and May, to return to that topic, the basis in other areas and at other times tends to strengthen or weaken.

Hedgers should pay attention to these basis patterns because it is possible to get on the wrong side of the basis. When this happens, hedge performance can fall well short of expectations. Consider two situations involving a long corn hedge, as illustrated in Table 5.

Table 5. Basis change matters

Scenario 1: The basis strengthens

	Cash corn			Corn futures	Basis
Sell cash	216	Buy futures		236	−20
Buy cash	236	Sell futures		252	−16
Result	20			16	4

Scenario 2: The basis weakens

Sell cash	224	Buy futures		236	−12
Buy cash	236	Sell futures		252	−16
Result	12			16	−4

This hedger is buying corn futures to protect against rising prices. In the first case, the basis strengthens 4 cents a bushel, and the futures position falls 4 cents a bushel short of matching the cash-market gain. In the second case, the basis weakens 4 cents a bushel, and the futures position covers the cash price change and 4 cents a bushel more. It actually generates a net gain. For a short-hedger who initially sells futures, the situation will be the reverse. The strengthening basis will generate the gain. The weakening basis will make the hedge less effective.

Note that, in both cases, the hedger is still better off than an unhedged counterpart. Still, awareness of basis dynamics can help grain and oilseed merchandisers and end users find extra opportunities and avoid pitfalls.

Grain merchants have become masterful basis traders. Because basis patterns are so regular and futures such reliable risk management tools, these merchants can, at certain times, assume risks they might not otherwise take in order to profit from managing them. For example, through the US corn- and soybean-growing areas, country elevators might offer extremely attractive terms in certain seasons to attract grain into the house. Anticipating a weakening basis, they use this grain to "short the basis" – sell cash and buy futures. The assumption is that the favourable basis change will more than compensate for unfavourable cash-market developments. Table 6 shows how such a strategy can work in the corn market.

Table 6. A short basis trade to enhance profits				
	Cash corn		Corn futures	Basis
Sell corn	225	Buy futures	240	−15
Buy corn	235	Sell futures	255	−20
Result	−10		+15	−5

In this example, the cash corn position lost 10 cents a bushel, yet the weakening basis caused the combined cash and futures positions to gain 5 cents a bushel. This would seem to be what Georges Andre was getting at when he said, "The secret of success in the grain business is to sell cheaper than you buy and still make money" (Morgan, 2000, p. 202). Journalists often take a jaundiced view of such remarks. They may not fully understand how grain merchants use the basis dynamic to generate income where, in the absence of a futures market, they could not do so.

The soybean crush spread

An especially interesting spread relationship is the soybean crush spread. This trade uses soybean, soy meal and soy oil futures to capture the gross margin of processing soybeans. Consider that a soybean processor buys beans at one end of the process and sells soybean meal and oil at the other. In between, something happens that should add value. The crush spread reflects the fact that a 60-pound bushel of soybeans yields 44 pounds of 48% protein meal and 11 pounds of soybean oil and tells spread watchers about the profitability of processing.

The spread calculation depends on the formula illustrated in Table 7. Note that it converts the dollars per ton of the meal contract and cents per pound of the oil contract into the cents per bushel of the bean contract and expresses the spread in cents per bushel.

Table 7. Calculating the crush					
Soybean meal	+	Soybean oil	−	Soybeans	=	Crush spread
(price × 0.022)	+	(price × 0.11)	−	price	=	spread
(172.70 × 0.022)	+	(20.56 × 0.11)	−	5.655	=	spread
3.7994	+	2.2616	−	5.655	=	0.41
The 41 cents per bushel represents the gross processing margin or the crush spread.					

Something around 40 cents a bushel gives a good industry-wide ballpark break-even figure. Obviously, that varies from place to place as local needs and conditions differ. And it can vary significantly during a year and from year to year.

The spread is narrowing when the cost of soybeans gains relative to the prices of the two products. The spread is widening when the prices of the products gain relative to the cost of the beans.

When risk managers track the crush, they need to consider whether the spread is "normal" for the time of year in light of recent history. A good chart helps with that. They should also develop a view concerning whether the spread is more likely to narrow or widen during the term of the hedge they contemplate. And they should determine whether the meal or the oil is driving the crush at that time.

Soybean producers have an obvious interest in those answers, but so do feed users. When meal demand is low, the crush typically reflects that fact. And anyone contemplating herd expansion might well pause to consider further.

For hedgers, crush spread developments may provide early warning of important basis changes. After all, when an activity promises to be especially profitable, people want to do more. Then processors may have to bid aggressively to attract beans. Conversely, when the margin narrows significantly, processing activity may slow. Prices will become less favourable. The basis will reflect that. But hedgers may at times see the crush shift before other signals emerge.

Options represent a new twist on old ideas

Options were a late arrival on the exchange-traded derivatives scene. The first options on agricultural futures began trading at the end of October 1984. The CBOT introduced options on soybean futures, and the New York Cotton Exchange introduced options on cotton futures. Options on corn futures began trading a year later, and options contracts on the rest of the grain and soy complex futures were phased in during the rest of the 1980s.

Options were not exactly a new idea. The theoretical work of Black, Scholes and Merton had been published in 1973, and equity options had begun trading at that time. Yet, while that theoretical work marks the beginning of modern options markets, the basic idea is an old one. At base, where a futures contract entails an obligation to make or take delivery, an option conveys to the holder (buyer) the right, but not the obligation, to buy (in the case of a call) or sell (in the case of a put) the underlying commodity or futures contract. During the tulip mania in Holland in the late 1600s, people entered into option-like contracts. Even the ancient Greeks seem to have had the basic idea – to wit, the story about the philosopher Thales buying the rights to all the olive presses in the region and then becoming wealthy when there was a bumper crop and growers needed the presses.

Both risk managers and traders can find options helpful because they allow market users to alter risk–reward profiles and to benefit from seasonal volatility patterns.

Reshaping risk–reward profiles

Physical commodities and futures on those commodities have symmetrical risk–reward profiles. Prices go up or down in essentially linear fashion, and market participants gain or lose accordingly. Options have asymmetrical risk–reward profiles. The holder of a call option can gain if prices rise, but the loss in a down market is limited to the premium paid. Where a futures or cash position can suffer seemingly endless losses, this feature of options strictly limits the loss potential – for the option buyer. Similarly, a put option holder can gain in a down market, but the loss in a rallying market is limited to the premium paid.

Further, traders and risk managers can combine cash or futures positions with option positions to create a variety of synthetic exposures. For example, a combination of short futures or cash and a long call will generate basically the same results as a long put position. Hence, such a complex position is a synthetic long put. A range of other such synthetics are possible.

Volatility creates opportunity

Options also allow traders to take positions based on their opinions about volatility. In fact, it is fair to say that, unless traders or risk managers have opinions about volatility, they have no business using options. That said, options can create extra benefits for risk managers.

In the agricultural markets, volatilities typically follow seasonal patterns with the periods of highest volatility occurring in late spring or early summer. The logic of this should be obvious. This is the time right after planting when the crops are in doubt. The unpredictability of weather and demand creates anxiety, and this translates into volatility. Once people know what the crop will be like – bumper or bust – the market calms. After harvest, it calms yet more.

Risk managers can use knowledge about volatility to design a variety of interesting strategies. For instance, consider the case of a wheat miller. To protect against rising prices, such a market user will typically enter into a forward contract or buy futures much as would the corn processor cited in the futures example. However, a combination of options can provide a good alternative.

Suppose that in late May, wheat futures are trading at US$3.34½ a bushel and the implied volatility of the December at-the-money call is 30.2%, which is rather high relative to the long-term mean of futures historical volatility. This wheat miller might be concerned that wheat prices will rise 20 or 30 cents a bushel in the next month but doubt that they'll go higher than US$3.70 a bushel.

Given this price outlook, and knowing that volatility tends to be mean reverting, this wheat miller might consider a three-legged option strategy. He can buy a near-the-money December call and sell an out-of-the-money December call. This short call leg limits the upside potential of the trade, but it also lowers the cost of the risk management strategy. In addition, the wheat miller can sell an out-of-the-money December put to help finance the trade. Table 8 shows the details of this strategy in which the miller buys the 340 December call, sells the 370 December call and sells the 310 December put. The exhibit also shows how this strategy will perform in situations where the futures price rises to US$3.60 and implied volatility (a) remains the same, (b) falls 10 percentage points or (c) falls 15 percentage points.

Table 8 shows that, at this price and volatility, the income from the two sold options is enough to allow putting on this trade at a net credit. Notice also that the more volatility drops, the better the trade will do. Curiously, the gains come from different parts of the trade.

Table 8. A three-legged wheat option strategy to reduce purchase prices

Scenario A

	Initial values (days to expiration: 173) (prices: cents/bushel)	Ending values (days to expiration: 158)	Results
Futures price	334.5	360	25.5
Implied volatility	30.2%	30.18%	
Options			
Buy 340 Dec call	−25	38.625	13.625
Sell 370 Dec call	16.25	−25.875	−9.625
Sell 310 Dec put	11	−4.75	6.25
Net	2.25	8	10.25
		Effective price	349.75

Scenario B

Futures price	334.5	360	25.5
Implied volatility	30.2%	20.02%	
Options			
Buy 340 Dec call	−25	29.875	4.875
Sell 370 Dec call	16.25	−14.5	1.75
Sell 310 Dec put	11	−2.75	8.25
Net	2.25	12.625	14.875
		Effective price	345.125

Scenario C

Futures price	334.5	360	25.5
Implied volatility	30.2%	14.97%	
Options			
Buy 340 Dec call	−25	25.875	0.875
Sell 370 Dec call	16.25	−9.875	6.375
Sell 310 Dec put	11	−0.875	10.125
Net	2.25	15.125	17.375
		Effective price	342.625

Scanning down the "Results" column, note that the long call accounts for most of the gain in Scenario A while the short call generates a loss and the short put generates a modest gain. The net gain is 10.25 cents a bushel. In Scenario B, where the volatility drops 10 percentage points, the long call made a more modest gain (almost 5 cents a bushel) while the short call made 1.75 cents and the short put made 8.25 cents. The net gain here is 14.875 cents a bushel. In Scenario C, where the volatility dropped 15 percentage points, the long call contributed less than a cent, but the short options made strong contributions for a 17.375 cents a bushel net gain.

This strategy lowered the cost of wheat anywhere from 10.25 cents a bushel to 17.375 cents a bushel. These amount to significant improvements on the US$3.60-a-bushel ending futures price. Yet the bulk of the gain from this strategy in Scenarios B and C results from the effect of the volatility change, not from the price change.

While this example only hints at the opportunities that options can make available, it should serve to show that options on futures give users more ways to achieve their risk management and trading goals than futures alone. Options allow users to capitalise on price changes, as do futures, but they also allow them to put volatility changes to work for them.

Looking forward in conclusion

People can control prices in one of two ways. They can turn to the government for price controls, or they can turn to the derivatives markets to manage the price risks of fluctuating commodity supply and demand. Dan Morgan, in *Merchants of Grain*, provides an especially telling comment on the efficacy of central planning in this regard. When the Soviet army invaded Czechoslovakia in 1968, Morgan reports, "Czechoslovaks looked so well-fed and prosperous that some of the occupying troops refused to believe that they had invaded a socialist country" (p. 11).

Indeed, more and more countries are at least exploring the idea of establishing futures and options exchanges. Market demographics are shifting. Factors such as the growth of the South American soybean crop and the re-emergence of Eastern Europe as a major centre of wheat production have been cited above. Further, the phasing out of price supports in Western Europe and major changes in the Asia-Pacific economies are exposing commodities users to increasing amounts of price risk. All of these developments will motivate the emergence of new exchanges. Or regional exchanges may form partnerships with larger, more globally oriented exchanges. These developments may lead to new contracts as well.

Much of the buzz in other markets concerns electronic trading. This has been slower to develop in the US agricultural markets. As more and more global market users enter the mix, and as demand for electronic access to these markets increases, this may change.

In sum, the need for futures to be invented is even greater than it was when futures were invented. Given the price risks that producers, merchants and users of agricultural commodities face, a world without agricultural futures and options is difficult to imagine.

BIBLIOGRAPHY

Morgan, D., 2000, *Merchants of Grain* (Lincoln, NE: Authors Guild Backprint.com).

Petzel, T. E., 1989, *Financial Futures and Options* (New York: Quorum).

4

OTC Instruments

Nigel Scott and Hendrik Wijnen

Rabobank; Cargill

The previous chapter described a range of exchange-traded instruments available to agricultural businesses who wish to manage their market price risk. However, exchange-traded instruments sometimes fail to meet all of these businesses' needs:

❑ The commodities underlying the exchange-traded contracts may always not be identical, in terms of location, quality or origin, to the commodities of interest to the businesses concerned.

❑ The structures of the exchange-traded contracts may not always be appropriate for the companies seeking protection. For example, an Australian wheat producer who is otherwise satisfied with Chicago futures and options as hedging instruments may require AU$-denominated rather than US$-denominated price protection to reflect his AU$ cost structure.

❑ Exchange-traded contracts typically require cash payments upfront for initial margin and variation margin, whereas in the agribusiness world cash may not always be available.

All these drawbacks could be remedied by moving away from exchange-traded instruments to over-the-counter (OTC) instruments. OTC instruments are individually negotiated, cash-settled contracts agreed between two parties with specific terms reflecting both parties' needs and desires. Their terms could be identical to those of exchange-traded instruments but need not necessarily be so. For example, the two parties could agree an OTC instrument linked to the price of Chicago wheat as translated to Australian dollars at the prevailing AU$–US$ exchange rate.

This chapter, therefore, outlines in more detail the potential applications of OTC derivatives. It contains the following sections:

1. A survey of the features of the global commodity markets as they impact on the use of exchange-traded or OTC derivatives to manage risk.
2. A description of a typical risk management problem facing a raw-cotton trader. The features and complexities of this problem will be used to illustrate some of the following sections.
3. An explanation of how OTC instruments work in practice.
4. A comparison of OTC and exchange-traded instruments, focusing on key benefits and features of OTC instruments.
5. Illustrations of potential difficulties with OTC instruments.

The chapter closes with a report on an innovative commodity risk management programme, which is introducing OTC hedging instruments, at fair market prices, to farmers in the developing world.

Features of the global commodity markets and their impact on OTC derivatives

The production, shipping and sale of agricultural commodities is incredibly diverse. With a large number of origins, qualities, grades and delivery locations, commodity prices vary considerably from place to place, origin to origin and quality to quality.

As a result of these numerous characteristics and the large numbers of combinations of these characteristics that determine commodity prices, different prices observed for the same commodity can vary enormously. For example, a high-micronaire, high-grade piece of cotton FOT Ex Gin Azerbaijan varies considerably in value from a piece of SJV cotton FOB the west coast of the US. Soft feed wheat FOB UK varies considerably in value from wheat for human consumption, eg, Hard Milling Wheat Rail-delivered Gulf, United States. All of these variations have a very real impact on the ability for a market participant to perfectly hedge an open commodity position in a highly variable underlying market.

The trading of commodities by producers, traders and consumers is mainly done through spot or forward fixed-price contracts. Bespoke in nature, and, by definition, off-exchange, these contracts are the primary method of hedging commodity contractual commitments. Should a contract or position be entered into where no equal and opposite contract exists or can be entered into, principals have few possibilities of matching off their liabilities.

In order to understand the hedging requirements of a commodity market participant, a complete understanding of the problems and concerns regarding physical commodity contracts is vital. The derivative utilised must of course perfectly mirror the market movements of the underlying, but additionally must be appropriately flexible to mirror the underlying contracting issues associated with physical commodity. Some of the main issues impacting the physical trade of raw commodity are described below.

SUPPLY – CAN BE UNRELIABLE

The responsibility of the deliverer or shipper is that they deliver or ship on time, in the right quantity at the right point of delivery. The term "delivered" is often regarded as synonymous with cost, insurance and freight in the international cargo trade. Generally, the seller's risks are greater in a delivered transaction because the buyer pays on the basis of landed quality/quantity, depending on the terms of the trade and commodity. Risk and title are borne by the seller until such time as the commodity passes from seller to buyer.

The impact of non-delivery or non-receipt of the commodity impacts both the buyer's and seller's positions, which has a knock-on effect on the derivatives either party has contracted. An example would be tenor – the delay of physical delivery could require the derivative to be rolled back a commensurate period of time.

QUALITY – CAN BE UNRELIABLE

Quality problems include commodity being the incorrect origin or grade, or other quality parameters. There could be evidence of extraneous matter within the delivery, or potential contamination through the use of inappropriate packaging, overageing or moisture retention. There could be damage to the wrapping or bagging.

Variation in quality has basis implications for the derivative hedge – for example, if the hedge is for FAQ feed barley, but the underlying is malting barley, the hedger is exposed to basis risk.

MARKET RISK – CAN LEAD ALSO TO CREDIT RISK

The risk of loss in value, due to adverse movements in price of commodity on a spot or forward basis, is commonly referred to as market risk. This is the main subject of this chapter.

But market movements also have the potential to create credit risk in the form of wilful contract default if the market moves sufficiently to give the counterparty an incentive to fail the trade and to seek a new trading partner at a new price. This kind of default can of course turn a derivative hedge position that perfectly matches, or is opposite to a physical position, into an outright speculative position. In this case a hedge would have to be immediately unwound, or else a flat-price position would remain, exposing the counterparty to market risk.

The best way of explaining how all of these risks effect a commodity transaction is to take an example.

A typical risk management problem in raw cotton

TANZANIAN ROLLER GINNED TYPE 1 (TANZ RG T 1) COTTON PURCHASED FROM A TANZANIAN COOPERATIVE BY A MERCHANT

In June, a merchant purchases 500 bales of Tanzanian Roller Ginned Type 1 cotton at US$0.70/lb for delivery free on truck (FOT) ex Gin Mwanza for December delivery, ie, six months after trade date.

The merchant takes on the obligation to make payment for the 500 bales in six months' time to the co-op, against receipt of the cotton by his chosen haulier.

He is exposed to the following risks:

❏ The supplier not delivering the requisite grade or the specified quantity at the contract stipulated date.
❏ The haulier not being able to transport the cotton from the gin to the port.
❏ The overall market price of cotton falling between June and December, with the result that he sells the cotton to its eventual consumer at a loss.
❏ The specific market price of Tanzanian RG T 1 at the port falling between June and December, even if the cotton market in general is stable, again resulting in the merchant taking a loss when the cotton is finally sold.
❏ Forex risk, if not a dollar-denominated company.

The first of these risks should properly be considered as credit or counterparty risk and is discussed in a later chapter of this book. The last two are market risks, which can be hedged only by market transactions, either in the physical market or in derivatives.

A physical hedge would simply take the form of a contract for the sale of the physical cotton in December. The merchant could contract this hedge with another trader or, perhaps, with the eventual processor. In this case he would run credit risk on both of his transactions: if market prices rose then his seller might have an incentive not to deliver, and if market prices fell then his buyer might decide not to pay.

Why might the merchant decide to hedge his market price risk via a derivative rather than via a physical contract?

❏ Speed: To hedge a physical position in the quickest possible time.
❏ Confidentiality: He may not wish to betray his position to the rest of the physical market.
❏ Liquidity: The physical market may be unattractively priced, or simply not bid or offered in volume, whereas the derivative market may be the opposite.
❏ Flexibility: In order to finesse the logistics until the last moment on a trade flow.
❏ Price: To take advantage of an arbitrage between the physical market and the derivative markets.
❏ Credit risk management: The physical forward carries credit risk, which he may prefer to take with a derivative house – which will typically be a well-rated bank, an exchange or a major trader – than with a local physical trader who may have no scruples about disclaiming the trade if prices fall and it becomes attractive for him to do so.

By trading a derivative, the merchant is effectively separating his physical ownership of the cotton from his economic risk. He retains the physical ownership, control over logistics and the choice of physical counterparty at the conclusion of the transaction. However, he trades away the economic price risk associated with this physical ownership.

How this works in practice is described in the next section.

How OTC instruments work in practice

HEDGING WITH COMMODITY SWAPS

If the merchant decided to trade away his price risk via an OTC derivative, the simplest instrument for him to use would be a swap. A commodity price swap is a forward price agreement between two counterparties who agree to settle the difference between:

❑ a fixed price, established on trade date by mutual consent; and
❑ a floating price index published by an independent third party, whose value will be examined at the end of the transaction on "fixing date".

Settlement would normally be made a few business days after fixing date.

The term "swap" is used because settling the difference between two price indices is analogous to "swapping" the prices. One party pays one index (or a fixed amount) and in exchange the other party pays another index. In practice, settlement is always made net by whichever party owes the larger amount.

The swap is called a "derivative" because it is a contract whose value is *derived* from the third-party, independent price source. The swap cannot reference the physical bales of Tanz RG T 1 traded by the merchant, free on truck ex gin or delivered to the port, but will instead reference an index such as the Cotlook "A index", which is the nearest widely traded index to Tanz RG T 1.

Because the merchant is long-cotton from his physical trade, he would wish to use the derivative to go short, in other words to notionally sell cotton at a fixed price. He might therefore contract as follows:

❑ To receive a fixed price of US$0.70/lb on a notional quantity of 500 bales.
❑ To pay the "A index" on the same notional quantity.

If the index rises over US$0.70/lb then he would make a market-related gain on the physical sale of his cotton but pay away the difference via the derivative. If the index falls below US$0.70/lb then the opposite would take place. In either situation his general price risk is zero.

Of course, the merchant has no guarantee that the price he achieves when making his physical sale will equate to the "A index" price when the swap matures. This difference between the real physical market and the index is known as "basis risk".

Basis risk is simply the risk of loss due to imperfect correlations between the derivative and the physical price. Traditionally, when derivatives were confined to exchange products, basis was described solely as the differential that exists at any time between the cash, or spot, price of a given commodity and the price of the nearest futures contract for the same or a related commodity. Today we may redefine basis to be the differential that exists at any time between the cash, or spot, price of a given commodity and the price of the nearest derivatives (OTC or exchange-based) contract for the same or a related commodity. Basis may reflect different time periods, product forms, qualities or locations.

It should be noted that with the multiplicity of qualities of different commodities, basis risk can generally not be completely removed. However, it can be significantly reduced through the choice of an appropriately narrowly defined index. However, there is always a trade-off between basis risk and liquidity – more broadly defined indices are of interest to more traders and are therefore more liquid, but in turn carry more basis risk, if it is not exactly the same index that represents the physical goods traded. This trade-off is a key difference between the exchange-traded and the OTC derivative markets – the exchange typically being more liquid in the near maturities but with an underlying that carries considerable basis risk versus any particular physical piece of commodity other than one deliverable into the contract.

Interestingly, there is a lower threshold of volume required to ensure that an OTC market succeeds than the higher volume required to ensure that an exchange-based market succeeds. This is often because the type of trades that occur on an exchange follow small-sized, frequent hedging patterns, while an OTC market in soft commodities is typified by infrequent or intermittent, large notional transactions. The former can sustain the costs involved in an exchange, if the small trades are done in sufficient volume. If not, the futures market fails. Frequently, the research performed that identifies the need for a futures market is justified – it is perhaps the daily volume, or pattern of trades, which is overestimated, resulting in the failure of an exchange-based market. It is the underlying, true rationale for a market that is often then picked up by an OTC market maker. The resulting OTC market formed can be successful where the futures market failed.

An example of the trade-off between basis risk and liquidity was seen in the fertiliser swaps markets. The CBOT futures market had failed as a result of lack of liquidity required to support an exchange-based product, and an OTC market was formed for DAP (diammonium phosphate), FOB Tampa. Then, in 1999, four granular-urea markets were formed, and three markets formed in prilled urea. All the markets had legitimate basis and market requirements for a derivative. However, only three, out of the total six, urea markets survived, because of liquidity challenges. The fertiliser swaps markets remain an interesting example of a swaps market experiencing some measure of success, following a futures market failure. This has been seen in cotton and the freight swaps markets (FFAs) as well.

In the final analysis, the merchant's profit margin must also depend on his skill in managing the logistics and his ability to negotiate with his two physical counterparties around the general market price. No amount of derivative financial engineering can replace these skills and abilities.

COMMODITY SWAPS DISSECTED

Characteristics to be specified in a swap agreement are the following:

❑ Which type of index or fixed price is to be received by each counterparty. The main indices used in commodity price swaps are the settlement prices of commodity futures or independent, published reference prices.
❑ The maturity of the swap, which would generally be from three months to five years.
❑ The frequency of the fixings, which can either replicate the first notice day of a future's strip or can be monthly, quarterly or annually. The example above was designed to hedge a single physical transaction and had only one fixing date, but a merchant with continuing supply over a number of months, or a processor with continual purchases over a number of months or years, might wish to trade a swap with multiple fixing days to match his business profile.
❑ The averaging method, if averaging is required. Many agricultural businesses are more exposed to the *average* price of their commodity over a period of days or months than to any particular price on a single fixing date. Averaging is therefore very common in commodity swaps and is one of the key advantages of OTC products as compared with exchange-traded ones.
❑ The level of the fixed price, determined at the outset of the transaction depending upon market conditions and the characteristics of the underlying transaction, which is effectively the level at which the counterparties notionally "buy" or "sell" commodity via the swap.
❑ The notional quantity to which the prices are applied, which might be quoted in MT, bales, bushels, lb or in "futures contract" equivalents. If the transaction has multiple fixings, the notional quantity may vary between fixing dates, in accordance with a schedule, which would be mutually agreed at the start of the transaction. The seasonal nature of agricultural production means that some kind of notional quantity schedule is a common feature of commodity swap contracts and the ability to tailor-make fixing dates and amounts per fixing is another key benefit of OTC as opposed to exchange-traded contracts.
❑ The currency in which settlement is to be made and the exchange rate. Some agricultural businesses will wish to receive a fixed price in their domestic currency

in order to hedge their domestic production costs. In this case their counterparty may have to trade a foreign-exchange-rate hedge as well as a commodity hedge in order to secure their positions.

❑ Upfront fee. If the swap is struck at market prices no upfront fee would be payable. However, an off-market commodity swap would require a fee payable at some point before maturity in order to bring its economic value back to fair value.

The cancellation of a commodity price swap remains possible throughout the transaction's lifetime, by transacting an identical but opposite swap. The replacement cost of this swap will be dependent on the market conditions prevailing at the date of cancellation.

In practice, banking counterparties prefer to transact commodity swaps under the master agreement of the International Swaps and Derivatives Association (ISDA), which has standard definitions for commodity swaps. However, other documents are used as well. The credit and documentation implications of using or not using ISDA are discussed in Chapter 10, which covers credit risk management.

COMMODITY OPTIONS

In the example above, the profits and losses on the commodity swap balanced almost exactly – basis risk excluded – against the profits and losses on the merchant's physical trade. What if the merchant wished to have the best of both worlds: to receive protection from his derivative if prices fell but to avoid paying away when price rose? In this case he would purchase a commodity put option: if prices fell his effective selling price would be flat because his derivative gains and physical losses would net to zero, while if prices rose his effective selling price would rise, too.

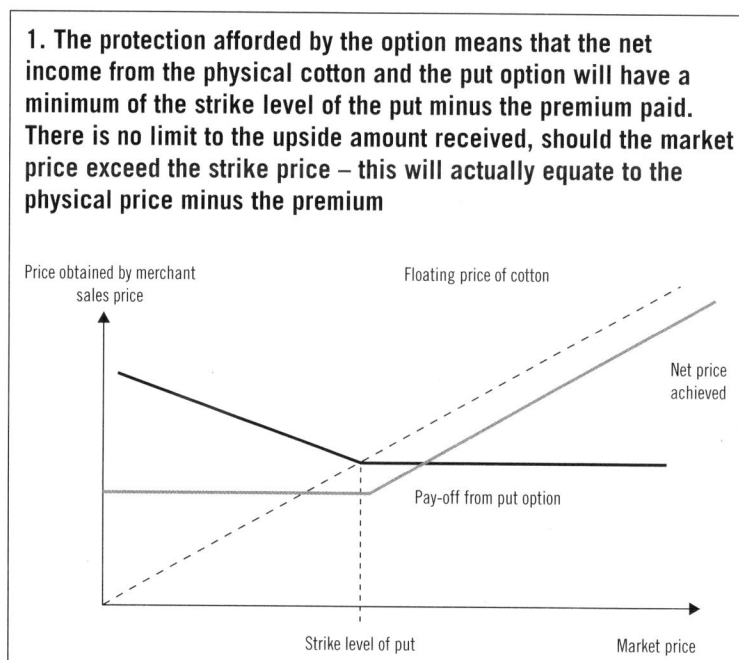

1. The protection afforded by the option means that the net income from the physical cotton and the put option will have a minimum of the strike level of the put minus the premium paid. There is no limit to the upside amount received, should the market price exceed the strike price – this will actually equate to the physical price minus the premium

Characteristics to be specified in an option agreement include all the characteristics required in a swap agreement as well the following.

❑ Which counterparty is the buyer of the commodity price option and which one is the seller.
❑ The premium amount, which is always paid by the buyer to the seller, and the premium settlement date, which is usually a few business days after trade date.
❑ The style of the option, which may be European if it can only be exercised at maturity or American if it can be exercised before maturity. Most exchange-traded options are American.

❏ The expiry date or dates, which replace the fixing dates in the swap contract.

❏ The option strike, which is determined at the outset of the transaction and corresponds to the fixed price of the swap.

OTC and exchange-traded instruments compared

HISTORICAL DEVELOPMENT OF EXCHANGE-TRADED AND OTC MARKETS

Commodity markets of today originated from simple farming markets and vary in their level of freedom. This has a direct impact on the requirement for a hedging programme – in an environment of a controlled or semi-controlled market there is arguably little need for hedging for any subsidised or protected parties. Interestingly, though, subsidised markets can, through the reference of the subsidy, provide additional or new ways of hedging an overall total return for trader, producer or consumer. For example, the US Farm Program provides such possibilities when combined with hedging instruments.

The Commodity Brokers' Association was formed in the beginning of the 19th century, which approximately coincided with the initiation of trading cotton futures in Chicago on the CBOT. The first cotton contract was traded in 1865 and was based on the Liverpool Commodity Exchange price of physical contracts. A migration ultimately occurred to New York, where the NYBOT and then the NYCE traded exchange-based futures and then options contracts. At the same time, contracts on grains and other agricultural products gained in volume and popularity.

It is not within the remit of this chapter to further discuss exchange-based instruments, but it is important to grasp the choices facing a holder of a physical position as to the hedge he or she employs for an opposite physical position. The choice of which derivative to use is up to the market counterparty, who should make an informed decision based on the underlying physical position held and the characteristics of the hedging instruments available.

Exchange-based derivatives are designed to appeal to the widest possible audience to achieve reasonable liquidity, so they are homogeneous in nature. In order to encourage the maximum number of transactions they are traded in one location for a specified number of hours. Information about the exchange, market information and prices are published on the Internet, with a slight delay, and in real time from international service providers. This ensures global availability to the knowledge of this market, and allows price discovery to take place.

But with this liquidity and price transparency has come a cost, namely that futures contract specifications have been designed, broadly speaking, for domestic US counterparties to hedge the majority or all of their risk, but not for other global counterparties with different qualities, origins and locations. Globally, the US futures exchanges have allowed only a section of market participants to hedge all of their risk. This has meant that counterparties have retained exposure to basis risk and, in some instances, the hedged risk has been largely offset or even exceeded by the additional risk introduced by the basis between the exchange-traded product and the physical commodity being hedged. This is clearly not a result that users would have desired when entering a derivative contract to hedge a physical commitment.

An Indonesian purchaser of grain who is a multi-origin purchaser of grain could hedge his short position through physical contracts, but, if he was unable to do this, may purchase futures on the CBOT or Kansas. In this case, he may actually end up purchasing grain from Australia or the US, or a variety of other origins, so he is well and truly exposed to basis risk.

Increasingly in grain markets, this is becoming an issue, as even traditional single-growth purchasers of US grain turn to other origins, for a variety of reasons. A good example would be Morocco, or even Egypt.

As a result of efforts to reduce basis risk in other commodities, mainly oil components, some OTC commodity swap markets began to develop in the 1980s. Next to be traded as OTC contracts were swaps in freight. Then, in the 1990s, soft-commodity OTC contracts began to be traded. These markets were based on the concept of a contract for difference, derivative markets that were cash-settled and derive their price reference from the price of physical commodity against which market participants are trying to hedge their risk. Interestingly, while swaps were traded in traditional exchange-based commodity markets, there were other, slightly more exotic, commodity underlyings traded, albeit in tiny volumes: for example, corn gluten feed pellets, CIF A/R (Amsterdam/Rotterdam). This was a natural progression for grain traders, used to trading "string" contracts, as they effectively had been trading "paper" markets anyway: there was little chance in a string contract of actually being the recipient of the cargo unless so desired. Commodity swaps form a small part of the overall financial OTC swaps markets, whose outstanding notional amounts are currently estimated to be valued at US$83 trillion.

EXCHANGE-TRADED OR OTC?

How would a market participant decide whether to use exchange-traded or OTC derivative products to hedge his price risk? Table 1 outlines the key features of commodity derivative contracts in general and illustrates how they are reflected in exchange-traded and OTC products.

It is clear from the Table 1 that they key benefits of the OTC products as against the exchange-traded ones are related to tailoring and specialisation. A few examples, which illustrate these features, are discussed in more detail in the rest of this section.

Table 1		
Feature	Exchange-traded	OTC
Price transparency	Excellent	Poor
Counterparty risk	Practically none	Significant (see Chapter 10)
Liquidity	Excellent for near months, can be difficult for longer maturities	Less liquid than the exchanges in the near months, more flexible otherwise
	Can be a barrier for a successful exchange market if insufficient daily volume	Can be successful with smaller daily volumes that an exchange market
Accounting, booking and valuation	Very transparent	Require derivative-specific skills
Cashflows and margin calls	Initial and variation margin required, can cause major liquidity problems for hedger if timing of margin calls on hedge fails to match cash received on core commodity transactions	Can be adjusted to match perfectly with cashflows of underlying physical business
Underlying price indices	Typically US-based, with the exception of London sugar/coffee/cocoa and Paris grain contracts	Any index in the world can be used provided it is calculated by a reliable independent third party
Tailoring	None possible other than selection of contract type, contract month and number of contracts to trade	Complete flexibility over quantity, maturity, settlement formula, averaging, foreign exchange components of the settlement index, etc
Brokerage	Small and transparent	Can be significant, and extent of bid–offer spread not always obvious to the end user
Cost-effectiveness overall	Excellent on brokerage, but client may end up buying more protection than he needs	Can be cheaper if tailored structure is a better match with client needs

CROSS-CURRENCY SWAPS AND OPTIONS

Most exchange-traded derivatives are priced in US$. But, with an OTC transaction, a bank can quote a producer (in the client's time zone) a fixed price in the producer's own currency. For example, he might quote AU$400 per metric tonne FOB NSW port on 20,000 tonnes of canola with an expiry in December 2004. This will automatically be closed at the nominated benchmark yielding an AU$ profit or loss. Otherwise, the producer would have had to trade futures on the Winnipeg Commodity Exchange and then transact separately the equivalent amount of foreign exchange, closing out the futures and foreign exchange separately to realise gains and/or losses.

A reasonably sophisticated Australian producer with 24-hour futures and foreign exchange trading capability would certainly be able to do the simultaneous foreign exchange and commodity trades himself. But an OTC market maker could also quote an option struck at the same fixed price in AU$. For the producer to replicate this himself would require continual night-time (in the Australian time zone) access to both the commodity and the foreign exchange markets as he adjusted his hedges. If he wanted to trade a very large volume, he may simply not be able to trade on the exchange at all. This level of operational activity would probably cost an ordinary producer more than any potential saving from using exchange-traded rather than OTC markets. The cross-currency commodity option, which is relatively easy to price and hedge, thus provides a powerful demonstration of added value that can be obtained from OTC market makers.

TERM STRUCTURE EXTENSION

A term structure extension swap consists of the provision of a commodity price swap beyond the term of the futures market between a fixed-price payer and a floating-price receiver. The fixed price is calculated by the bank and, at each fixing of the floating reference price, the level established is compared to this fixed price.

This product is designed for producers and consumers who are seeking to guarantee the price of a future unpriced physical sale or purchase beyond the term of the futures market and of course does not involve the physical sale or purchase of physical commodity. So swaps can be structured for periods of time significantly beyond where exchange-traded products stop trading, and this is the other particular area where swaps have developed. Banks make prices to commodity clients for tenors far in advance of traded months on futures or options exchanges. The Australian and Asian markets have been particularly focused on these products, an indication of the combination of the sophistication of the investors, the longer-term view of markets held by the participants therein and the lack of subsidies that forces producers' minds to focus on longer-dated price protection strategies.

In the previous example of canola, an OTC market maker could quote a swap based on canola prices in AU$ three years hence, and could quote for a greater volume,

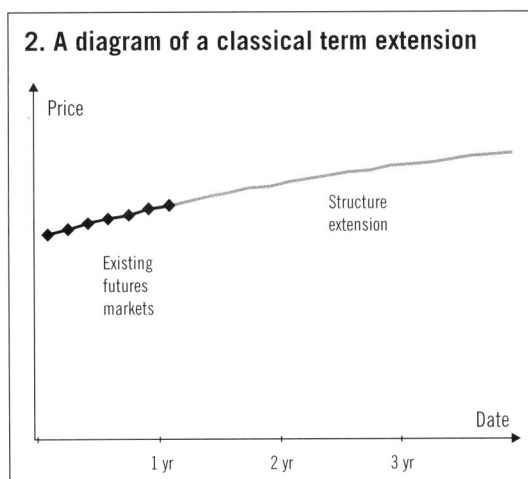

2. A diagram of a classical term extension

Price

Structure extension

Existing futures markets

Date

1 yr   2 yr   3 yr

or a longer tenor (term extension) than currently traded on the exchange. The producer could not replicate this himself. If he wanted a long tenor, or to trade a very large volume, he may simply not be able to trade on the exchange at all.

Since the turn of this century, coffee roasters have locked in long-term (3–5-year) low forward prices of coffee, textile mills have locked in long-term (2-year) low prices of cotton, and cocoa producers have locked in long-term (3-year) high forward prices of cocoa.

In summary, an OTC product applied properly can take some market or basis risk away from the grower, trader or consumer that is inherent in futures products. These risks are transferred to the provider of the OTC product.

Exchange-traded futures will not disappear. In fact, the gradual take up of OTC products may add to the liquidity of futures markets as they provide an ultimate clearing mechanism. The NYBOT has fully understood this and encouraged swaps use through Exchange For Swaps (EFS), whereby swaps positions can be migrated onto the board. It is possible, however, that over time the OTC product will become the product of choice by producers or consumers in some markets, liquidity and regulatory environment permitting.

Cost is clearly a driving force for change – OTC products allow the customer, who is often unable to pay up large sums, to pay only for the protection they really need. In some cases this cost saving can be significant over exchange-based products. If transacted through an institution that is providing credit already, such as a bank, OTC products don't necessarily require daily margining, potentially until the ability to pay the cash flow arrives (a producer sells his crop, for instance).

Potential difficulties with OTC instruments

LIQUIDITY

A market is said to be "liquid" when it has a high level of trading activity and open interest. Liquidity risk is the risk of loss due to inability to sell a derivative at a reasonable price and volume in a timely manner.

The commodity swaps market suffers from liquidity problems, which arise when market players utilise the market intermittently for large volumes. This is in contrast to the futures markets, where small regular transactions are executed by a wide range of players on a daily basis. Open interest is thus immediately visible. Liquidity risk has remained high throughout the life of the commodity swaps market. This has been exacerbated by some overly complex derivatives sold to some corporations – in certain parts of the world this has diminished the reputation of OTC derivatives in markets such as sugar. Liquidity risk should be clearly explained by the seller of derivative products, and this should be clearly understood by the "clients". The FSA in the UK, which governs (from a regulatory perspective) UK providers of soft commodity derivatives, has distinguished itself from other regulatory bodies globally in actively policing this aspect of capacity of counterparts to trade.

CREDIT

Credit issues will be addressed in Chapter 10, but it should be mentioned at this point that credit availability is one of the key drawbacks of the OTC derivative markets. Because of the provision of initial and variation margin, credit losses in the exchange-traded market are practically unknown. But credit losses in the OTC market are reasonably frequent and cause serious damage when they occur. As commodity markets tend to be more volatile than other financial markets, and counterparty credit quality tends to be lower, credit is a more dangerous issue in commodity markets than in other OTC derivative markets.

Credit problems can of course be reduced for market participants if they trade with a company that is well rated – preferably AA or above. And the credit risk of commodity derivatives should be seen in the context of the poor credit quality of many commodity players: it would certainly be preferable for most commodity merchants to trade long-dated price risk with a bank or OTC market maker, even one rated below AA, than to trade long-dated physical with a producer, unless the producer could come up with a letter of credit or bank guarantee. This is the reason, historically, that OTC swaps markets have evolved to banks and financial institutions that possess a good credit rating.

CONTRARIAN RISK

The seasonal nature of the world's commodity production, along with the function of buyers' and sellers' buying and selling habits, dictates the level of contrarian risk. An Ivorian cocoa producer is always technically long, a chocolate manufacturer is always technically short. Thus, contrarian risk naturally exists. The diversity of the global market – where commodities are produced in dozens of countries and traded in many more, with the ensuing variety of seasonal requirements – ensures, in theory at least, a natural spread of continuous contrarian risk.

Postscript: risk management using OTC instruments in the developing world

The majority of commodity producers in developing countries are, in general, unable to access derivative markets at all:

❑ The minimum size of contracts traded on organised exchanges may exceed the annual quantity of production of individual small and medium-sized producers.
❑ Small producers often lack knowledge of derivatives.
❑ Sellers of such instruments are often unwilling to engage with a new and unfamiliar customer base of small-scale producers, characterised by high transaction costs, diminished access to credit and increased performance risk.

They therefore suffer disproportionately from the effects of market price volatility and, as a result, are unable to access the credit resources they need to invest in and improve their operations and manage their risk more professionally.

One approach to mitigating the impact of price volatility on these small developing country farmers is to give them preferential access to risk management instruments available otherwise through international markets.[1] In 1999, the World Bank – with support from several donor governments, and in collaboration with other international organisations and private-sector representatives – started a project called the International Task Force (ITF) to make price risk management instruments available to farmers in the developing world, particularly the small ones, through cooperatives, producer organisations, banks and rural financial institutions, and traders.[2]

The role of the World Bank is that of a facilitator, providing technical assistance and capacity building to farmers and intermediary institutions that link farmers to risk management markets. Hedging transactions are carried out strictly on commercial terms and are transacted directly between the local intermediary and an OTC market maker in commodity price risk management instruments.

In 2002, the project entered into the implementation phase and several hedging transactions have now been concluded involving local producer organisations in Nicaragua, Tanzania and Uganda, and OTC market makers (one major international bank, Rabobank International, and one major trade house, Volcafe) in Europe and the USA. These pilot transactions in coffee assisted 250 farmers in Nicaragua, about 450 farmers in Uganda and a few thousand farmers in the case of Tanzania.

It is clear from anecdotal evidence in the trial transactions, that, in the future, price hedging via the international derivative markets will become a more regular feature of agriculture in developing countries and that this, in turn, will free up access to credit, to investment and to growth for farmers in these countries.

OTC INSTRUMENTS

1 *Some local hedging markets may also be good candidates for use of risk management, such as Argentina, Brazil, Hungary, India, Malaysia, South Africa.*
2 *Namely the European Union, and the governments of The Netherlands and Switzerland.*

RISK MANAGEMENT TOOLS AND INSTRUMENTS: THE PARTICIPANTS

5

Why Hedge?

Shawn Mills

Maple Leaf

Why hedge? There are numerous reasons for producers and purchasers of agricultural commodity products to consider hedging. Hedging can be used to lock in profits or minimise losses. Hedging can be used to ensure that your business is protected from drastic moves in the market and can ensure your business has a proper cashflow. And hedging can be used to remove the worry of price management and allow managers to focus on other aspects of the business such as production or marketing. All of these are great reasons to hedge and would lead you to ask the question "if you are *not* hedging, then why not?". Well, hedging tools are rarely perfectly correlated to the commodity to be protected and often, over time, the relationship of hedging tools to the commodity change – and as a result sometimes hedges do not work out as expected.

Introduction

This chapter will take a closer look at reasons for hedging, the tools available for hedging and how the effectiveness of these tools can change over time and why it is important to be mindful of the changes. We will also look at using the vertical co-ordination model to hedge and mitigate risks.

REASONS TO HEDGE

As outlined above there are a number of good economics reasons to hedge. One of the best examples as to why an agribusiness should hedge can be found when looking at the US live hog production sector. Figure 1 illustrates the profitability of the US hog production market by showing the US live hog market and the cost of production for US hogs.

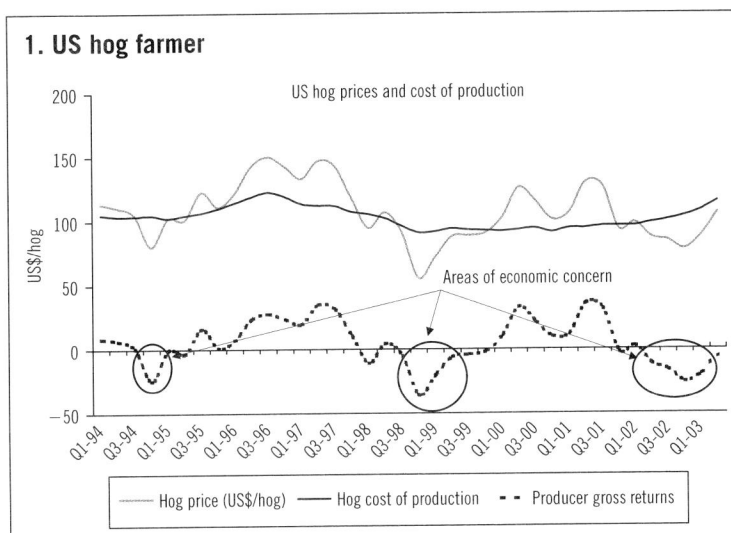

1. US hog farmer

US hog prices and cost of production

Areas of economic concern

Legend: —— Hog price (US$/hog) —— Hog cost of production - - Producer gross returns

If we take a closer look at Figure 1 we will see that in the Autumn of 1998 live hog prices dropped drastically below cost of production (break even) levels. During this period of time US hog farmers lost up to US$100/hog and many family farms went out of business. Could this have been avoided? If we look at the CME lean hog futures as a hedging vehicle then the answer to this question would be yes.

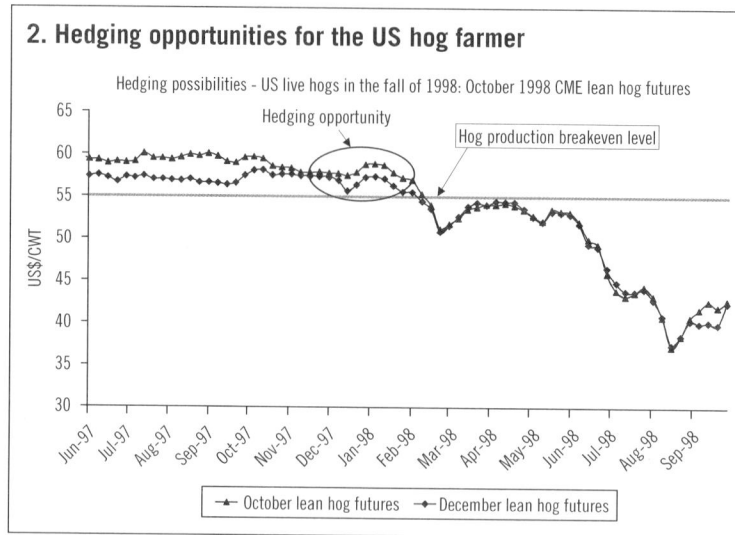

2. Hedging opportunities for the US hog farmer

Prior to the release of the USDA's June 1998 Hog and Pig Report, the CME live hog futures price for the October and December contracts were at levels that could be construed as breakeven to somewhat profitable levels. Figure 2 illustrates the CME hog contract price levels. Had US hog producers short hedged prior to 30th of June it might have been possible to hedge profits for the fourth quarter of 1998. At the very least, short hedgers could have limited the losses that would have subsequently occurred.

DEFINING RISK

The first step to hedging is to properly define your commodity risk exposure. The simplest way to define the commodities that impact your business would be to process map the commodities that you purchase and the commodities that you sell. For instance in the US hog production industry has considerable commodity risk exposure, both from a cost standpoint and a revenue perspective. Hog finishing operations need to purchase feedgrains (corn) and proteins (soybean meal). These are the critical commodity inputs that define the cost side of the business. The operation then sells market-weight pigs. The hog producers primary concern when it comes to commodity markets is that the commodity price for his/her market-weight pigs will not be enough to support the inputs costs (feedgrains and proteins). To mitigate against these commodity price risks the hog producer could enter into a series of contracts that define the feed costs and market pig prices to lock in a margin for the hogs.

If we return to Figure 1 we can see that there appears to be little relationship, in the short run, between the cost of production and the market price. However, if we look at hog costs versus hog price over a longer period of time we would see that there is a lag between these values. That is to say, that if feed costs were to rise, then cost of production would increase which, in the past, has led to a decrease in the number of hogs produced. This reduction in hog numbers ultimately leads to higher hog prices. It can then be said that higher grain prices will lead to higher pig prices and lower grain prices will lead to lower pig prices. This is an important inter-relationship to understand when thinking about long-term strategies.

CHOOSING AN EFFECTIVE HEDGING TOOL

There are a number of risks associated with hedging and in particular with improper use of hedging tools and the use of ineffective hedging tools. A major issue to be aware of in hedging is properly matching your commodity risk exposure with an appropriate hedging tool (ie, financial derivative). Some commodities do not have publicly traded derivatives to use and sometimes the paper market is so poorly correlated to the physical market that the hedger is trying to protect that the hedge becomes inefficient. This inefficiency can lead to basis risk, which can in turn compound potential losses. This section will look at using regression analysis to match your underlying physical commodity risk to the proper financial derivative.

Regression analysis is used to compare the variability of the price of the physical commodity and that of the financial derivative and accordingly, determine if that variability is related. Put another way, regression analysis attempts to prove or disprove that the change in the price of the financial derivative is the result of the change in the price of the physical commodity it is intended to protect. In keeping with our US hog producer, we can examine the CME lean hog futures and determine its effectiveness as a hedging tool for live hog prices.

It is apparent from Figure 3 that the CME lean hog futures price in the US is closely related to the cash price for US hogs and it appears that the CME futures would act as an effective hedge for hog prices. However, not until the completion of regression analysis can this be confirmed. From regression analysis we see that the two price series have an r-square value of 92.9% and a p-value of zero, which fits the definition for an effective hedge.

3. US cash hog price versus CME futures price

US lean hog futures versus the cash hog price

Regression equation:
Lean hog price $= 3.91 + 0.955^*$ NBC, r-sq $= 92.9\%$

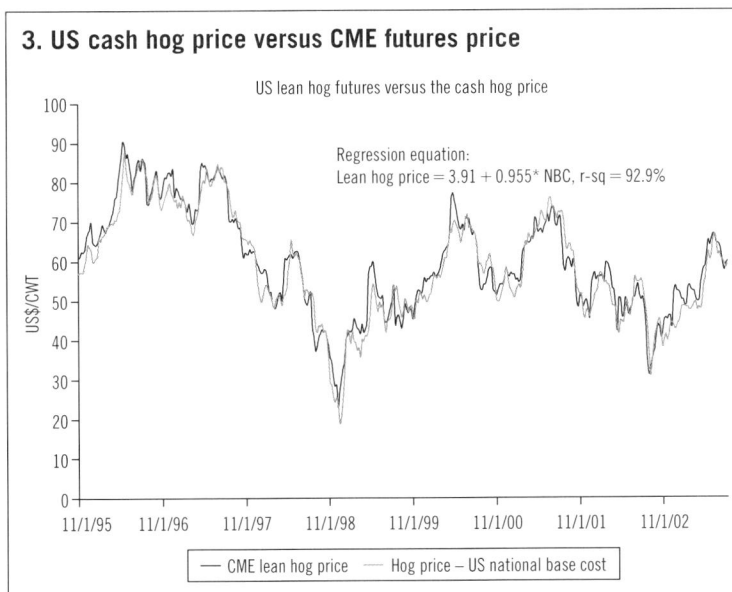

— CME lean hog price   — Hog price – US national base cost

Vertical co-ordination/integration as a hedging tool

Vertical co-ordination is often confused with vertical integration but there are a few major differences between the two models of ownership structure. The main concept that both vertical co-ordination and vertical integration share is that they both attempt to control multiple vertical levels of the industry that they participate in. For instance, in the pork industry an example of vertical integration or co-ordination would be controlling hog production, feed production, rendering assets and primary and secondary pork processing.

Further, the defining difference between the two models is that vertical integration uses physical ownership to gain control, while vertical co-ordination attempts to set contractual agreements to control the levels. Advocates for integration claim that ownership provides greater control and greater ability to make changes swiftly. Advocates of co-ordination claim that because ownership is retained at various levels, the owners are better motivated to produce high quality outputs and they will initiate changes much faster than their corporate-owned equivalents. Regardless of which is the better model, in the author's opinion one thing is for certain. The co-ordination model requires much less capital investment than the integration model, which potentially leaves vertically co-ordinated companies with more capital to spend in other areas of the company, such as in risk management.

4. Hog production and pork processing returns

US pork processor and US hog producer returns

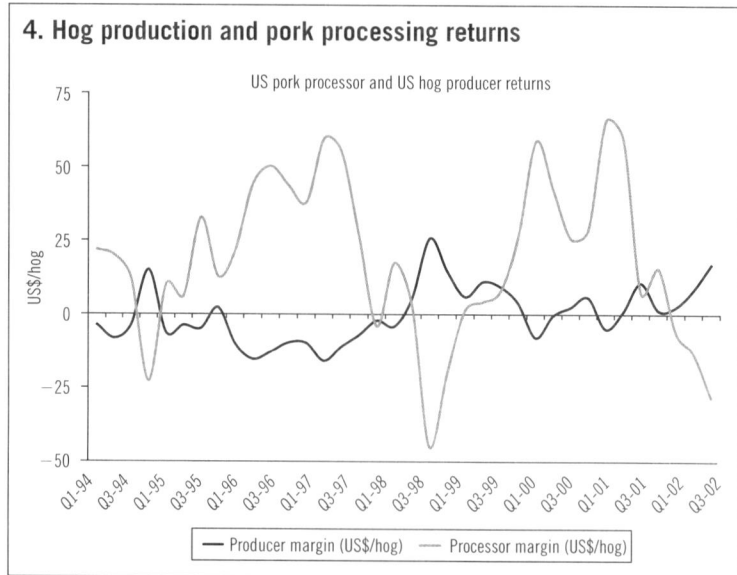

To illustrate how the vertical co-ordination or integration model can be used to hedge against commodity risk we once again return to the pork market. In this example we will look at a vertically co-ordinated/integrated company that has ownership in both hog production and primary pork processing. From Figure 4 we can see that, for the most part, the change in returns in the hog industry is almost exactly opposite to the change in returns in the pork processing industry. This reasoning provides a good argument for the need to combine the two businesses in order to hedge the returns of the organisation.

Figure 5 displays the expected margin from combining effective hog ownership with primary pork processing. The return is based on owning enough hogs to fill 25% of the

5. Vertically co-ordinated returns – hog production and pork processing returns combined

US pork processor and US hog producer returns
combining pork processing and hog production

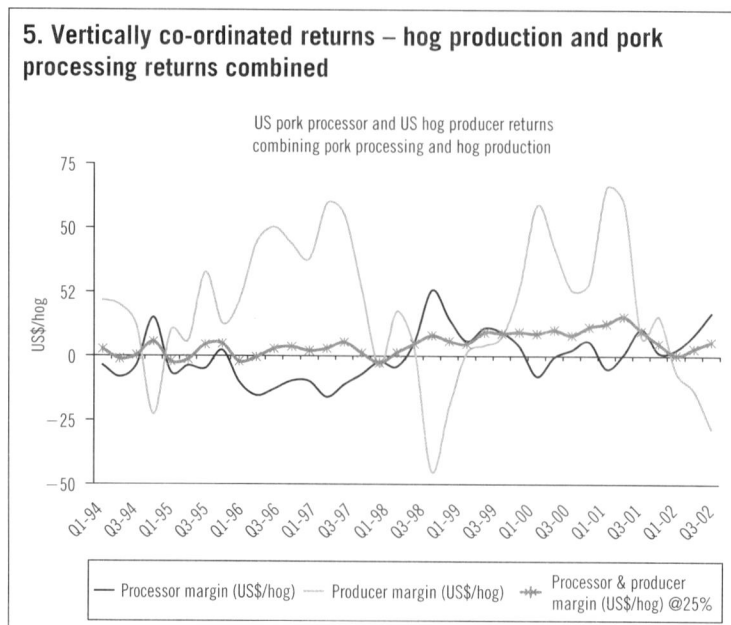

primary pork processing requirements. As is seen by the combined ownership margin line, the consistency of achieving profitable results is improved when there is ownership in one segment or the other. Additionally, volatility of the earnings is drastically reduced.

REASONS FOR CHANGES IN THE EFFECTIVENESS OF HEDGING TOOLS

Over time the effectiveness of hedging instruments can change. Productivity gains, technological changes and government policy can dramatically shape commodity prices and price volatility, which in turn can impact the effectiveness of hedging instruments. This section will discuss the reasons why hedging tools can gain or lose their effectiveness and why it is important to monitor changes.

Agricultural commodity markets are notoriously volatile and this volatility can lead to changes in the relationship between hedging tools and the commodity to be protected. These changes often lead to a decrease in the effectiveness of the hedge. Commodity markets are dramatically affected by uncontrollable events such as weather problems, disease outbreaks and also by government policy. Over the years commodity markets have become more vulnerable to world events as agriculture has become more global in nature.

Production problems can dramatically affect the ability to hedge. For producers who plan on providing physical delivery of a commodity, production risks can enter into the equation when hedging. For instance, if for some uncontrollable circumstance the hedger were unable to produce the physical commodity (ie, due to weather or disease problems) then in essence one half of the hedge position would be removed, leaving the hedger susceptible to losses in the derivative position.

Effectiveness of hedging tools is impacted by technological advancements in productivity and efficiency in gains in commodity production. These technological changes have led to dramatic impacts on price discovery for commodities. For instance, technological advancements have increased the yields of crops and efficiencies of feed conversions in livestock. Technology has allowed countries that formally couldn't produce crops and animals, because of climate or costs, to be agricultural leaders. China, for example, has historically been a net importer of agricultural commodities but now is a major exporter of commodities such as corn. This has led to a major shift in how the prices of agricultural commodities are derived. Now the crop growing conditions in countries such as China and Brazil are having almost as great an impact on the price of corn and soybeans as growing conditions in the US. While US corn futures are still an effective way for producers and users of corn to hedge, in the future this may not be the case.

New uses for agricultural products has also changed the way commodity prices are set in hedging relationships. Commodities such as grains can now be processed to produce ethanol to power gas combustion vehicles. Animal fats in the rendering business can also be further processed to create alternative fuel sources. Theses new uses create new demands and as a result impact commodity prices. For instance, if a world shortage of oil were to develop further processing of agricultural commodities into fuel would increase creating a price increase in these commodities. In the case of grains, US futures are still an effective way to hedge costs and revenues, but again, the relationship may deteriorate as a result of the mentioned new and diverse issues for crops.

Livestock diseases can have profound impacts on hedging and hedging tool efficiency. For instance, in recent years the outbreak of Bovine Spongieform Encephalopathy (aka. Mad Cow disease) has led to the ban on using any animal by-products in animal feeds in Europe. This ban has effectively displaced animal based proteins and fats for vegetable derived equivalents in Europe and has led other countries such the US and Canada to follow suit to a certain degree. As a result, there are now fewer end markets for animal based feed additives and accordingly, the price relationship between vegetable-based feed additives (such as Soybean meal and animal based feed additives, eg, meat and bonemeal (MBM)), has been drastically reduced. A further result has been the removal of the ability to effectively hedge MBM by using Chicago Board of Trade (CBOT) traded financial derivatives. Prior to the beginning of 1999, the price relationship of MBM from US renderers to CBOT traded soybean meal had an r-square value of 81.3% and a correlation of 90%, which made soybean meal an effective hedging instrument. Since the beginning of 1999 additional cases of BSE in the UK and cases of BSE in mainland Europe, Japan and Canada, – along with other disease events such as Foot and Mouth – have reduced the price relationship of MBM to soybean meal. The r-square value of the relationship between MBM and CBOT soybean meal has more recently been 59.4%, which is no longer at a level to be considered an effective hedging instrument.

Conclusion

There are a number of sound financial reasons for hedging, from guarding against bankruptcy to capturing profits. However, before entering into any hedging activity it is critical to accurately define and map out your company's commodity risks. It is also crucial to define any price inter-relationships in the case of multiple commodity exposure.

Vertical co-ordination or integration is a structural way for agribusinesses to mitigate commodity risk exposures. This method of risk mitigation looks at combining counter-cyclical returns of different segments in the same industry in order to maximise and reduce volatility of the company's earnings.

When contemplating hedging it is also important to understand that the marketplace is dynamic and that the hedging effectiveness of financial instruments that you might be using may also be changing. One should ensure that they fully understand the key drivers of the instrument that is used and that one is aware of any changes that may reduce its efficacy to a level where the instrument is no longer useful. Ultimately, using ineffective hedging tools can compound losses and lead to even greater financial distress.

6

The Australian Cotton Industry

Cliff White

Queensland Cotton

The success story of Australian cotton is one of tenacity and ingenuity; of agricultural innovation; irrigation and technological improvements. It is a little-known fact, however, that cotton was being promoted as having the potential to become one of Australia's staple crops as early as the 1840s.

However, the real development of the Australian cotton industry has occurred only in the past 30 years, and in particular major advancement during the past 15 years. Today, cotton is produced in the Emerald, Dawson Callide, Darling Downs, Macintyre Valley, Gwydir Valley, Namoi Valley, Macquarie Valley, Bourke and Hillston regions. Australian cotton has built its reputation on quality, lack of contamination, and delivery reliability, with each factor contributing value to a premium that has been established in the market. Subject to production constraints, cotton has become one of Australia's largest rural exports. Australia has also become one of the world's largest cotton exporters and as such can have an influence on price. The world export trade of cotton is approximately 30 million bales with Australia in normal seasons representing roughly 10% of this figure.

Unfortunately, our ability to produce is directly linked to water availability and in the past couple of seasons this has become a major issue. After we had established ourselves as producers of 3-million-bale-plus crops, severe drought reduced 2003 production to approximately 1.5 million bales. This drastic decline in production introduces many other issues to the marketing of Australian cotton, not least of which is a reduced supply-reliability factor. In turn this has the potential to impact a portion of the premium Australian cotton received in the international marketplace.

Marketing alternatives available to Australian cotton growers

Australian cotton producers market their product without benefit from government subsidies or tariff protection. For this reason, Australian cotton producers pay particular attention to the price they receive for their cotton and they are arguably the most advanced cotton producers in the world.

The need to maximise returns has in turn pressured Australian cotton marketers into providing highly competitive marketing contracts. These contracts are usually available up to three years ahead, and, as a consequence, over the past decade, a large proportion of risk (both production and price risk) has moved from the grower to the merchant.

The lack of regulation in the cotton industry means there is a strong relationship between the physical cotton market and the New York futures market. Merchants utilise New York futures and options in pricing strategies and offer a wide variety of contract alternatives. Generally, these contracts can be defined as *fixed-bale contracts* and *area contracts*.

FIXED-BALE CONTRACTS

Fixed-bale contracts allow growers to contract a fixed number of bales. It is normal practice to contract in multiples of 100 bales, except for when the ginning season produces smaller and/or spot lots. Contracts may be based in either Australian dollars or US dollars depending on the individual grower's choice. As contracts are for a fixed number of bales, growers are required to deliver all cotton nominated on the contract.

Fixed-price contracts

These are the simplest and most often used contracts. The relevant amount of cotton is contracted on the day at the price on that day. The price on the contract is final.

On-call contracts

On-call contracts are used by growers who wish to fix the three legs of their contract price (futures, exchange rate and basis) at different times. Growers may wish to do this to take advantage of ideal levels that may occur at different times for each of the different legs. Any leg can be fixed at any time and in any order. Once all legs are fixed the price is finalised.

Call-pool contracts

The call-pool contract is the most flexible of contracts. It is used by growers who wish to fully manage their cotton contract. As with on-call contracts, this contract enables growers to fix various legs of the contract as they wish. Call-pool contracts have the added advantage of allowing growers to trade cotton options and futures against the contract.

Pool

Growers have the option of contracting fixed bales to a pool managed by individual merchants. Pools are commonly used by growers who wish to delegate the time-consuming job of marketing to various merchants.

AREA CONTRACTS

Area contracts allow growers to contract a definable area (whole of farm, for instance, or whole of field) and so the cotton produced from this area. Growers may also elect to withhold a fixed number of bales to be sold against a separate contract and so use the area contract as a balance-of-crop contract. If no cotton is withheld, each and every bale grown from that area is committed to the contract.

Fixed-price contracts

Growers receive a fixed price for each and every bale delivered from a nominated area. Price is usually at a discount to the cash price of the day.

Call-pool contracts

Growers may wish to nominate an area rather than fixed bales to the call pool. As in the fixed-bale case, the management of the contract price is totally at the grower's discretion.

Pools

In any one season Australian merchants offer a number of area pools. Pools offer an indicative price and assume total production risk from the grower.

Marketing alternatives available to Australian cotton producers are not limited to the above. Depending on market and seasonal conditions, guaranteed minimum-price contracts, price-enhancer contracts and grade-bonus contracts have been offered, to name a few. These contracts essentially utilise New York cotton options to manage price risk.

Prices offered to cotton producers are all established on a base grade of "middling" with fibre length (staple) of $1-^3/_{32}''$ and a micronaire (fineness and maturity) of 3.5–4.9.

The value of quality delivered is determined by a premium and discount schedule, which means that growers can virtually deliver any grade of cotton against their contract.

Forward market makers

Forward purchasing has always been a part of the Australian cotton business. Forward selling by producers has provided farmers with certainty of cashflow and therefore allowed them to prepare strong business cases for expansion. Prices offered to the Australian cotton growers are traditionally quoted in Australian dollars per bale but the grower is fully conversant in how that price is derived. A daily price sheet will typically show a US-cents-per-lb quote converted at the day's US$–AU$ exchange rate.

As the Australian cotton industry has matured, so too has the appetite for risk. Daily cash prices are issued to cotton producers with offers being given for up to three years in advance. At the same time, international mills have shown an increasing tendency to be prepared to purchase cotton as far forward as possible, principally under "on-call" terms, whereby the final contract price is finalised in the majority of cases closer to the shipment period. Clearly, by offering cotton so far forward to both producers and consumers increases risk. "Time is a risk" and the increased length of time to market exposure is compounded by counterparty risk. Client management and understanding of clients' requirements and behaviour is an extremely important aspect of risk management, as the best hedging strategies in the world can be blown away in the event of a contract default. (Contract sanctity is an increasing issue in today's international cotton market.)

When contemplating forward contracting, serious consideration has to be given to the following:

❑ counterparty risk;
❑ country risk; and
❑ price risk.

While we can make subjective assessments on the first two, it is price risk that has to be managed. The Australian cotton industry relies heavily on "hedging" its exposures.

Basis traders

The Australian cotton industry is defined by its "basis" trading and so has developed a close (but not perfect) relationship with the New York cotton futures market. Indeed, outside of the United States the Australian industry represents the largest non-US participant in the futures market. Typically, the cotton trade refers to the Australian basis as being the difference between the relevant futures contract (predominantly the May or July contracts) and a cash-price-based cost-and-freight Far Eastern destination. Likewise, the Australian producer is familiar with his basis being the difference between New York futures and his cash price Ex gin. In the majority of times, New York futures provide an adequate hedge for Australian cotton; however, price divergence can occur and traders have to be ever conscious of the fact that New York reflects only the US cotton situation.

HEDGING

The Australian cotton industry has two major exposures: price-risk and currency-risk. Although it has always been possible to limit the exposure to each of these risks, the alternatives were either very limited or nonexistent.

Price could be hedged through the New York cotton futures market, which was at least an established market. The industry's US$/AU$ exposure was hedged through the banks on straightforward FECs. The advent of the derivatives market has changed the risk management alternatives available quite dramatically. The introduction of over-the-counter (OTC) options has opened up a completely new ball game in the risk management of both the commodity and foreign exchange exposure. Today we utilise the following risk management tools:

❑ New York cotton futures;
❑ New York cotton options;
❑ over-the-counter options; and
❑ swaps market.

These tools can also be described as limiting or non-limiting hedging instruments. Limiting instruments provide the buyer/seller with price protection at a specified level but at the same time limit the potential to profit from favourable movements. Swaps and NY futures contracts are examples of these instruments.

Non-Limiting instruments, such as NY and OTC options, also provide the buyer with price protection but do not limit the potential to profit from favourable movements.

Obviously non-limiting instruments would be the preferable hedging instrument. However, as the saying goes, you do not get anything for free and careful consideration has to be given for each instrument. The risk-to-reward evaluation is one that always has to be made. Can your position stand the consequences in a worst-case scenario?

Liquidity in the market place is always an issue and likewise, while risk management alternatives to straightforward futures trading can look attractive, the difficulty in getting positions established at prices that make sense for your trading book is a factor that can make these alternatives unattractive.

The financial requirements and demands of today's cotton trade have led the financiers of the industry to stipulate that price exposures must be closely monitored and trading policies established. Models based on earnings at risk (EAR), for example, are now increasingly required by financial institutions as evidence of sound risk management practices.

ACTIVE/PASSIVE HEDGING

To hedge or not to hedge? That is the question! Once a physical position is established, the decision has to be made about whether a "hedge" should be placed and therefore the market player has to determine if he wants to be an active or passive hedger.

The main tenet of "passive management" is that all price risk is hedged immediately and therefore futures are bought or sold on the opening of the cotton exchange in response to physical cash sales or purchases. This style of price risk management clearly limits a trader's opportunities. However, for the more conservative and risk-averse, it is a satisfactory direction to pursue.

For the more adventurous there is "active management", which, as the name suggests, promotes a more proactive approach to risk management. However, to pursue this direction requires more of a "view" to price direction, which can be derived from either a fundamental or technical approach or possibly a combination of the two. While the fundamentals of supply and demand will ultimately determine price direction, the introduction of increased position limits for the speculative element in the New York cotton futures market has introduced a significant degree of more volatility.

A trader who undertakes "active management" is seeking to improve the effective hedge rate and therefore reduce the buy basis or increase the selling basis. This can be accomplished by using options instead of futures or by delaying the futures trade until the price has moved favourably.

For example, a trader may sell 1,000 bales to a mill at 65.00 US cents/lb based off the current futures price of 60.00 US cents/lb. A passive trader will hedge this by buying futures at 60.00 US cents/lb when the market opens, thereby locking in the sales basis at 5.00 US cents/lb on – there is a slight risk that the opening price will be different, but this is unavoidable.

An active trader, however, may do one of the following:

❑ If he believes the market is likely to trade lower during the day he may place an order to buy futures at 59.00 c/lb rather than on the open. He obviously faces the risk that his view is wrong. However, if he is correct and the order is filled, he has improved the selling basis to 6.00 c/lb.

❑ If he is very bearish, he may buy a call option at a cost of 2.00 c/lb. If over time the market falls to 50.00 c/lb, then he can buy the futures at 50.00 c/lb and has now increased his selling basis to 13.00 c/lb (65.00 − 50.00 − 2.00). If he is wrong, however, his buy basis falls by the cost of the option to 3.00 c/lb on.

The Australian cotton industry is probably unique in the fact that the vast majority of its cotton is forward-sold for a number of crop years rather than when it is physically produced. Risk management is therefore very important to all players in the Australian industry, as price movement and exposure can be very dramatic. In order to recognise the importance of risk management to both producers and consumers in the world cotton industry it is necessary only to look back at the history of New York cotton futures prices over the past 10 years.

The interesting aspect of risk management adoption has been the fact that cotton producers in Australia have picked up and utilised the risk management tools available far more readily than cotton spinners. Why is this? Is it because the cotton grower has a more pressing requirement to protect his break-even cost rather than the cotton spinner, who is more dependent on the yarn price for his profitability?

Since 1992 the New York cotton futures price has averaged 65 c/lb, which historically has been a price that appeals to both growers and mills. However, the average yearly range has been 22 c/lb, and even more disturbing is the fact that, during the last 10 years, the cotton market has had a range of 87 c/lb, trading between a 30-year low of 28.20 c/lb and an all-time high of 115.20 c/lb.

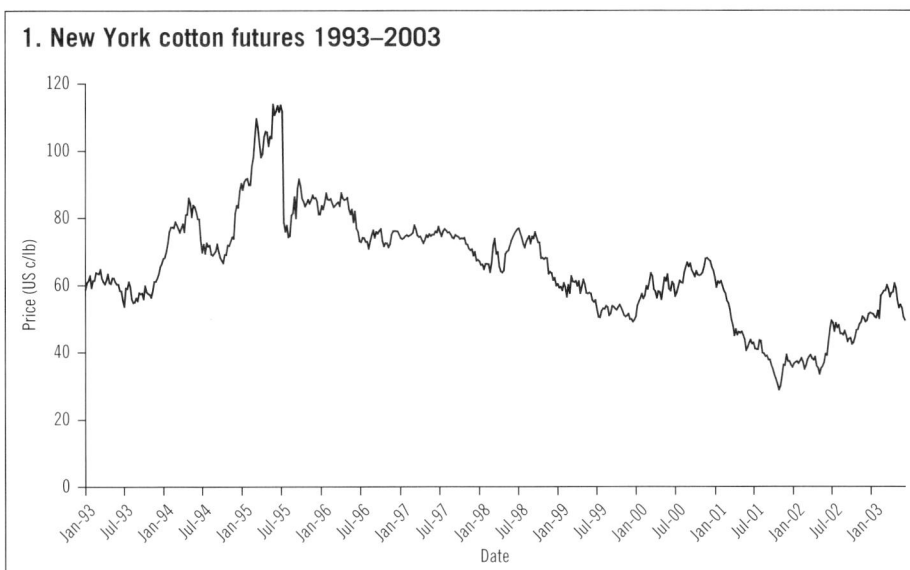

1. New York cotton futures 1993–2003

The numbers in Figure 1 demonstrate the high volatility of the cotton market and it is easy to imagine the large amount of money that could be lost or gained during these large price moves, especially since at the extremes cotton prices were well outside break-even levels for the producer and mill. It is during these times that the producers, consumers and merchants who had clearly defined risk management strategies fared much better than those who didn't.

Below are two case studies showing how a farmer and a mill used risk management strategies to protect their business during the 2001 season. The 2001 season was selected because it was a year that tested all members of the industry. Growers had to contend with a market that initially offered very attractive forward prices before beginning an unprecedented and relentless decline to 30-year lows and prices that most believed impossible, while mills had to cope with a market that, after rising for the whole of 2000, fell back to what had historically been good buying levels before, then declining to be half that value at the time of delivery. This decline is shown in Figure 2, which plots the New York cotton futures price during 2000 and 2001.

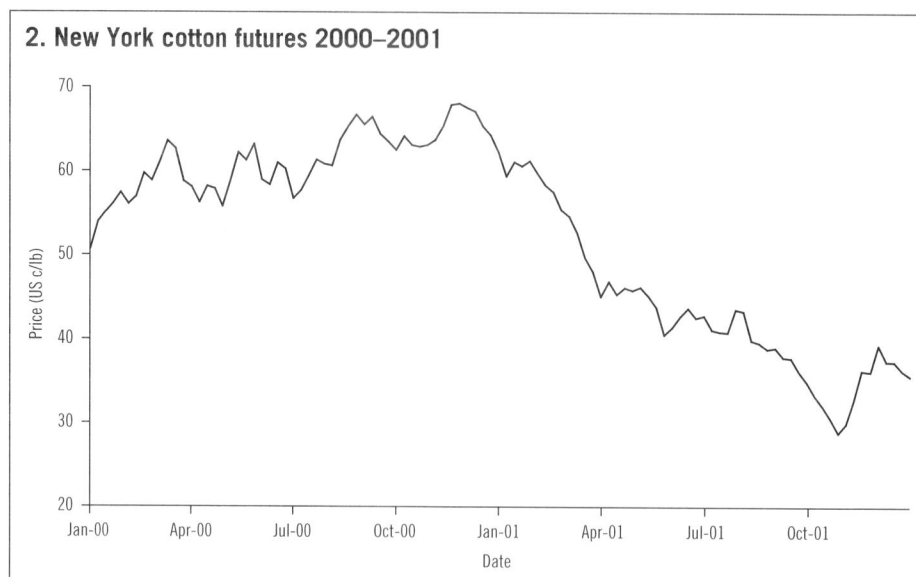

2. New York cotton futures 2000–2001

CASE STUDY: THE FARMER

There are a number of risks that a farmer must address when planning and implementing a risk management strategy however the main two are:

❑ Production: Despite being a mainly irrigated crop, droughts, hail and floods have taught the Australian grower that yearly production is never certain and therefore care must always be taken when committing to fixed-price sales.
❑ Falling price: Obviously this is a major risk and the one that risk management seeks to protect against. However, the risk is not simply that the price falls but that it falls below some important level that may be related to the grower's budget, debt levels or simply his break-even level. It is essential that this level be identified prior to his developing the strategy.

Australian cotton merchants offer growers numerous marketing alternatives. However, they generally fall into the following categories;

❑ Cash: The grower commits a fixed number of bales to the merchant and receives a fixed price per bale.
❑ Pool: The grower commits a fixed area but only an indicative number of bales and in return for this flexibility is given only an indicative price at the time of contract. This price may vary from the actual price received.
❑ Options: The grower uses cotton options to lock in a minimum New York futures price without having to commit fixed bales.

Our farmer usually grows 500 hectares of irrigated cotton and has averaged 8.50 bales per hectare for the last five years, giving an estimated production of 4,250 bales. He is an experienced grower and marketer and will often commit bales forward if the price is above A$500 per bale, since it is above his break-even of A$400 per bale and his budget of A$450.

Figure 3 shows the 2001 cash price.

February 2000: The price reaches A$500 for the first time, so grower sells 1,000 bales at AUS$500 per bale and is tempted to commit more. However, it is still seven months until planting and water supply is not yet assured, so he decides to wait.

3. Cash price 2001

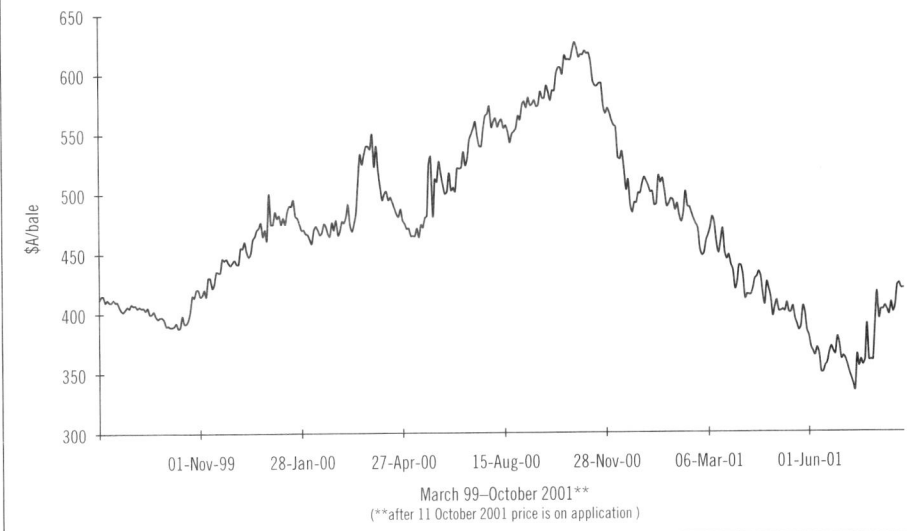

March 99–October 2001**
(**after 11 October 2001 price is on application)

1. September 2000: Sells 1,000 bales at A$570. Water supply is guaranteed and planting conditions are good, so he is confident in his production estimate of 4,250 bales. Fundaments appear bullish, so he does not commit any more.

2. January 2001: Although fundamental news remains generally positive, the market has fallen over 10 c/lb (A$90/bale) in the past month. At under 50% hedged, the grower is still overly exposed to a price fall but is reluctant to sell at current levels. Accordingly, he decides to hedge most of the crop by buying 20 May 60 c put options for 200 points (A$18/bale). The put options will lock in a minimum NYF price of 58 c/lb and still allow the grower to participate in any increase in the market.

3. April 2001: The crop is progressing very well and the initial estimate of 4,250 bales looks realistic. The grower's market view was wrong and the market has continued to fall, with cash prices now A$400 per bale. However, fortunately, the put options are now worth 14.00 c/lb (A$140/bale). Since the options are about to expire, the grower decides to sell them and at the same time sells 2,000 bales.

4. June 2001: The crop has been harvested and total production was a little better than expected at 4,700 bales. The grower still has 700 bales to market and can either sell the cotton or store it and sell at a later date. As this will incur additional charges, the grower decides to sell the 700 bales at the cash price of A$380 per bale. However, he also decides to purchase 7 December 44 c call options for 2.00 c/lb (A$18/bale) just in case the market rallies later in the year.

5. November 2001: December continued to fall during the year, so the call options expired worthless.

Results

❑ Sold physical cotton, 1,000 bales at A$500, 1,000 bales at A$570, 2,000 bales at A$400, 700 bales at A$380. Average price A$454.

❑ Bought 20 May 60 c puts at 200 points (A$18/bl)

❑ Sold at 1,400 points and generated a profit of A$244,000.

❑ Bought 7 December 44 c calls at 200 points (A$18/bl)

❑ Expired worthless – cost: A$12,600.

In summary, the grower's decision to purchase put options was an excellent idea. His physical sales averaged only A$454/bale. However, the option trades increased this to A$503/bale.

CASE STUDY: THE MILL

There are some similarities and some differences in the risks that mills must consider when devising their risk management strategy:

❑ Securing supply: Mills need to compare the risk of buying cotton far ahead of when they anticipate using it, against waiting and possibly being unable to secure supply.
❑ Rising price: If the mill elects to buy the cotton "on call", then it obviously runs the risk of a rising price in the future and having to pay more for the cotton. This risk may be offset, however, by an increase in the yarn price.
❑ Falling price: Because the mill is often unable to forward-sell its yarn, it also faces an additional risk that the grower does not. If it fixes its cotton price and the price then falls, there is a likelihood that it will be at a competitive disadvantage compared with mills that did not price their cotton, or may have to sell its yarn at a lower price than it expected when it fixed the contract price.

Mills have two different contract types as well as being able to use options:

❑ Fixed-price contract: The mill purchases a set quantity and quality of cotton at a fixed price for a specified delivery date.
❑ On-call contract: In this contract, rather than fix the contract price, the mill simply locks in the "basis" and the price remains floating and can be fixed at any time prior to the expiry of that futures month.
❑ Options: The mill can use cotton options to lock in a maximum New York futures price while still being able to participate in any falls in the price.

This mill uses 100 MT (440 bales) of Australian high-grade cotton every month. As it has specific quality requirements it prefers to secure the cotton by entering into a contract well in advance of the delivery.

1. April 2000: The mill decides it must secure its supply by buying 5,280 bales. It can buy either at a fixed price of 67.00 c/lb or at an on-call basis of 5.00 c/lb. Because it does not have any yarn sales contracted for 2001 it is unwilling to lock in the cotton price and therefore buy 5,280 bales of cotton for delivery April 2001 through to March 2002 at 5.00 c/lb on the futures month.
2. February 2001: As first delivery approaches and the May futures price falls below 60 c/lb for the first time in one year, the mill fixes the A/M/J portion of the contract (1,320 bales) at 59 c/lb plus basis of 5 c/lb (64.00 c/lb).
3. March 2001: The price continues to fall and, although the mill believes that prices are good value at these levels. (July New York futures is 53.00 cents but the mill has not yet sold the yarn so is reluctant to fix the price.) To protect itself it instead buys 13 July 55 calls at 1.50 c/lb and 13 December 55 calls at 2.50 c/lb. This means that two-thirds of the contract is now protected from increases in the price while the call options mean that the mill can still benefit from a fall in prices on those bales.
4. June 2001: The July futures price has continued to fall, so at option expiry the July calls expire worthless and the mill fixes the 1,320 bales at the current price of 42 c/lb plus basis (47.00 c/lb).
5. November 2001: The cotton price has continued to fall and, although prices have rallied over 20% from the lows, at 35 c/lb they are still well below the call options. The mill lets the options expire worthless and fixes its O/N/D portions at 35.00 c/lb plus basis (40.00 c/lb).
6. December 2001: Prices appear to have stabilised in the last two months and seem more likely to rise than fall. Therefore, despite not having fixed the yarn price of its last shipments, the mill believes the price is low enough to offset this risk, so fixes the last 1,320 bales at 37.00 c/lb plus basis (42.00 c/lb).

Results

- ❏ 1,320 bales fixed at 64.00 US cents per lb.
- ❏ 1,320 bales fixed at 47.00 US cents per lb.
- ❏ 1,320 bales fixed at 40.00 US cents per lb.
- ❏ 1,320 bales fixed at 42.00 US cents per lb
- ❏ Bought 13 July 55 cent calls at 150 US cent points per lb.
- ❏ Bought 13 December 55 cent calls at US 250 cent points per lb.
- ❏ Both sets of options expired worthless as market continued to fall.

In summary, the mill has ended up with an average contract price of 47.75 c/lb, while the 26 call options cost 1.00 c/lb over the entire contract, making the final price to the mill 48.75 c/lb. This is nearly US$100 per bale better than the fixed price it was offered in April 2000 (67.00 against final price 48.75), and, although the options were not used, they did provide the mill security against any possible price increase.

7

What Drives Actual Hedging Behaviour? Developing Risk Management Instruments

Joost M.E Pennings

University of Illinois at Urbana-Champaign and
Wageningen University, The Netherlands

In the last forty years economists have made great progress in developing optimal risk management strategies. Various authors have formulated optimal hedging models that maximise the decision maker's utility by explicitly taking the risk-return trade-off into account. While these models seem helpful, the actual behaviour of firms does not seem in line with the optimal strategies proposed by the models. This mismatch is partly caused by neglecting alternative motivations to hedge.

In this chapter I show the relationship between the firm's focus on shareholder value and hedging behaviour. Furthermore, this mismatch is caused by neglecting the beliefs and perceptions structure of managers. This mismatch between optimal and actual risk management behaviour has great consequences for firms facing risk, as well as for financial institutions, such as banks and exchanges, attempting to develop risk management policies. A product-development model for risk management services is proposed that integrates the findings of behavioural decision-making models and optimal hedging models.

Motivations for hedging: a brief review

Historically, several explanations have been given as to why managers use futures markets. I will briefly review them here. The term "hedging", used here, refers to taking a selling or buying position in the futures market.

In the 1930s, Hoffman (1932) stated that "hedging is risk shifting", thereby voicing the then dominant opinion that futures markets existed for the transfer of risk. This perspective on hedging as a kind of insurance, where risk is transferred from one market participant to another, was not new. Already, in 1919, the prominent economist Marshall (1919, p. 260) had claimed that "the hedger does not speculate: he insures". The "insurance perspective" was dominant until after World War Two, when resistance grew.

Working (1953) claimed that hedging did have a profit motive, through the exploitation of (expected) changes of the basis (local cash price minus futures price). Thus, profit opportunities arise from anticipated price fluctuations in the futures market versus the spot market. In this view, hedging was first and foremost a kind of *arbitrage*, entered into only if the hedger perceived a promising profit opportunity. According to the portfolio theory, first introduced by Markowitz (1959), Johnson (1960) and Stein (1961), a hedger maximises the expected utility of a portfolio consisting of spot and futures contracts. In this framework, the hedger explicitly weighs risk and return against one another. The portfolio theory makes risk the central concept in futures contract usage. Telser (1981) shifted this perspective by contrasting the properties of futures contracts and forward contracts. He postulated that contracts at organised futures markets are superior to informal forward contracts in several respects: futures contracts are based on an organised market with an elaborate set of written rules, arbitration boards and limited market membership. Through their standardisation and rules, futures contracts ensure liquidity and eliminate the counterparty default risk. In contrast, forward contracts are based on mutual trust. In Telser's view, the use of futures contracts no longer primarily depends on a company's objective to reduce its risks, but also on the properties of the futures market as an institution.

Recently, managers have been urged to focus on shareholder value. Shareholders evaluate a company's performance on how its actions contribute to shareholder value, the outcome of which is usually reflected in the stock price of the company (Woolridge and Snow, 1990; Srivastava, Shervani, and Fahey, 1998). Since there is a link between increased shareholder value and managers' salaries (Woolridge and Snow, 1990), the stock market is in fact rewarding managers for developing strategies that increase shareholder value, and stock return is partly driven by cashflow expectations (Vuolteenaho, 2002).

The next section shows how the use of futures contracts can enhance shareholder value, and how it may solve conflicts over different contract preferences between companies in commodity-marketing channels. Shareholder value has in fact become an alternative motivation to hedge.

Hedging and the creation of shareholder value
AN ALTERNATIVE MOTIVATION TO HEDGE

There is a converging interest in how shareholder value relates to market activities and how the increased use of financial services can fundamentally alter markets and contractual behaviour (Boatler, 1998). Despite this interest, there has been little empirical guidance as to how a focus on shareholder value can effectively or systematically translate into managerial action. By neglecting to study the rapid development of financial facilitating services, such as securities, agribusiness managers may have missed a key piece to link their marketing and management decisions to financial objectives and performance.

The difficulty in translating a firm's focus on shareholder value into marketing decisions can be overcome by focusing on the cashflow consequences of contracts. Shareholders evaluate a company's performance on how its actions contribute to shareholder value. The outcome is usually reflected in the company's stock price. Shareholder value can be seen as a forecast cash flow, discounted by the risk-adjusted cost of capital. Rappaport (1986) showed that shareholder value can be enhanced in four ways: accelerating cashflows, increasing their level, enhancing their residual value or reducing their volatility.

In this section, I focus exclusively on cashflow volatility as one of the drivers of shareholder value. A decrease in cashflow volatility cuts the firm's cost of capital, therewith enhancing its shareholder value. That is, more stable cash flows generate higher net present values, creating more shareholder value. This notion implies that companies that focus on shareholder value prefer forward contract relationships over cash transactions all other things being equal. Whether the company's preferred contract relationship will be realised depends on the other company's contract preference. The final outcome depends on the interdependence between the companies. The degree of interdependence affects each party's motivation, behaviour and perceptions in the exchange. Interdependent channel members will continue to interact or exchange only if both parties benefit.

When highly interdependent channel members disagree on the contract relationship, a conflict situation might arise. Futures contracts can solve these conflicts, through their ability to enhance shareholder value by complementing the cashflow consequences of contract relationships. By thus reducing the cash volatility of the contract relationship between the channel members, the once-disputed contract becomes amenable to both parties. For example: a processor might use the hedging services offered by one of the Chicago exchanges to complement the cash transaction relationship preferred by a wholesaler. Hedging can then be redefined as a service that offers one party (eg, the processor) the opportunity to buy products forward at a fixed price, without restricting it to engage in a cash contract relationship with the other (eg, the wholesaler).

These findings shed an interesting light on the current debate in the US and Europe about power imbalances in the agricultural marketing channel due to different contract preferences and concentration in the agribusiness. Our results indicate that power imbalances, assuming that they do exist, might be counterbalanced by futures trade. Recently, an empirical study in the meat complex by Pennings and Wansink (2003) has confirmed the use of futures to enhance shareholder value and to solve conflicts caused by incongruent contract preferences.

Hedging effectiveness and ratios: the role of market liquidity risk

With the reasons for hedging given above, agribusiness companies have to decide on the optimal hedge ratio, ie, how many futures contracts to use. This raises the issues of the hedging effectiveness of futures and market depth or liquidity. A futures market is considered liquid when market participants can buy or sell futures contracts quickly, with little by way of price effects resulting from their transactions. Since many (of the small and especially new) commodity futures markets are thin markets, hedgers face liquidity risks that have to be taken into account when evaluating hedging effectiveness. In thin markets, the transactions of individual hedgers may have significant price effects and result in substantial transaction costs (Pennings *et al*, 1998).

Most hedging effectiveness measures so far have disregarded liquidity and focused extensively on basis risk (the uncertainty about the basis at the time a hedge is lifted). Since the agribusiness faces substantial market depth costs, I propose an extended version of the Ederington (1979) measure to include market depth risk. This new hedging effectiveness measure can be expressed as:

$$HE = -\frac{b^{*2}\left(\sigma_f^2 + \sigma_{md}^2 - 2\sigma_{fmd}\right) + b^*(-2\sigma_{sf} + 2\sigma_{smd})}{\sigma_s^2} \tag{1}$$

where σ_s^2, σ_f^2, σ_{sf}, σ_{fmd}, and σ_{smd} represent the variances and the covariances of the prices (subscript s and f denote spot and futures prices respectively), and market depth cost changes (denoted by md) from time 1 to time 2, and b^* is the risk-minimising hedge ratio with

$$b^* = \frac{\sigma_{sf} - \sigma_{smd}}{\sigma_f^2 + \sigma_{md}^2 - 2\sigma_{fmd}}$$

Market depth costs are calculated as the area between the downward-sloping price path (selling order imbalance) and the price at which the participant enters the futures market (2),

$$MD = PF^1 \cdot N - \sum_{i=1}^{N} (PF^i) \tag{2}$$

where PF^1 is the futures price at which the participant enters the market, PF^i is the price of the i-th futures contract, and N the total order flow, or as the area between the upward-sloping price path (buying order imbalance) and the price at which the participant enters the futures market (3):

$$MD = \sum_{i=1}^{N} (PF^i) - PF^1 \cdot N \tag{3}$$

The measure from (1) guides agribusiness companies in evaluating different commodity futures exchanges on their risk-reduction capacities. At the same time, it provides information about the optimal hedge ratios. To use the measure effectively, companies need detailed futures and cash-price data. First, the company needs a data infrastructure that provides cash prices paid or charged for commodities. Second, to calculate the market depth costs and hence σ_{fmd}, and σ_{smd}, transaction-specific data should be obtained from the futures exchange. Obtaining them requires an initial investment from the agribusiness company.

Optimal hedging models and revealed behaviour

Optimal hedging models have long been normative models, showing users (eg, agribusiness companies) how they *should* behave. By nature, normative models are meant to describe and predict *ideal* situations, which are not necessarily the *actual* ones. However, if optimal hedging models neither describe nor predict actual behaviour, their practical usefulness might be questioned, when there is a large gap between norm and reality. The issue of ideal and real behaviour is relevant to the users of hedging services and certainly to the institutions that design them (eg, futures exchanges, banks and agribusiness companies). Futures contracts designed according to optimal hedging models, ie, with ideal user behaviour in mind, might not succeed in a market based on real behaviour.

When comparing the optimal hedge ratios to the actual hedge ratios, Hartzmark (1987), Peck and Nahmias (1989) and Pennings and Garcia (2004) concluded that the two differ significantly. This difference can be explained by investigating the underlying decision-making structure of decision makers. Pennings and Leuthold (2000) and Pennings and Garcia (2001) have found that, in order to understand actual hedging behaviour, psychological constructs should be taken into account, as well as the heterogeneity of companies with respect to their decision-making behaviour.

Both factors are discussed below to gain more insight into actual hedging behaviour and hence into the gap between actual and optimal hedging ratios, which is in fact a behavioural issue.

ADOPTION OF FUTURES

In psychological frameworks for risk management behaviour, beliefs and perceptions play a crucial role. Beliefs pertain to the degree to which an object (eg, futures contracts) may have particular consequences, and perceptions reflect the interpretation of these consequences. Managers' perceptions and beliefs regarding futures contracts are driving their choices. Based on Pennings and Leuthold (2000) and Pennings, Candel and Egelkraut (2003), I introduce a conceptual decision-making model.

Managers of agribusiness companies do not always consider futures contracts relevant to their operation. That is, futures contracts are not always considered a part of the business of conduct (see Pennings and Smidts, 2004). Before a manager enters the futures market, the futures contract must be part of the manager's toolbox, and hence be considered a relevant marketing tool by an owner-manager. In the adoption phase, managers decide whether or not futures contracts can contribute to their enterprise. In this chapter, I use the multi-attribute attitude theory (eg, Ajzen and Fishbein, 1980).

In the multi-attribute attitude framework, attitude is assumed to be decomposable as a sum of the products of beliefs and evaluations. The beliefs reflect the degree to which a futures contract may have particular consequences, for example, risk reduction, and the evaluations reflect the importance of these consequences. Similar beliefs are grouped into components and the evaluation of these components may influence each manager's attitude differently. These belief components and their evaluations are referred to as the *subjective criteria components* (SCC). Each manager uses these SCCs when deciding whether or not to make futures a part of his/her toolbox.

Pennings and Leuthold (2001) have shown that, in the adoption phase of futures, the SSC *perceived performance* of futures exchanges (risk reduction, speculation or other functions) plays a role. Perceived performance may differ from the actual performance as reflected by hedging effectiveness measures as given by Equation (1). The perception managers have of the futures market's performance is central. In this section, I do not focus solely on the risk-reduction and speculation services of futures exchanges. Instead, I view customer perception of futures exchange performance as a driver of customer behaviour.

Working (1953) claimed that the use of futures gave managers greater freedom for business action. He argued that the freedom thus gained could be used to make a sale or purchase that would otherwise not have been possible. This is in line with recent findings that managers value instruments that increase their "freedom of action" in the marketplace (eg, Brandstätter, 1997). Thus, we may expect the SCC *entrepreneurship* to play a role in making futures part of the business of conduct. Several researchers, Ennew *et al* (1992), among others, have shown that managers perceive futures trade as complex and difficult. This perceived complexity implies extra costs, eg, of information gathering, which inhibits the adoption of futures. Therefore, we expect SSC *ease of use* to be another important component for owner-managers in adding futures to their toolbox. Though the manager is the primary decision maker, the decision to use futures is often influenced by advisers, employees and other important people. These people form the *decision-making unit* (DMU). Recent findings suggest that the DMU has a significant influence on major decisions (Dholakia, *et al* 1993). Furthermore, we expect *risk attitude* to drive hedging behaviour (Pennings and Smidts, 2000, Pennings and Garcia, 2001).

PULLING THE TRIGGER

While the adoption phase explains how managers weigh the usefulness of futures contracts as a tool, it does not explain the manager's decision on whether or not to initiate futures positions in a concrete choice situation. This is the second phase, where futures contracts are already in the manager's toolbox. In a concrete choice situation, the manager has two options: to initiate a futures position or not (the latter could mean a delay). Any manager deciding whether or not to initiate a futures position takes the consequences of this action into account.

Initiating a futures position has two important consequences. First, by fixing the price in advance (s)he reduces his/her spot market risk. Secondly, fixing the price in advance at a certain price level is inherent to taking a futures position. From the decision literature it is well known that decision makers use anchor points to evaluate a stimulus, in our case, futures prices (Payne, Laughhunn and Grum, 1980). Tversky and Kahneman (1981) showed that decision makers perceive outcomes (such as futures prices) in terms of gains or losses. Gains and losses are defined relative to the manager's reference point.

Therefore, managers compare the futures price level to their reference price, whereby the reference price is defined as the manager's internal price that (s)he uses as an anchor to judge other prices. The further the futures price exceeds the manager's reference price, the more attractive it becomes for him/her to take a futures position. And, conversely, the further the reference price exceeds the futures price, the less attractive it becomes to take a futures position. In the context of an agribusiness company deciding on a futures position, the reference price may be closely related to the production costs of the underlying commodity. Pennings (2002) showed that *risk attitude* and the *ratio of the futures price level to the reference price* play a role in a manager's behaviour in initiating a futures position.

HETEROGENEITY IN HEDGING BEHAVIOUR

The motivations of agribusiness companies to use derivatives as a hedging tool may not be homogeneous. Firms from different regions or with different organisational structures may face dissimilar economic constraints and conditions that might lead to a different choice of derivatives. Particularly in agribusiness, the variety in organisational structures is wide. Similarly, managers may have different objectives and motivations that can also result in different derivative decisions. Furthermore, managers may themselves have different risk attitudes and risk perceptions, resulting in firms behaving differently (eg, Pennings and Smidts, 2000). Consequently, we may expect the factors that influence a firm's choice of financial instrument to vary across the segments of an industry, and common factors to influence firms differently.

Clearly, this heterogeneity impacts the efforts of financial institutions in developing appropriate derivatives, particularly customised products. Heterogeneity posits two interrelated ideas that are central to our understanding of hedging behaviour. The first notion is that not all managers respond similarly to a given change in the determinants of derivative use, but that segments may exist of managers who behave similarly. The second notion is that these segments are not directly observable, prior to the analysis. Rather, they are determined by grouping together managers who reveal a similar relationship between the determinants of derivative use and their hedging behaviour.

Pennings and Garcia (2004) investigated the issue of heterogeneity in the meat complex. They found three segments of managers, demonstrating the existence of multiple-industry segments with different relationships between manager and firm characteristics and derivative use. In Segment 1, which contained 48.9% of the producers, 36.0% of the wholesalers and 3.3% of the processors, and constitutes 44.1% of their sample, risk exposure, firm size, the influence of the decision-making unit (DMU) and the manager's risk perception showed significant association with derivative use. Moreover, the interaction between risk attitude and risk perception is significantly associated with derivative usage. Compared with the other two segments, this segment used the fewest derivatives.

Segment 2 contained 28.9% of the producers, 42.0% of the wholesalers and 20.0% of the processors, and constituted 29.8% of their sample. It revealed significant effects of risk exposure, firm size and level of education on hedging behaviour. In this segment, the use of derivatives is modest: higher than in Segment 1, yet lower than in Segment 3. Interestingly, the fundamental determinants, risk attitude, risk perception and their interaction, are not significantly related to derivative usage in this segment.

Segment 3 was the smallest, containing 26.1% of their sample, 22.2% of the producers, 22.0% of the wholesalers, and 76.6% of the processors. In contrast, risk perception, risk attitude and their interaction were significantly related to derivative usage. Here, the terms can be clearly interpreted: a risk-averse manager uses relatively more derivatives to reduce price risk. When a manager perceives a large price risk (ie, high-risk perception), derivative usage will be more prominent. A risk-averse manager with high-risk perception relies on derivatives more heavily. Moreover, other financial determinants, such as leverage, are also significantly related to derivative use in this segment, as are the level of education and the influence of the DMU.

Pennings and Garcia's findings have a clear economic interpretation. Segment 1 consists of companies whose decision regarding derivative use depends on their risk exposure and the opinions of members of the decision-making unit. This segment is dominated by relatively small firms that do not use derivatives extensively. In contrast, the hedging behaviour of the firms in Segment 3 is driven by the fundamental drivers, risk attitude, risk perception and their interaction. It is consistent with Pratt and Arrow's models and economic theory suggesting that risk attitude and risk perception are important concepts in determining optimal hedging positions (Holthausen, 1979). Furthermore, other financial determinants, such as leverage, are significant in these managers' decisions.

The fact that the three segments are not homogeneous as to firm type (producers, wholesalers or processors) further substantiates that the heterogeneity emerges from the influence of the determinants of derivative use, rather than from a single observable variable (eg, company type). Had Pennings and Garcia ignored *latent* heterogeneity, and used a variable such as company type as the classifying criterion instead, they would have overlooked the heterogeneity present within these groups and found the same relationship between the factors and hedging behaviour within each group for all producers, wholesalers or processors. The only dissimilarities found would then have been between the company types, inconsistent with Pennings and Garcia's actual findings.

The heterogeneity in derivative usage suggests that financial institutions need to use different tools to attract different segments. Identifying the segments is a challenge. With this information, financial institutions are able to target their marketing efforts and design customised financial products. Fridson (1992), and Nesbitt and Reynolds (1997) show the importance of customising financial services. Based on the characteristics of the different segments, financial institutions can select a group of potential customers, to whom they offer risk-reduction services, designed to match their derivative usage profile. This implies a differentiation of the services offered by financial institutions. Having identified the segments and gained information about their profiles, the financial institution can target these segments and design securities that better fit their needs.

Designing risk management instruments: challenges for agribusiness companies

The behavioural models discussed above teach us that risk reduction is not necessarily the main driver of futures contracts usage. Many different factors drive actual hedging behaviour and the influence of these factors may not be the same for all managers. This has great implications for optimal hedging models that assist managers in their risk management decisions. Clearly these models must be adjusted to managers' preference structures. What these preference structures are cannot be answered easily. The management literature shows that managers have difficulties articulating their objectives. The optimal hedge models from the literature and the one presented in Equation (1) assume risk minimisation or risk reduction to be the main objective. These models need extending in the near future, to reflect better the objectives of agribusiness managers. Perhaps behavioural models should play a role in this process. Behavioural models may also help agribusiness companies to develop OTC products to substitute futures trade. Thus, agribusiness companies become financial service providers.

The behavioural approach outlined above attempts to determine whether the hedging services provided satisfy potential customers' needs. Customer needs concerning risk management services are divided into *instrumental needs* and *convenience needs*. Customers will choose that "service-product" (futures, options, etc) that best satisfies both their needs, instrumental and convenience, at an acceptable price. *Instrumental needs* are the needs for price-risk reduction. Hedgers wish to reduce, or, if possible, eliminate portfolio risks at low costs. The instrumental needs are related to the core service of financial service providers: reducing price variability for the customer. Not only do hedgers wish to reduce price risk, they also desire flexibility in doing business, easy access to the market and an efficient clearing system. These are called *convenience needs*. They deal with the customer's need to be able to use the core service provided with relative ease. The extent to which the financial service provider is able to satisfy convenience needs determines the process quality. The service offering is not restricted to the core service, but has to be complemented by so-called peripheral services. The core plus peripheral services constitute the augmented service offering. An example of a peripheral service is the efficient and correct conclusion of transactions.

A financial service provider can meet both types of needs by setting up a "trading component or execution component" and a "clearing component". The "trading component" handles the actual transactions and is the place that mainly meets instrumental needs. After the execution, the clearing component handles the financial settlement and ensures that the commodities delivered meet the contract specifications. The clearing component mainly meets the convenience needs.

After analysing customer needs, the marketing process continues by designing the service and developing service delivery. Both *service design* and *service delivery* affect the customer's service experience (Parasuraman, Zeihaml and Berry, 1985). Service design is mainly linked to the instrumental needs, service delivery to the convenience needs. In most cases, more than one instrument will be available to meet a firm's needs for price-risk reduction. This makes it interesting to know *how* a firm chooses between these competing alternatives. The behavioural models outlined above can be very helpful in this respect.

The results of the behavioural model, as described above have important managerial implications for developing and evaluating risk management services. For example, the fact that managers evaluate different price-risk management instruments on a dimension like entrepreneurial freedom makes it interesting to position risk management services as a tool for more freedom of action.

Moreover, to reduce the psychological distance to risk management services, financial institutions might develop training programmes for managers, thereby increasing understanding and ease of use. The performance of risk management instruments can be increased by using a more appealing standardisation procedure of the underlying commodity. Relaxation of some of the standards may help in this respect.

The behavioural approach, in its preoccupation with customer needs, tends to pay only limited attention to issues of technical feasibility when creating a particular service, whereas the traditional optimal hedging approach (as described above) tends to under-value customer needs in favour of the technical aspects of a particular service. Therefore, the development of new risk management services might profit from an integration of the behavioural approach (with its stress on desirability from a customer perspective) and the optimal hedge approach (with its focus on the technical feasibility of a service).

The behavioural approach draws on *customer-specific information*. This includes time preferences, choice criteria, investment opportunities and the risk preferences of individual economic agents. Customer-specific information is essential for determining market needs and profit opportunities. A problem of financial institutions and customers may be information asymmetries, such as hidden information and hidden action, which might result in adverse selection and moral hazard. The costs of information asymmetry can be reduced by marketing research, if the expected value of perfect information is positive. Customer-specific information is also useful in selecting target markets. Targeting market segments and designing effective positioning strategies requires managers to have insight into how the attributes of a service-product are valued by current and prospective customers. Customer-specific information can provide that insight. Defining a commodity derivative from the point of view of customer needs might conflict with technical feasibility and vice versa.

It is often difficult to derive the successful functional and technical properties of financial services from the behavioural approach alone. On the other hand, it remains unclear whether the feasible properties of financial services as determined in the optimal hedge approach generate sufficient demand. It seems, therefore, that the optimal hedge and behavioural approach to financial services, whether from the perspective of supply or demand side, are complementary in developing, producing and marketing financial services.

Both approaches feed each other with information and provide feedback as given in Figure 1. Thus, the behavioural approach furnishes information about the characteristics that make risk management instruments attractive to firms, whereas the optimal hedge approach determines the technical feasibility of such characteristics. This information then becomes the basis for a first concept of service design and service delivery. This concept is adapted and improved, after being tested on target customers and financial experts. Then, the improved concept may, in turn, be improved by another round of testing and so on. This development process of risk management instruments implies a full integration of the optimal hedge and behavioural approach. The integrative product-development approach is desirable to acquire insight into the *necessary* and *sufficient* conditions for successful risk management instruments.

1. Designing risk management instrument

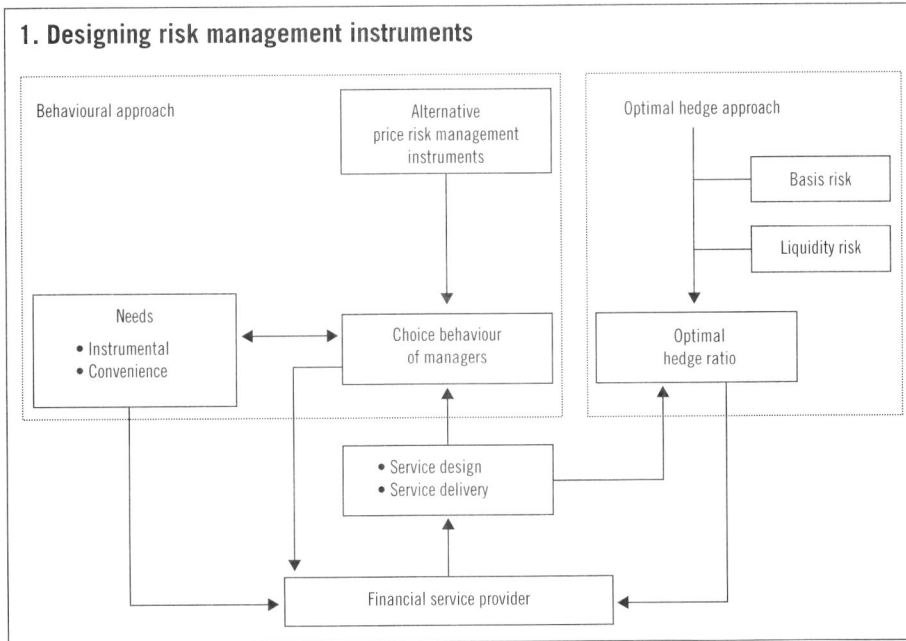

In order to benefit optimally from the integration, the optimal hedge approach needs a shift of perspective from portfolios to financial service provider management. This means, for example, that the measures developed within the finance approach should also provide the exchange management with information on how to improve hedging efficiency (Pennings and Meulenberg, 1997). The behavioural approach should focus particularly on a better understanding of the decision-making process of firms, as far as the use of price-risk management instruments is concerned.

The proposed integrated approach towards the development of price-risk management instruments provides insight into the success factors of a risk management instrument, divided into two groups: factors with a technical character (referred to as the "optimal hedge approach") and factors dealing with the decision-making process of managers concerning hedging (referred to as the "behavioural approach"). Secondly, it provides a methodology for organising the product-development process of risk management instruments, through the integration of both technical and behavioural factors. Because this approach contains all the relevant aspects, it is a powerful tool for drawing conclusions about the viability of commodity risk management instruments.

BIBLIOGRAPHY

Ajzen, I., and M. Fishbein, 1980, "Understanding Attitudes and Predicting Social Behavior" (Englewood Cliffs, NJ: Prentice-Hall).

Boatler, R.W., 1998, "Capital Markets and Institutions: A Global View," *Journal of Finance*, 53, October, pp. 1829–30.

Brandstätter, H., 1997, "Becoming an Entrepreneur: A Question of Personality Structure", *Journal of Economic Psychology*, 18, pp. 157–77.

Dholakia, R.R., J.L. Johnson, A.J. Della Bitta, and N. Dholakia, 1993, "Decision-making Time in Organizational Buying Behavior: An Investigation of Its Antecedents", *Journal of the Academy of Marketing Science*, 21, pp. 281–92.

Ederington, L.H., 1979, "The Hedging Performance of the New Futures Market", *Journal of Finance*, 34(1), pp. 157–70

Ennew, T.C., W. Morgan, and T. Rayner, 1992, "Role of Attitudes in the Decision to Use Futures Markets: The Case of the London Potato Futures Market", *Agribusiness: An International Journal*, 8, pp. 561–73.

Fridson, M.S., 1992, "High-yield Indexes and Benchmark Portfolios", *Journal of Portfolio Management*, 18, pp. 77-83.

Hartzmark, M. L., 1987, "Returns to Individual Traders of Futures: Aggregate Results", *Journal of Political Economy*, 95, pp. 1292-1306.

Hoffman, G.W., 1932, *Futures Trading upon Organized Commodity Markets in the United States* (Philadelphia: University of Pennsylvania Press).

Holthausen, D.M., 1979, "Hedging and the Competitive Firm under Price Uncertainty", *American Economic Review*, 69, pp. 989-95.

Johnson, L., 1960, "The Theory of Hedging and Speculation in Commodity Futures", *Review of Economic Studies*, 27, pp. 139-51.

Markowitz, H. M., 1959, *Portfolio Selection: Efficient Diversification of Investments* (New York: John Wiley & Sons).

Marshall, A., 1919, *Industry and Trade* (London: Macmillan).

Nesbitt, S.L., and H.W. Reynolds, 1997, "Benchmarks for Private Market Investments", *Journal of Portfolio Management*, 23, pp. 85-90.

Parasuraman, A., V. Zeithaml, and L. Berry, 1985, "A Conceptual Model of Service Quality and Its Implications for Future Research", *Journal of Marketing*, 49(4), pp. 41-50.

Payne, J. W., D.J. Laughhunn, and R. Grum, 1980, "Translation of Gambles and Aspiration Level Effects in Risky Choices Behavior", *Management Science*, 26, pp. 1039-60.

Peck, A.E., and A.M. Nahmias, 1989, "Hedging Your Advice: Do Portfolio Models Explain Hedging?", *Food Research Institute Studies*, 21, pp. 193-204.

Pennings, J.M.E., and M.T.G. Meulenberg, 1997, "Hedging Efficiency: A Futures Exchange Management Approach", *Journal of Futures Markets*, 17(5), pp. 599-615.

Pennings, J.M.E., W.E. Kuiper, F. ter Hofstede, and M.T.G. Meulenberg, 1998, "The Price Path Due to Order Imbalances: Evidence from the Amsterdam Agricultural Futures Exchange", *European Financial Management*, 4(1), pp. 47-64.

Pennings, J.M.E., and A. Smidts, 2000, "Assessing the Construct Validity of Risk Attitude", *Management Science*, 46(10), pp. 1337-48.

Pennings, J.M.E., and R.M. Leuthold, 2000, "The Role of Farmers' Behavioral Attitudes and Heterogeneity in Futures Contracts Usage", *American Journal of Agricultural Economics*, 82(4), pp. 908-19.

Pennings, J.M.E., and P. Garcia, 2001, "Measuring Producers' Risk Preferences: A Global Risk Attitude Construct", *American Journal of Agricultural Economics*, 83, November, pp. 993-1009.

Pennings, J.M.E., and R.M. Leuthold, 2001, "A Behavioral Approach towards Futures Contract Usage", *Australian Economic Papers*, 40, December, pp. 461-78.

Pennings, J.M.E., 2002, "Pulling the Trigger or Not: Factors Affecting Behavior of Initiating a Position in Derivatives Markets", *Journal of Economic Psychology*, 23, April, pp. 263-78.

Pennings, J.M.E., and B. Wansink, 2003, "Channel Contract Behavior: The Role of Risk Attitudes, Risk Perceptions, and Channel Members' Market Structures", forthcoming, *Journal of Business*.

Pennings, J.M.E., M.J.J.M. Candel, and T.M. Egelkraut, 2003, "A Behavioral Decision Making Modeling Approach Towards Hedging Services", forthcoming, *Journal of Behavioral Finance*.

Pennings, J.M.E., and P. Garcia, 2004, "Hedging Behavior in Small and Medium-sized Enterprises: The Role of Unobserved Heterogeneity", forthcoming, *Journal of Banking & Finance*.

Pennings, J.M.E., and A. Smidts, 2004, "The Shape of Utility Functions & Organizational Behavior", forthcoming, *Management Science*.

Rappaport, A., 1986, *Creating Shareholder Value: The New Standard for Business Performance* (New York: Free Press).

Stein, J.L., 1961, "The Simultaneous Determination of Spot and Futures Prices", *American Economic Review*, 51, pp. 1012-25.

Srivastava, R.K., T.A. Shervani, and L. Fahey, 1998, "Market–Based Assets and Shareholder Value: A Framework for Analysis", *Journal of Marketing*, 62, January, pp. 2-18.

Telser, L.G., 1981, "Why There are Organized Futures Markets", *Journal of Law & Economics*, 24, pp. 1-22.

Tversky, A., and D. Kahneman, 1981, "The Framing of Decisions and the Psychology of Choice", *Science*, 211, pp. 453-8.

Vuolteenaho, T., 2002, "What Drives Firm-Level Stock Returns?", *Journal of Finance*, 57, February, pp. 233-64.

Woolridge, J.R., and C.C. Snow, 1990, "Stock Market Reaction to Strategic Investment Decisions" *Strategic Management Journal*, 11, September, pp. 353-63.

Working, H., 1953, "Hedging reconsidered", *Journal of Farm Economics*, 35, pp. 544-61.

8

The Roles of Market Participants and their Influence on Risk Management in the Agricultural Sector

Daniel Day-Robinson

Day Robinson International Ltd

Introduction

The commodity markets involve many different players: the producer, merchant, trader, exchange, shipper and the consumer. Risks can be quantified at every level relating to the activity of every type of market participant. In this chapter, I look at the roles and influence of a range of market participants, including producers, traders, brokers, exchanges, warehouses, collateral managers and governments in overall commodity risk management.

Producers

Producers, together with the lobbies supporting them, greatly affect risk management markets. Whether in developing countries, where risk management influences come from governments and aid agencies, or in developed economies, where they come from exchanges and private-sector activities, we must not underestimate the influence and demands of the producers in the agribusiness risk management sector. The problems surrounding producers in developing countries, together with risk management issues, have been testing banks, trading firms, brokers and the donor community for some time, gathering momentum in recent years. Many observers are aware of the frightening statistic that over 1 billion people in developing countries are earning less than a dollar a day. Since a large number of these people are involved in the rural economy and agricultural production, which in the poorest countries is focused on producing staple commodities for export to Western markets, we need to ask about the stake of these producers in risk management. We also need to know how, with so few financial resources, farmers in developing countries manage risk. The answer is that there are few institutional mechanisms to support them; they do not have adequate financial resources; the private sector is unable to enter the risk management market on any great scale; ands the risk of default is too large. Further, even if a more conducive environment were to be created, it would probably still mean high volumes of transactions involving small financial considerations – not the ideal scenario for anyone seriously considering risk management as a business.

THE ROLES OF
MARKET
PARTICIPANTS AND
THEIR INFLUENCE ON
RISK MANAGEMENT IN
THE AGRICULTURAL
SECTOR

The developing country farmer has to deal with two main types of risk to anticipate and manage. These relate on one hand to price volatility (it is difficult to forecast the selling price of the commodity produced) and on the other to physical risk, ie, loss or damage to the crop arising from adverse or even extreme weather conditions, storage, handling, etc.

While there are few remedies for risk mitigation in developing countries, there are a wide number of solutions available in the risk management market to developed country producers. These producers face the same set of risks, but they are supported by government minimum-price, set-aside and other similar sorts of support schemes, which may go a long way to protect their basic incomes. Government support schemes are limited to richer countries and are driven not just by the need to mitigate producers' risks, but also by the need to respond to international trade and WTO issues. For example, government schemes to support prices through intervention schemes limit the downside to farmers by providing a threshold below which prices cannot fall. This is risk mitigation in itself. Many UK farmers will remember with great affection EU feed wheat intervention prices of the 1980s, which set support prices at over US$50 above world prices for the same commodity. Farmers at that time were comforted by the certain knowledge that the price floor offered by government covered both cost of production and a large margin of profit.

Similarly, governments are involved in schemes offering much-needed producer risk management through their own over-the-counter derivatives. For example, the US Department of Agriculture (USDA) offers the US dairy industry a scheme whereby US milk producers are offered a subsidy to pay for the cost of a put option for their milk sales – enabling them to fix prices for future sales. The farmer is able to mitigate downside price risk. This type of scheme is replicated in proposals for poor countries being considered by the International Task Force for Commodity Risk Management (ITF), a group hosted by the World Bank in Washington, DC. ITF is funded from a number of sources, including the Dutch and Swiss governments and the European Union.

Producers can use insurance to manage risk. As well as producers' cover for standard risks – fire, storm damage, etc – revenue-risk insurance protects farmers from the combined risks of yield shortfalls and price drops. Ideally, revenue-risk insurance insures the revenue of the entire farm rather than the individual crop by guaranteeing a percentage of average gross farm income over the past few years. However, in practice, commodity insurance payouts to producers may be based on indices (average yields and price) rather than on the farmer's revenue outcome or declaration, so avoiding moral issues among would-be claimants. There are some pilot schemes available in the US and – although this type of insurance is virtually unobtainable outside the OECD – it is again a focus of attention among some donors, and particularly the World Bank at present.

As well as on-exchange futures markets products, to protect against price volatility or weather risks, cash market derivatives offer solutions for farmers as well. For example, producers can hedge risk using OTC cash and forward cash market products offered by leading firms. Some banks, brokerage houses and trading houses offer a range of products directed at producers. These are either exchange based or over-the-counter cash market products, which enable the farmer to assess different and fairly unique hedging and marketing alternatives. The great advantage of these tools is that they don't offer just price risk management, but also offer the producer some credit enhancement, eg, the ability to receive favourable financing terms from lenders. Most of the products fulfil two objectives for the provider of the instruments: they encourage the farmer to deliver the commodity, and they enable the merchant to hedge these transactions. Providers of exchange-based agricultural market risk management instruments include all the major soft-commodity brokers. Providers of over-the-counter (OTC) agricultural market risk management instruments include all the major trade houses (such as Dreyfus, Glencore, ADM, Cargill, Ecom, Volcafe, Barry Callebaut, Touton, Bunge) and a few specialist soft-commodity banks (Rabobank, McQuarie and NAB). Schemes vary in size and may be applied to larger individual producers or cooperatives representing a larger number of small-scale producers. Coverage of these products varies and there are only one or two price providers that could be considered global – one international trade house and one international bank.

Traders & brokers

In some countries suffering from the effects of economic shock, trading firms can use their knowledge of risk management to influence the wider market to adopt novel schemes or to simply revive old methods. Recently, for example, the motor manufacturer Daimler Chrysler teamed up with the grain-trading firm Louis Dreyfus to barter cars for grain in Argentina. This innovation overcame difficult trading conditions in Argentina, brought about by the extremely volatile economic climate. As a result of the financial collapse there, around half the population in 2002 were living below the poverty line and inflation was between 50% and 70%. There was a substantial devaluation of the peso and following the collapse of several major banks it was almost impossible to arrange credit.

Not surprisingly, total industry sales of motor vehicles slumped from 307,000 in 2000 to 70,000 in 2002. However, farmers continued to produce large crops of soybeans and wheat and prices in a climate of rising world prices. The scheme, called Plan Cereals, enabled farmers to swap soybeans or wheat for cars or trucks. Under the scheme, farmers could sell their crops to Louis Dreyfus, who then paid Daimler Chrysler for the cost of a vehicle. Daimler Chrysler then invoiced the farmer and supplied him with the vehicle. A farm truck could be exchanged for 200 tons of soybeans and a Mercedes saloon would be priced at 400 tons. The advantages of the system were that it was quite simple and it reduced the cost of transactions and related risks. There is now some talk of similar plans for wool, fruit and honey.

In the case of the barter product described above, Louis Dreyfus took most of the risk. However, there will always be circumstances when traders or borrowers – and the banks that serve them – will be unwilling or unable to take on high levels of physical risk. During this process, they may look to brokers to provide them with price- and risk-management-related information.

Part of the value of a good broker is that he will provide not only information about prices and deals, but snippets of gossip about who is doing what – and why. Traders are always focused on supply-and-demand aspects of physical commodities in which they trade and as well as the larger macroeconomic picture, so it is important to assess what other competitors, are doing in the market. Some brokers are giving a lot of value-added service in not only providing price information but offering lots of ideas on the economic backdrop, current and future price trends, etc. Whether brokers are futures brokers or deal in physical transactions, the tendency has been for many of them to become principals. Traders can be sceptical about the information given by brokers, particularly if they feel it has been influenced by the broker's own relationship with another position taker – either inside his own group or elsewhere. However, since brokers are largely looking to commission as a way of earning money for the company – and their own commissions – this may be a somewhat churlish position to take. Nonetheless, brokers play a key role in augmenting price transparency alongside the international and domestic commodity exchanges.

Exchanges

The principal role of exchanges is to regulate and control futures and derivatives trading through a membership system. Commodity futures date back to the trading of rice futures in Japan in the 1600s – but the underlying principles of commodity futures go back a long way further. Commodity markets have been around for some thousands of years and the degree of their formality has been dependent on the political, social and economic environment prevailing at the time.

The trading of futures is relied upon these days by producers, traders and speculators, and high volumes of transactions on the major exchanges illustrate both the size of their role and the level of influence they have on the market in general. Futures markets help overcome difficult challenges faced in balancing supply and demand and exchange products. Derivatives, futures and options provide several economic benefits, including primarily the provision to mitigate the inevitable risk of price volatility. Since the 1990s, in an environment of liberalisation and following the collapse of many commodity boards in Africa, the role of exchanges has been enhanced.

The presence of exchanges and the development of futures and options markets have influenced the development of the commodity swap market. At present, although the commodity swap market is very small in comparison with the currency swap market, it is growing. For comparison, there was an amount outstanding of US$598 billion for commodity derivates in December 2001 by comparison with US$69 trillion in the interest-rate and currency swap market at the end of the same period. Most of the commodity swap transactions were for OTC contracts – about 40%, according to the Bank of International Settlements.

In recent years, we have seen the growth of existing exchanges and the emergence of new ones. There are major commodity futures exchanges in over 20 countries, including Australia, Brazil, France, Germany, Japan, Korea, Singapore, the US and the UK. A large number of new exchanges were created during the past decade in developing countries; not all of them have progressed to the level of futures trading, and many have rapidly disappeared again.

PANEL 1

WAREHOUSES

Commodity exchanges are inevitably linked to warehouses. Since a proportion, albeit a small proportion, of futures contracts are tendered into the futures stores, it follows that the development of a properly regulated warehouse system must be important. Warehouse receipts, covered in Chapter 14 of this volume, influence the market by providing evidence of collateral to lenders, as well as purchasers of the commodity itself.

Warehouse receipts are a crucial element for risk mitigation, enabling a financier to lend to a borrower. The borrower's buyer then reimburses these funds to the bank, usually directly. Using warehouse receipt finance, a bank or trader relies on goods in an independently controlled warehouse to secure financing. Usually, provided (among many things) there is an off-taker and that there are other forms of recourse (the borrower's balance sheet, for example), banks will lend against commodities stored in a reliable warehouse that have been properly pledged to them in a sound legislative environment. So warehouse receipts provide for a degree of physical risk mitigation and, in support of an exchange-based trading system, they are important for underpinning futures.

Accordingly, warehouse operators can act as key influencers of risk management. If they are able to issue warehouse receipts, which can be used as collateral by banks, they may use this as a way of encouraging deliverers of commodities to move stocks into their facilities. Warehouse operators receive goods into the warehouse and issue "receipts" showing the goods have been received into the store. Among other things, the receipts themselves contain information about the quality and type of the commodity taken into store. The receipts are for the information of the depositor of the goods or, if he is a borrower, for his bank. However, these receipts are not negotiable documents of title, ie, the

79

**THE ROLES OF
MARKET
PARTICIPANTS AND
THEIR INFLUENCE ON
RISK MANAGEMENT IN
THE AGRICULTURAL
SECTOR**

title to the goods themselves may not transfer from one to another person via the passing of the related warehouse receipt.

Herein lies the potential for some degree of confusion. The term "warehouse receipt" means different things to different groups of people around the planet. For example, in the United States, the term "warehouse receipt" is used for a document evidencing storage of a commodity in a warehouse. Unlike elsewhere, it is a document of title, supported by legislation – in this case the US Warehouse Receipts Act of 2000, which replaced a piece of legislation enacted in the US in 1916. By contrast, in the United Kingdom, a warehouse receipt is a non-negotiable instrument simply notifying that at a certain moment in time a certain amount and quality of a commodity was delivered into a warehouse. In the UK, a negotiable form is represented by a warehouse "warrant" of the type issued by London Metal Exchange-nominated warehouses.

The main advantages of warehouse receipt financing from a risk management perspective are that:

❑ The identity of the collateral is less contestable and the intention of the borrower to pledge it is clear, avoiding ownership disputes and competing claims.
❑ The collateral can be auctioned or sold promptly and at low cost if there is a loan default.
❑ A lender holding a warehouse receipt can claim against the issuer (the warehouse company) as well as the borrower in the event that the collateral should go missing.
❑ In a bankruptcy scenario a document of title can cut off the claims of competing creditors.

Warehouse receipts can be negotiable or non-negotiable. A non-negotiable warehouse receipt is made out to a specific party (a person or an institution). Only this party may authorise release of goods from the warehouse. He may also transfer or assign the goods to another party: for example, a bank. The warehouse company must be so notified by the transferor before the transfer or assignment becomes effective.

The non-negotiable warehouse receipt in itself does not convey title and, if it is in the name of, for example, a trading firm, it needs to be issued in the name of, or transferred to, the bank in order for the bank to obtain more than just a security interest. A security interest is much less attractive to a bank than if it has what is called *possessory collateral* – that is to say it has direct recourse to the warehouse where the goods are stored and, in the event of a default or similar, it is easy for the bank to sell the commodities in a shorter time frame.

Collateral managers

Issuers of non-negotiable warehouse receipts include collateral managers. They are becoming increasingly important, with companies like ACE, Cotecna, Control Union, Drum and SGS rolling out collateral management products to serve a growing international market. Notwithstanding the fact that most bankers, borrowers and warehousemen say they find collateral management "just too expensive", their desire to use the services of collateral management companies is increasing. In the absence of totally secure, physical commodity-storage facilities and resulting from the risks in moving commodities about, banks are obliged to find other structures for protection against physical risks. The collateral management agreement (CMA) offered by a number of global firms offers one such solution.

The CMA is a tripartite arrangement between the banker, the borrower and the collateral manager and it is important to remember the CMA is a bespoke agreement. This means it can be time-consuming and expensive. The CMA is designed uniquely for

80

**THE ROLES OF
MARKET
PARTICIPANTS AND
THEIR INFLUENCE ON
RISK MANAGEMENT IN
THE AGRICULTURAL
SECTOR**

each transaction and the collateral manager will bargain for fees – for the transaction itself, and for participants in the commodity system. In Chapter 13 of this volume you can read in detail about collateral management, but the key influence collateral managers have on the system is that they:

❑ oblige an understanding, through their agreements among borrowers, of the risks faced by lenders;
❑ impose a system on warehouses to comply with rigorous standards (particularly important in developing countries);
❑ manage issues of quality and provide value-added services for quality/other considerations;
❑ define, through the CMA, complex issues such as commingling and lien over commingled goods;
❑ issue non-negotiable warehouse receipts;
❑ impose controls through the legal discipline of the CMA;
❑ impose controls and on-the-ground discipline as the commodity moves through the supply chain; and
❑ Provide insurance.

Some collateral managers make a play of the role of their global insurance cover. There are smaller collateral management firms who depend on this cover, possibly because their balance sheets are not large enough to provide comfort for the bank in the event of a large-scale default. The most efficient collateral managers in the developing world are those who are able to offer local services, make local decisions and sign the CMAs without recourse to the HQ in Europe or elsewhere.

Governments

After collateral management, we can look at the need by governments and legislators to address market infrastructure needs. Through regulation, governments deputise their responsibilities to national bodies (such as national regulatory organisations, whether enshrined in legislation or self-regulating) and international bodies (such as WTO or BIS).

Typically, government influence in risk management markets includes:

❑ supervising the regulatory environment;
❑ authorising commodity exchanges;
❑ enacting tax laws;
❑ imposing foreign exchange regulations;
❑ imposing price support or stabilisation schemes;
❑ imposing tariffs or quotas;
❑ directing public-sector and public-utility commodity-related activities; and
❑ actions by the central bank.

In developing countries, donors play a substantial role in influencing the development of local marketing structures by attempting to develop and promote an appropriate legal and policy framework to facilitate commodities trading. However, some countries have outright restrictions, which impede the use of market-based risk management instruments. The reasons underlying such restrictions are often related to factors such as fear of uncontrolled speculation, limited knowledge of complex instruments (or at least instruments that are perceived to be complex), misconceptions (confusing hedging with speculation, for instance), worries about adverse media coverage, worries about foreign exchange losses and so on. Or the problem could simply be with ideology. The obvious examples are Russia, which quickly embraced risk management after *perestroika*, and India, where deregulation has gathered pace only recently and the use of overseas futures and options exchanges was not permitted till late 1998. But there are a lot of other examples of government interventions around the planet in recent years.

81

THE ROLES OF
MARKET
PARTICIPANTS AND
THEIR INFLUENCE ON
RISK MANAGEMENT IN
THE AGRICULTURAL
SECTOR

Conclusion

In this short chapter, I have attempted a whistle-stop tour of some of the key market participants and their roles in risk management. From producers through to governments, everyone interacts with differing degrees of complexity. Producers, carrying some of the greatest risks, have to deal with price volatility and weather risk. They influence the market through their associations and lobbies, or, in the case of developing countries, through the donors and aid agencies.

Large trading firms are probably the most influential in the market, simply through their purchasing programmes and shipping activities. Trading in agricultural products around the planet is dominated by just a few large players. They are able to build private financing schemes for producers and offer incentives at farm-gate level to trade. The large trade houses also participate in OTC markets, driving price efficiencies and developing sophisticated arbitrage techniques. In particular, the development of the swap market is an exciting theme. The largest players can also use their trading muscle to mitigate risks even in very hostile environments, such as in Argentina in recent times, beset by economic woes that would otherwise have resulted in a cessation of international trade.

Agricultural risk management is complex and diverse. At an international conference a leading lawyer said recently that often frauds don't start out as frauds, but simply as exploitable mistakes. The banker faces the consequences of physical risk and collateral loss. The "disappearance" of consignments requires the lender to carefully consider ways of preventing fraud and, in the event of a default scenario, getting recourse to collateral. This is where warehouse receipts schemes and the role of the collateral manager play their part.

Agribusiness risk management is an issue for all players in the market, whether they are confronting price volatility or physical loss or damage. Using a range of techniques to handle both physical and price risks is the challenge for all market participants and the institutions that support them.

BIBLIOGRAPHY

Budd, N., 1994, "A brief description of the field warehouse pledge as an appropriate security device for developing countries and the new market economies", presented at the UNIDROIT/International Bar Association conference on current trends in the modernisation of the law governing personal property security, Rome.

Claessens, S., and R. C. Duncan, 1993, *Managing Commodity Price Risk in Developing Countries*, published for the World Bank (Baltimore, MD: Johns Hopkins University Press).

JP Morgan & Co Incorporated, 1992, *Commodity-Linked Finance* (London: Euromoney Publications PLC).

Mellor, J. W., 1978, "Food Policy and Income Distribution in Low-Income Countries", *Economic Development and Cultural Change*, 27(1).

Varangis, P., and D. Larson, 1996, "Dealing with Commodity Price Uncertainty", policy research working paper number 1667, World Bank.

9

Innovative Approaches for Managing Agricultural Risks

Panos Varangis, Ulrich Hess and Erin Bryla

World Bank

Farmers face a spectrum of risks, and each of these risks – along with how farmers manage them – impacts farm income, productivity and access to credit. Farm-level surveys have indicated that the most frequently cited risks are price, crop/weather and health. These risks among others lower farmers' anticipated income and have negative effects on their standard of living, ability to provide for themselves and their families, ability to build capital and ability to access credit from lenders. Without being able to predict the minimum level of income that they will receive for their crops, they have difficulty optimally managing their farms.

To deal with these risks in the past, several countries have attempted to guarantee commodity prices and provide crop insurance and/or disaster relief. With regard to price risk, attempts to stabilise prices using stabilisation funds and buffer stocks have defied market forces and resulted in unsustainable programmes and substantial losses to treasuries.[1] All major international commodity agreements have collapsed while in many countries and commodities national governments have liberalised their marketing regimes exposing farmers to the full fluctuations of international markets.

With regard to yield risk, traditional crop insurance has been unable to deliver protection to farmers against unfavourable weather events because of moral hazard, adverse selection and high administrative costs. Traditional crop insurance programmes require significant subsidies to be effective, which puts pressure on the government's fiscal situation, and makes them too expensive for most developing countries to implement. Because of the high costs of this insurance in addition to the difficulties associated with its administration, crop insurance programmes have faced little take-up and are in place only when heavy subsidies are maintained by national governments.

In light of these failures, farmers have been provided few alternatives to deal with price and weather risk. They have resorted to dealing with these risks at the farm level through sub-optimal coping strategies to mitigate them. They are unable to take advantage of economies of scale associated with producing high-risk cash crops and rather invest in low-risk, low-yield production that helps them self-insure against price and weather events and ensure a minimum income.[2] These production patterns come at the expense of high-risk, high-return production that could create income growth and the build-up of capital.

Community-level attempts to deal with risk have had little success because of the covariant nature of agricultural risks. While it would seem that community-level risk pooling could be a means to deal with these risks, because both price and weather risks are not individual or idiosyncratic risk – rather, they are correlated systemic risks – community and regional risk pooling is not sufficiently diverse to be effective. Price and weather risk typically affect a large system of producers at once and informal insurance arrangements at the local community level often break down in the face of large systemic risks such as the collapse in commodity prices.

This chapter discusses innovative ways to deal with both price and yield risk in order to give smallholders greater access to finance. It looks primarily at the use of market-based price-risk management instruments and index-based weather insurance as alternatives to traditional methods for dealing with these risks. For small-scale farmers, reduction of the vulnerability associated with the risk of falling prices and falling yields can potentially provide a number of benefits.[3] The use of price-risk management instruments and index-based weather insurance provides producers with greater certainty about the minimum income they will receive from their crop and allows them to make better farm-management decisions regarding purchased inputs and labour use. Qualitative benefits alluded to by farmers in interviews on the subject include greater certainty and peace of mind.

Impacts of risk on lending

Lending institutions have looked for a variety of ways to expand their portfolio into agriculture, but, because of the risks associated with lending to farmers who lack traditional forms of collateral and face price falls and yield risk, these inroads have been limited. The traditional arrangements that commercial banks and other financiers use to extend lending are not well suited on their own to provide lending to the agriculture sector. In lieu of private involvement in agricultural lending, the state has often set up financing facilities (mainly in the form of state-owned agricultural banks) at highly subsidised rates that often face very high default rates. It is often argued that this intervention is necessary because farmers are such poor risks (partly due to the unpredictably nature of agricultural prices and yields) that commercial credit institutions will not lend to them. It is an empirical question to determine to what extent price- and weather/yield-related risks impede or constrain lending for agricultural commodities, and it is expected that this depends on a case-by-case basis. Nevertheless, some empirical evidence indicates that these are important risks that lenders for agriculture face.

Smallholders and creditors alike would benefit from the mitigation of price and yield risk, thereby making some formerly uncreditworthy producers lending candidates. The diagram below shows the way in which price and yield risk make agricultural producers uncreditworthy and how the elimination or mitigation of these risk could improve their risk profile and make them better lending candidates in the eyes of banks.

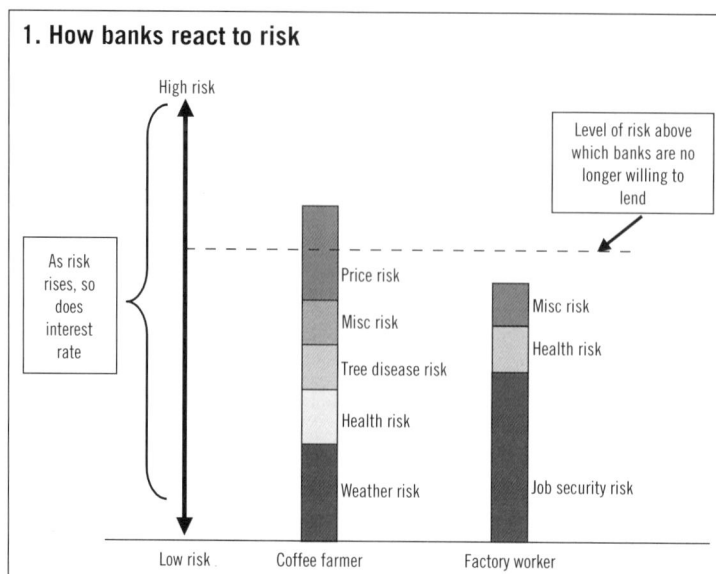

1. How banks react to risk

The use of market-based price-risk management instruments in mitigating risk for farmers and lenders

IMPACT OF PRICE VOLATILITY ON FARMERS

Price volatility significantly impacts the incomes of farmers and the macroeconomic health of their countries. From 1983 to 1998, the price of many commodities fluctuated from below 50% to above 150% of their average prices.[4] In the past, many countries used marketing boards to guarantee farmers a minimum price for their production. But government policy that attempted to separate domestic commodity prices from international prices has proven financially unsustainable. With liberalisation, many countries have abandoned marketing boards that were common to coffee, cocoa and other import crops, thereby eliminating the smoothing effects this guaranteed minimum income had for farmers.[5]

In light of this, farmers are exposed to price fluctuations over the course of the season, creating uncertainty about the price they will receive for their product when they take it to be sold. At the farm level, this uncertainty in commodity prices makes it difficult for producers to allocate resources efficiently, limits their access to credit for productivity-enhancing inputs and leads them to adopt low-yield, low-risk production technologies, thereby lowering average incomes. At the macro level, commodity price volatility affects governments' fiscal revenues, trade balance, exchange rate and creditworthiness.[6]

While market-based tools (futures and options) that insulate producers from the negative effects of short-term price volatility are widely used in high-income countries, the vast majority of agricultural producers in developing countries are, in general, unable to access these markets. In lieu of these alternatives, farmers take steps to mitigate their own risks.[7] In the absence of markets for price-hedging instruments, farmers try to cope with price risks by: (a) self-insuring through asset accumulation, savings and access to credit, (b) income diversification and (c) informal insurance arrangements. In most poor commodity-dependent countries and for most poor farmers, credit and savings markets are imperfect and asset accumulation is never enough in times of a crisis. Diversification to other activities is difficult because farmers lack skills, information and capital to do something else. Many farmers adopt low-risk and low-yield crop and production patterns to ensure a minimum income. These production patterns come at the expense of perhaps riskier but higher-return production that could create income growth and the accumulation of capital.

Finally, informal insurance arrangements at the local community level often break down in the face of large systemic risks such as the collapse in commodity prices. The use of market-based price-risk management instruments to mitigate this price risk would provide farmers with new alternatives and allow them greater certainty in planning their on-farm activities and possibly provide greater access to credit.[8]

Eliminating an important reason for non-repayment of loans, falling commodity prices could substantially reduce the risk exposure of agricultural finance programmes. The use of market-based price instruments is likely to result in improved access to credit for small-scale producers and a healthier loan portfolio for creditors. Coupling price-risk management instruments with a loan agreement lowers the risk of default that banks face because of falling commodity prices and substantially reduces transaction costs for the creditor and the borrowing producer. This type of joint product could serve to extend lending to producers who had not previously been deemed creditworthy, as well as increasing the average value of the loan because of the additional financing of the insurance premium, thereby allowing better absorption of the creditor's fixed costs.[9]

Financial institutions could combine hedging with lending in three main ways. The first is hedging the exposure of their overall portfolio to commodity prices. This could allow financial institutions to restructure their portfolio, extend repayments, or even forgive part of the interest and/or principal repayments when a severe price shock occurs. The second way is hedging on behalf of their borrowers, thus attaching a hedge to each loan, and the third is requiring that borrowers provide evidence of price protection when they come to negotiate a loan. A reasonable hypothesis is that banks will be able to expand their agricultural loan portfolios, and farmers will have better access to credit and/or opportunity to borrow at better terms. Microfinance institutions and credit unions may also prove feasible vehicles for delivery of price-risk management instruments, and are likely to have better access to smallholder farmers.

THE IMPLEMENTATION OF PRICE-RISK MANAGEMENT PROGRAMMES

While market-based tools (futures and options) that insulate producers from the negative effects of short-term price volatility are widely used in high-income countries, the vast majority of agricultural producers in developing countries are, in general, unable to access these markets. Some traditional barriers to entry have prevented small-holders from accessing these tools. The minimum size of contracts traded on organised exchanges far exceeds the annual quantity of production of individual small and medium-sized producers. In addition, small producers, as well as many market inter-mediaries in developing countries, lack knowledge of such market-based price insur-ance instruments and an understanding of how to use them. Finally, sellers of such instruments, generally international banks and brokerage houses, are often unwilling to engage with a new and unfamiliar customer base of small-scale producers, characterised by high transaction costs, diminished access to credit and performance risk.[10]

The World Bank – with support from several donor governments, and in collaboration with international organisations and private-sector representatives – has been working as a facilitator, providing technical assistance and capacity building to allow producers in developing countries and local intermediary institutions with links to producers to access these instruments. To date, seven transactions have been completed between developing-country clients (in Uganda, Tanzania and Nicaragua) and international providers (mainly major international banks in Europe and the US).

These transactions provided price protection for tonnages ranging from as low as 50 tons to as much as 700 tons. Transactions provided price protection for sales that were made in as short a period as one month in advance up to seven months in advance. The range of premiums paid for price protection varied from around 3% of the value of the commodity to as much as 9%, with most transactions involving premium payments of around 3–5%.[11] Several transactions were part of an overall hedging strategy in which the organisation that hedged aimed at improving its access to credit and reducing its borrowing costs.

HOW PRICE-RISK MANAGEMENT INSTRUMENTS WORK

A parallel can be drawn between hedging instruments for price risk and typical insur-ance products. Producers' organisations, local banks or exporters can purchase deriva-tives that are traded on international exchanges (or based off these exchanges), in most cases a simple put option, on behalf of their producers. When combined with physical sales these financial instruments will guarantee a minimum price level based on an international price (not a local price) for a given commodity for a number of months. In order to purchase this financial product, producers must pay a market-related fee or a premium. In the case of put option's, when price rises during the option contract period, the producer receives no payout from the contract but can still sell his physical product for the market price in order to benefit from the rising prices. However, when the price falls during this period, the producer receives a payout equal to the difference between the price the producer chose to insure with the price-risk management contract and the international market price on the last date of the option coverage.

Because of the size of these contracts it is necessary to aggregate producer demand for these products. A diversity of different types of organisations could serve this role as an intermediary. A domestic bank or other financial institution could integrate these products into its services.

Put option's are just one example of a price-risk management scheme that could be implemented. Each intermediary will have different ends based on the patterns of

2. Net price received vs net price received with hedging

The price *falls* and the farmer is not hedged

Price received = market price

Planting Harvest Sale

The price *falls* and the farmer is hedged

Price received

Insurance level

Market price

Planting Harvest Sale

Source: CRMG, World Bank, "Commodity Price Risk Management for Producers, A Training Guide"

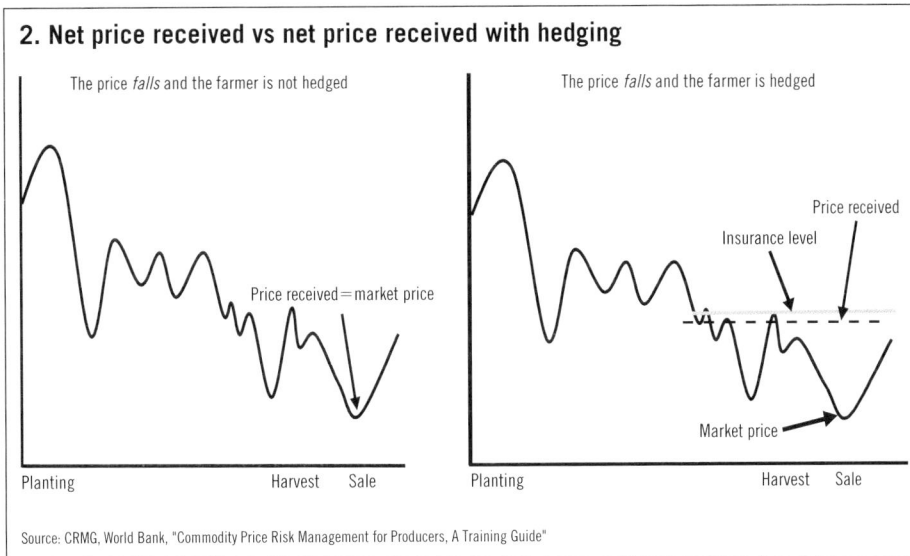

production of their farmers and their marketing strategies. Many alternatives exist in terms of the type and shape of price-risk management instruments farmers can utilise, and, as farmers become more experienced with these instruments, they can look at other instruments such as calls, collars and pops.

LESSONS LEARNED FROM CASE STUDIES TO DATE
The initial transactions that the World Bank has facilitated in addition to the past feasibility work have brought to light five major areas that must be addressed in order to overcome traditional obstacles such as contract size and knowledge gaps.[12] These areas highlight the necessary preconditions for establishing a price risk-management programme and carrying out its operations. The five primary "lessons learned" from this work to date are:

1. *The policy and regulatory environment* directly influences the use of these instruments and ability of smallholders to access price-risk instruments.
2. *Limited basis risk* is necessary for these instruments to effectively provide farmers a guarantee.
3. *Technical assistance and training* are necessary to "bridge the gap" between buyers and sellers of risk management instruments and complete transactions.
4. *The type of local client* dictates the nature of technical assistance and the implementation of a risk management programme.
5. *Private-sector providers* need intensive efforts in order to acclimatise them to transacting with clients in developing countries.

Policy and regulatory environment
The policy environment has an impact on the incentives for producers to manage price risks and makes it pivotal to investigate and analyse the domestic and international policy and regulatory environment in the countries where price-risk management instruments will be used. The environment that is most conducive to the use of hedging instruments in a country has liberalised markets, little to no direct government intervention in pricing and well-functioning private marketing institutions. Government interventions to artificially stabilise prices pre-empt the development of a market-based price-risk management system. In some cases the use of price-risk management instruments could allow governments to disengage from costly and distortionary stabilisation policies.

But it is not only minimum price policies that can preclude the development of a price-risk management scheme. In some countries – for example, India – current regulations prohibit the use of options by non-exporters; and, in other countries, it is difficult to transfer money abroad to purchase hedging instruments. International policies can also preclude the development of a price-risk management programme. Several developing countries sell their sugar into quota markets at a fixed preferential price, causing farm gate price to fluctuate relatively little and mitigating price risks for producers.

In addition, foreign exchange regulations can limit the operation of a price-risk management programme. Because price-risk management instruments are traded on international markets in dollars or pounds, distinct types of taxation on foreign exchange and limitations on business dealing in foreign currency can stymie the ability of organisations to undertake a price-risk management programme.

Basis risk
It would be impractical to establish a price-risk management programme in those countries where farmers face a high degree of basis risk between local prices and international prices and where local prices do not move concordantly with international prices. If there are no linkages in movement between international prices and local prices, price-risk management instruments will not be able to sufficiently hedge the risk a farmer faces. Because price-risk management instruments pay out according to international price movements, their usage hedges farmers' risk only when the international price falls, not when the local price falls. This could leave farmers exposed should their local prices fall when international prices are rising. Additionally, farmers whose countries face a high degree of currency risk might not be able to benefit from price-risk management instruments. Because these instruments are priced in dollars and pounds, farmers would take on the costs of any adverse movements in currency values.

Technical assistance and training
Because this is a completely new line of business, even for relatively sophisticated users such as managers and staff of producer organisations, the understanding of how hedging functions and the capacity to manage the transactions are low. Therefore, organisations' staff – both management and technical – must undertake sufficient training and capacity building in order to gain a very thorough understanding of risk management procedures before their organisations become clients.

Technical assistance must include assisting each producer organisation individually in making a comprehensive and coherent risk assessment. This analysis needs to compare/contrast risks involved in their operations with and without hedging. Risk assessment is a critical tool for local management, who must have the capacity to make informed decisions on how to proceed with implementation and specific transactions.

Technical assistance should also cover important areas such as internal procedures, and include participatory training activities such as mock trade sessions and different market scenarios and outcomes. The efforts to focus on training with management should run parallel with efforts to adapt these training sessions so that they will enable farmers to understand the basic mechanics of hedging and costs and benefits of participation.

Local clients
Given the small production volumes of most individual farmers, it is necessary to involve an intermediary institution that can aggregate the demands of individual farmers for a risk management instrument into the minimum size traded on international markets. Because of the diversified types of organisations that undertake marketing and provide services to producers, any of a number of different organisations could in principle play this role. There are three types of organisations – cooperatives, financial institutions and traders – that are, in general, best positioned to act as local intermediaries in providing risk management services.

Cooperatives are interested in combining risk management with the contract to purchase commodities from members. This increases the service offerings they provide to their members and makes them more competitive in relation to commercial exporters and other cooperatives.

Banks and other financial institutions are interested in linking loans to price-risk management tools, thus protecting their own risk profile. Financial institutions could combine hedging with lending in three main ways: (a) hedging for themselves the exposure of their overall portfolio to commodity prices, which could allow financial institutions to restructure their portfolio, extend repayments or even forgive part of the interest and/or principal repayments when a severe price shock occurs; (b) hedging on behalf of their borrowers, thus attaching a hedge to each loan; and (c) requiring that borrowers provide evidence of price protection when they come to negotiate a loan. A reasonable hypothesis is that the banks will be able to expand their agricultural loan portfolios, and the farmers will have better access to credit and/or opportunity to borrow at better terms. Microfinance institutions and credit unions may also prove feasible vehicles for delivery of price-risk management instruments, and are likely to have better access to smallholder farmers.

In principle, local traders, including exporters and warehouse operators, could be intermediaries in order to increase the services they offer. But the majority of traders do not necessarily have an incentive to increase the capacity, sophistication and market knowledge of the producers. In addition, most traders hedge their price exposure already (back-to-back sales, use of forward and futures markets) and they may find little incentive to develop risk management instruments for farmers who have different price exposure than they (traders) have. Also, a trader linking risk management instruments to the physical sales of the product faces a higher default risk than he does when offering straightforward purchase contracts. If prices rise, the purchase contract with the embedded risk management instrument pays a lower net price to the producer than competing purchase offers without risk management, creating a disincentive to fulfil the contract.[13] On the other hand, traders may find that embedding price protection (eg, minimum price) into their physical contracts will improve the services they provide to farmers and may attract more business.

Private-sector providers

It was initially assumed that, once clients in developing countries had the technical skills to design a price-risk management programme, it would take limited work to identify and establish a relationship with a private sector provider for these clients. But, contrary to this assumption, most providers of price-risk management instruments are not completely prepared to transact with entities in developing countries, particularly with organisations of small-scale producers.

One of the main reasons is that providers lack familiarity with the policy and regulatory issues involved in doing business with international partners and lack experience of working with clients from developing countries. Additionally, before providers are ready to do business, they must also fulfil the stringent regulatory requirements that precede taking on a new client, including performing due diligence to look at money laundering, evaluating clients' understanding of risk management and fulfilling general "know-your-counterpart" guidelines.

Another issue that slows providers from entering into these transactions is a worry that the volumes of transactions could be too small for providers to have adequate margins and sustain their interest in the long run. Providers understand that all new business development starts small; but, when taking on a new client, providers must also consider the potential of that client's transactions to increase over time in order to make that client a viable business partner for the provider.

CASE STUDY: TANZANIAN COFFEE

In 2001 and 2002, coffee price fell to 40-year lows. Coffee is 20% of Tanzania's export earnings and this fall has affected more than 400,000 low-income coffee households in Tanzania. The coffee sector in Tanzania was liberalised in 1993 and as a result there is competitive buying at the village level, where coffee is purchased by both private traders and cooperatives. Liberalisation has exposed farmers and their marketing organisations to price fluctuations over the course of the season, which has made it difficult for farmers to optimise production technology, timing of sales and use of assets that could eventually result in higher household incomes.[14] Exposure to price volatility coupled with absolute low prices for coffee has greatly diminished the overall welfare of coffee farmers.

While the long-term trend of declining prices cannot be stopped without some overall structural changes in the world coffee market, to confront the negative effects of short-term price volatility one of the largest coffee cooperatives in Tanzania has begun working with the World Bank to utilise price-risk management instruments to hedge their price risk. This cooperative union has a large number of smallholder-producer members whose average production is 20–100 kg per farmer.

Like many other cooperatives in Tanzania, the cooperative union utilises a pricing system that consists of multiple payments to farmers throughout the year. Cooperative members receive a uniform minimum price for their coffee when they deliver it to the union, and then, later in the season – depending on sales and market performance overall – farmers may receive subsequent payments for their product. The uniform minimum price, which is called the "first payment", is established months in advance of the actual selling season and agreed at the annual general meeting of the producers. The guaranteed first payment is viewed as a service to the farmers and provides them with some form of price stability, but it can have disastrous financial impacts on the cooperative overall. If cooperatives guarantee a low first payment at the beginning of the season, they run the risk that market prices will rise and farmers will sell to traders instead of to the cooperative (local traders compete with the cooperatives by paying full market price for coffee, in cash, at the time of delivery of the product). If cooperatives guarantee a high first payment at the beginning of the season, they run the risk that market prices will fall, and they will make losses on the negative margin between purchase price to farmers and actual sales prices on the market. Since the first payment price is established well ahead of the selling season at a time when sales prices are not yet known, the cooperative union is essentially taking a long position on coffee, which is in effect from the time they set the first payment until the time they conclude all sales of coffee at the end of the season, a period that can stretch up to 10 months.

There are other negative impacts of the first payment pricing system as well. In years past, in order to maintain the first payment price in the face of falling market prices during the sales period, the cooperative union would rely on premiums received for quality coffees with high positive differentials. This is proving not to be an effective strategy, however, since quality premiums are volatile and vary from season to season, and since the system creates disincentives for farmers to produce quality coffee. Because the union's policy is to pay the first payment price to all producers uniformly, those producers who sell quality coffee have very little incentive to sell to the cooperative. Any premium that the cooperative union does receive for sales of quality product is essentially diluted across all members to help guarantee the first payment and contribute to any subsequent payments.

For long-term survival and to assure continued financing year to year, it was important for the cooperative union to develop new ways to manage a number of very difficult, sometimes conflicting goals, including:

1. Maintaining the tiered pricing system that gave farmer members a first payment price at the beginning of the season. This is considered to be a valuable service of the cooperative union, since the system provides price stability that helps farmers plan individual production and family budgets.
2. Finding a way to protect overall profitability from the often disastrous effects of setting first payment price high at the beginning of the season and having to sell low when prices fell later in the season.

3. Maintaining the union's ability to attract coffee supply large enough to meet forecasted sales obligations (ie, not lose supply to traders).
4. Maintaining the union's ability to attract high-quality coffee product in order to maximise high premium coffee sales.

In past years, the cooperative union had received funding for its operations at the beginning of the season in the form of a loan from a local commercial bank. Going forward, however, the loan agreements and the union's access to financing were in serious jeopardy due to a history of poor financial performance, which related in large part to the pricing problems described above. Since the coffee sector is very important to the economic and social structure of Tanzania, in the past the government had supported many of the cooperative unions through difficult times, but was indicating an impatience to continue doing so indefinitely.

The management of the cooperative union was determined to try to save the organisation so that it could continue to provide services to its thousands of farmer members. Management began an aggressive export marketing drive and was able to improve the volume of export sales, which often receive Fair Trade prices and high-quality premiums, but the majority of sales volume continued to be problematic and at risk. In order to assist the cooperative's own attempts to strengthen its marketing operations, the World Bank began working with the union to help it protect its prices with market-based hedging instruments.

The services provided by the World Bank's Commodity Risk Management Group consisted of technical assistance in the form of training and education about price-risk management markets, principles and products. The training with the cooperative union focused on four primary areas: (1) global markets, activities and risk management products for producers; (2) risk assessment and design of price-risk management programme; (3) membership awareness and adoption of programme; and (4) account opening and mechanics of trading.

Work with the cooperative union began in the summer of 2001, when the team provided the cooperative, the local bank and other players in the Tanzanian coffee sector with an overview of price-risk management markets and instruments, and their application for producers. Information on the price-risk management strategy was then distributed through society-level training sessions administered by the cooperative staff. While these sessions did not get into details on options and derivatives markets, they did provide society leaders with a needed basic understanding of how hedging instruments work and the costs and benefits of using them. Once the union's management accepted the project, it was presented at the annual general meeting for approval (1) to move forward with such a programme and (2) to allocate funds to pay premiums for these instruments. After completion of this step, the project team provided more in-depth training, held collaborative work sessions with the management team and proceeded with implementation. Using put option's, the cooperative union designed a hedging strategy that matched its risk profile and was able to put in price floors on the international market to protect against declining prices. The objectives of the strategy were to protect the union's break-even position and guarantee a first payment to farmers.

One of the main challenges associated with implementing this programme was the opening of an account to trade with the international bank acting as provider.[15] It was initially assumed that, once clients in developing countries had the technical skills to design a hedging strategy, it would take limited work to identify and establish a relationship with a provider. However, most providers of price-risk management instruments are not completely prepared to transact with entities in developing countries, particularly with organisations of small-scale producers. A key issue for the providers was the need to prove knowledge of the client, including ensuring that the client understood the risk management products he/she was purchasing. Providers of financial products and services have intense due-diligence requirements that include, among other things, the need to provide detailed information about ownership, structure, financial status and trading history of the cooperative union. With anti-money-laundering laws getting particularly stringent, this part of the process took on added importance, and a great deal of time. Eventually, the cooperative was approved as a new client and was able enter the market and hedge its price risk. The union took its first hedge position by buying a put option in October and it continued with market activity (which consisted of reselling the option when it no longer had exposure in a given month, and purchasing new option contracts to cover upcoming months) through to the end of the selling season in March.

From the provider's perspective, the technical assistance provided by the Commodity Risk Management Group was critical. Without such technical assistance, private-sector participants have indicated that they would not have been willing and able to transact with such new clients in developing countries. For the cooperative, although conclusive impacts of the risk management strategy are not yet entirely known, since the season is just now ending at the time of writing (April 2003), there were a number of positive effects:

1. The union improved its relationship with its local bank, which included a loan for premiums to cover the cost of hedging instruments in the total loan package given at the beginning of the year. In fact, partly due to hedging, the local bank reduced the interest rate it offered on new loans to the union by about five percentage points.
2. The union improved its overall financial state, including its debt position, and management of the union had a clear view of overall financial status throughout the season, without having to worry about the impact of prices falling below a certain level on the global market. They were able to communicate results with confidence to the local bank and government ministers, who were monitoring progress.
3. Improved financial transparency helped the union make better and more strategic selling decisions.
4. The union was able to pay farmers a second and third payment, since there were periods of relatively higher market prices during some months of the selling season. In the past, any positive returns from high-priced sales would have been held by the union until the end of the season to protect against future losses. With hedging, the price floor created by the option allowed the union to disperse revenue at the time it was earned.

Each of the impacts listed above bodes well for the union's ability to continue to strengthen its relationship with its lenders and improve its access to credit. In a very short period, the union has moved from being a very high-risk enterprise to a much more stable operation. Price risk management has contributed to that growing stability and the union's managers have indicated that they are very pleased to have knowledge and access to such tools.

The use of index-based yield insurance in mitigating risk for farmers and lenders

IMPACT OF WEATHER RISK ON FARMERS[16]

While farm yields can be affected in a number of ways – bad farming practices, shortage of labour, ageing and diseased plants – most of these things can be controlled through proper farm management and agricultural technology. But the ability of farmers to mitigate the impact of weather events such as droughts, floods, frosts and hurricanes on their income is limited. Weather events are a pervasive characteristic of agricultural production. Some of the ways farmers deal with weather risk are similar to their mechanisms for dealing with price risk through activities such self-insurance, diversification and adoption of low-risk, low-return production practices, but farmers also undertake additional risk management practices such as irrigation and conservation tillage to protect soil and add moisture.

Weather risks are covariant and typically shock entire regions at once. If one farmer is suffering from some sort of weather problem, it is likely that all of his neighbours are also. This makes it very difficult to set up local insurance schemes that have sufficient diversity in their portfolio to deal with the covariant risks. This bankrupts and makes ineffective "risk pools" and other local insurance schemes in the time of a weather crisis in a given area because all farmers must be paid at once.[17]

Limitations on agricultural lending are in large part due to the inability of farmers to control yields in light of possible weather events. By nature, weather events are generally hard to predict and can be devastating to a farmer's anticipated income and ability to repay debts. Because of this unpredictability, banks are hesitant to lend to farmers who could suffer loses due to weather. Weather risk, like price risk, has been one of the justifications for supporting state-owned agricultural banks to provide lending to farmers. Some developed and developing countries have adopted crop insurance programmes to deal with yield variations, identifying crop insurance as a way to protect agricultural credit. In many cases, banks have linked crop insurance policies to the farmers' credit requests. Brazil, India, Mexico and Morocco, among few other developing countries, have tried to link agricultural credit to some form of yield insurance, usually traditional crop insurance. However, traditional crop insurance has several problems, including moral hazard, adverse selection and high administrative costs.[18] These problems are much higher when it comes to small producers in developing countries, with weak information systems, lack of experience in insurance and weak financial/ insurance institutions. Because of the problems with traditional crop insurance, many of these efforts linking credit to insurance have encountered serious limitations (eg, limited coverage) and high costs. Governments and local private companies are looking into new approaches for linking credit to some form of output or weather insurance.[19]

HOW INDEX-BASED WEATHER INSURANCE WORKS

Risk management products based on weather events avoid the problems of traditional crop insurance because they rely on objective observations of specific weather events that are outside the control of either farmers or insurance companies. They are also less costly to administer because they do not require individual contracts and on-field inspections and loss adjustments. Although these are often called index-based weather insurance products, they are strictly risk management tools rather than traditional insurance.

Index-based weather insurance compares a measurable, objective, correlated risk (eg, rainfall, temperature, wind speed) to yields.[20] In the case of rainfall as the correlated risk, historical data gathered from regional weather stations are used to determine the mean rainfall for a given period in the farmer's area. Once the appropriate period has been selected, the issue becomes one of structuring the rainfall index.[21]

A weather (rainfall) "index" should be carefully designed to weight the more important periods for rainfall in the crop cycle more heavily and than those periods where rainfall is not as important to production. Precipitation in different stages contributes in different measures to plant growth and an excess of rain may be of no use for production. Hence, it is useful to develop a weighting system that allows for differentiation in the importance of rainfall in different growth periods and to shape the model so as to take into account the fact that excess rain may be wasted without contributing to plant growth. The final value of the index (the value that, when compared with the threshold, indicates whether or not the insured should be granted an indemnity) is calculated by summing the values obtained by multiplying rainfall levels in each period by the specific weight assigned to the period.[22]

Once a sufficient degree of correlation is established between rainfall and yield, and the index has been weighted properly, an agricultural producer can hedge his production risk by purchasing a contract that pays in the case that rainfall falls below a certain threshold. Farmers can elect coverage for a given period, taking into consideration the crop cycle and the marketing cycle. Using this historical index, the programme is designed as a European put, where the option premium is the cost of the coverage and the strike is the rainfall threshold below which indemnity is triggered. The insurance is set up on a proportional basis, allowing farmers to choose their rainfall trigger level or threshold.[23]

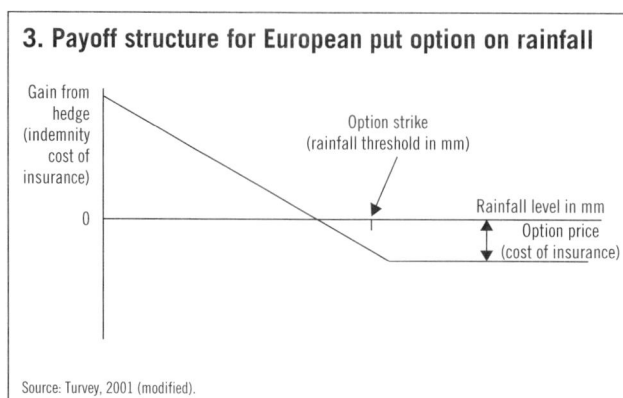

3. Payoff structure for European put option on rainfall

Gain from hedge (indemnity cost of insurance)

Option strike (rainfall threshold in mm)

Rainfall level in mm
Option price (cost of insurance)

0

Source: Turvey, 2001 (modified).

Customers participating receive a payment if the rainfall index level falls below the threshold. The higher the threshold set for the contract, the better the coverage provided, the trade-off being the higher the threshold, the higher the cost of the coverage. In essence a farmer can elect a lower trigger amount of rainfall in order to lower his premium or he can elect a much higher trigger that will give him greater protection but will cost more in premium. Customers can also elect the comprehension of their insurance so they can partially or fully insure their revenue.

Their payment from the insurance is ultimately determined by the combination of these two factors – the rainfall threshold that they wish to be their trigger and the comprehensiveness of the coverage they want. Payment is equivalent to the percentage of rainfall-index shortage multiplied by the level of coverage selected. In the case where rainfall does not fall below the trigger, no payment is made to the farmer and the premium is not returned.

NECESSARY PRECONDITIONS FOR THE USE OF THESE INSTRUMENTS
Index-based weather-risk management programmes have shown many advantages over traditional crop insurance. They do not suffer from the same type of moral hazard and their administration costs are significantly cheaper. But there are a few preconditions that must be met before a index-based weather-risk management can be established.

1. *A measurable, correlated risk* must be present in order that a comparable index can be established.
2. *Reliable weather and yield data* need to exist. There is also a need for weather-measuring infrastructure that is reliable and tamperproof.
3. *Policy and regulatory environment* in a country must allow for the use of index-based weather-risk management programmes.
4. *Risk levels* must be acceptable for reinsurers in order that premiums do not become unaffordable.

Measurable objective risk and reliable weather data
An index-based weather-risk management programme is contingent on the ability to establish a measurable index. Using rainfall as an example, if either rainfall could not be accurately measured or there was insufficient historical data to establish an index, it would be impossible to establish this type of insurance. In many countries, historical weather data are insufficient to determine whether a correlation exists between yield and weather. In those cases where data are sufficient and a correlation can be established between yield and another measurable weather factor, it is necessary that accurate and timely weather data can be gathered. This would include the ability of personnel to take accurate measurements and the prevention of tampering with weather stations and data.

Although verification mechanisms such as fallback stations and even satellite data might be used, the primary data have to be highly reliable and accurate.

Policy and regulatory environment

A second major precondition in establishing a weather-risk management programme is to ensure the presence of the proper regulatory framework. Limitations on the usage of insurance could inhibit the use of these types of markets. But a more common policy issue that effects the establishment of a weather-risk management programme is the crowding-out effect associated with emergency aid and frequent bailouts in the cases of severe weather events. Governments who frequently give aid in times of climatic problems create disincentives for participation in weather-risk management programmes. Farmers prefer to keep the money they would spend on the premium and hope for government relief in times of emergency. This requires that governments establish clear rules of providing emergency assistance following predefined catastrophic weather events.[24]

Acceptable levels of risk

The third major precondition applies to whether there are acceptable levels of risk for reinsurers to be interested in participating in the risk management programme. Some producers face unfavourable weather events frequently, and, while these events are devastating to farmers' production, their frequency limits the ability of reinsurance markets to take them on. The frequency coupled with the severity of these events drives up the premium levels for coverage, often making them unaffordable and impractical for producers.

CASE STUDY: RAINFALL RISK IN INDIA

The World Bank, in conjunction with a number of Indian partners, is implementing two index-based weather insurance projects to help farmers deal with weather risk during the monsoon season. Weather risk is the most pervasive factor in monsoon-season production. Low rainfall is the primary factor affecting *kharif*, or monsoon-season crop production, in India. In the past, the magnitude of decline in production during this season has varied depending upon the severity of the drought. In 2002–2003, poor rainfall caused the largest drop in food production since 1972–73 even when compared with other poor rainfall years. During the 2002–2003 season, India received the lowest rainfall ever for the month of July (49%), normally the rainiest and most crucial month of the season for *kharif* crops.

Table 1.

Deficient rainfall years	Monsoon rainfall % departure from normal	Rainfall in July %	*Kharif* food-grain production % fall
1972–73	−24	−31	−7
1974–75	−12	−4	−13
1979–80	−19	−16	−19
1982–83	−14	−23	−12
1986–87	−13	−14	−6
1987–88	−19	−29	−7
2002–03	−19	−49	−19

Source: GoI, Economic Survey 2002–2003, p. 157.

This severe drought in 2002–2003 caused a 3.1% decline in agricultural GDP and is likely to reduce overall GDP growth from 5.6% in 2002 to 4.4% in 2003. In addition to monsoon risk in certain states, such as Andhra Pradesh, there is flood and cyclone risk. This shows the pervasive nature of weather risk in parts of India, exemplified by a 2003 survey of coffee farmers in Karnataka, which identified weather volatility as the single most important risk faced according to the respondents.[25]

CHALLENGES FOR GOVERNMENT PROGRAMMES

This drought problem has certainly not gone unnoticed by the government, who have reacted to drought risk by beginning to offer an area index-based crop insurance scheme through state-owned insurance companies. The objective of the government scheme is to insure the farmer's crop loan exposure against drought risk. The National Agricultural Insurance Scheme (NAIS) covers credit default risk for most crops at premium rates of 1.5–3.5% of the loan amount, with small farmers receiving a 50% premium subsidy. The agriculture insurance corporation implemented this scheme and collected premiums of Rs2.5 billion covering an area of 1.3 million hectares, a negligible fraction of Indian cultivated land. Total claims on this insurance were Rs4.7 billion, resulting in a claims ratio of almost 200% in a normal year.

Because of this high cost, this scheme has been unsuccessful in providing farmers with security against weather risks that affect their production. As stated in Parchure (2002),

> *The performance of the crop insurance scheme in India can only be judged as disappointing on all counts; financial, economic and administrative. … from 1985–6 through 1999 the total premiums collected were Rs. 402 crores (US$80 million) and the total claims paid Rs. 2305.0 crores (US$461 million) with a sum insured of Rs. 24,921 crores (US$5 billion). The loss ratio excluding huge management expenses stands at 5.72. From an economic point of view average per annum claims paid were Rs. 233 crores which if compared to the sum-at-risk ie, the agricultural output of the country worth Rs. 6,50,000 crores is hardly 0.035% and when compared to the total farm loans of Rs. 58,000 crores is only 0.40%.*

The following tables also reveal that premiums and claims do not seem to be "equitably" distributed across crops and states.

Table 2. Lending to Indian agriculture

Table 2a. Cropwise premiums and claims: origin and destination (1985–6 to 1999)

	Premium		Claims		Loss Ratio
	Rs. Cr.	%	Rs. Cr.	%	
Paddy	217.52	54	576.26	25	2.65
Wheat	52.36	13	46.10	2	0.88
Groundnut	60.42	15	1,221.68	53	20.22
Jowar	36.25	9	184.40	8	5.08
Bajra	24.16	6	184.40	8	7.63
Pulses	4.02	1	23.05	1	5.73
Others	8.04	2	69.15	3	8.60

Table 2b. Statewise premium and claims: origin and destination (1985–6 to 1999)

	Premium		Claims		Loss Ratio
	Rs. Cr.	%	Rs. Cr.	%	
Gujarat	64.45	16	1,336.93	58	20.74
Maharashtra	60.42	15	253.55	11	4.19
Andhra Pradesh	100.70	25	322.70	14	3.20
Others*	177.24	44	391.86	17	2.21

*include 22 states and UT's excluding Punjab, Haryana and North-Eastern states.

According to a leading microfinance practitioner in India (see Mahajan, 2001), due to the small average size of transactions and distance of the branches from the villages, the transaction costs of savings in formal institutions were as high as 10% for the rural poor. Most of the poor do not have access to the banking system for the purposes of lending, either. A study by PriceWaterhouseCoopers in 1997 indicated that the dependence of the low-income households on the informal sources of finance is as high as 78%. India's formal financial intermediaries – through their commercial lending programmes – reportedly meet merely 2.5% of the credit needs of the unorganised sector.[26] This lack of access is aggravated by the risk profile of farmers, in particular rain-fed farmers. Additionally, formal finance institutions are limited from lending to farmers because caps on interest rates and government regulations restrict them from charging the interest rates necessary to account for this risk and recover their costs. Finally, banks are hesitant to lend to farmers because of what is perceived as a culture of default in the case of crop failures, coupled with the fact that political pressures for debt forgiveness tend to rise in drought years.

The proposed weather-risk management programme apportioned with a crop loan seeks to transfer risk of nonpayment as a result of a monsoon from the farmer–bank relationship into insurance markets and minimise the "excuses" for non-repayment. By combining a weather-risk management instrument with a crop loan, farmers will be given greater ability to access credit and repay that credit in times of weather calamity. The scheme outlined below aims to significantly increase access to crop loans in rural areas, particularly in rain-fed areas.

TWO PROPOSED PROGRAMMES TO DEAL WITH WEATHER RISK FROM MONSOONS
Monsoon insurance contracts are written against specific rainfall outcomes (eg, drought or flood, recorded at a local weather station) that are highly correlated with the value of regional agricultural production or income. For example, an insured event might be that rainfall during the most critical month of the growing season falls 70% below normal. In years when the insured event occurs, all the people who purchased the insurance receive the same payment per unit. In all other years, no payments are made (see Skees/Hazell, 2002). In the Indian case, the insurance event is defined as cumulative weighted rainfall dropping below a certain threshold of 75% up to 85% of the normal rainfall measured at the nearest weather station. Contract periods and payout dates depend on the particular crop cycle. Payouts are proportional to the measured rainfall deficit below the threshold and occur in the form of crop loan interest and principal relief.[27]

Two pilots are being set up in India to meld index-based crop insurance into two established programmes that have already had a good deal of success in delivering financial services to producers.

Mahindra Shubhlab cooperation with ICICI
The first of these pilots will be with the producers who obtain lending from ICICI Bank, India's second-largest bank with total assets of about Rs1 trillion (US$20 billion) and a network of about 540 branches and offices and more than 1,000 ATMs. ICICI Bank offers banking products and financial services to corporate and retail customers through its specialised subsidiaries and affiliates in the areas of investment banking, life and non-life insurance, venture capital, asset management and information technology. In order to expand its services to the rural sector ICICI is looking to find a means to limit its exposure to non-repayment. Index-based weather insurance is seen as a means to insure against this risk.

ICICI Bank already has a strong presence in the rural sector. ICICI innovated in the rural sector, lending by effectively delegating a large part of the lending and collection process to de facto agents such as traders or agricultural service providers or local brokers that are close to the farmer by the nature of their business. These local brokers operate service centres that provide inputs and extension in addition to credit.

In the ICICI model, the bank identifies an integrated agricultural services provider (IASP) that has a good relationship with the farmer and provides genuine and timely information through extension services to act as partners in credit distributions. ICICI enters into a tripartite agreement with the IASP and the output buyer. In this arrangement, ICICI provides credit to the farmers on the recommendation of the IASP, the farmer pledges his produce to the output buyer, and the IASP provides inputs to the farmer. Loan processing, disbursement and collection are effectively done by the IASP, while the credit decision remains nominally with ICICI Bank. At the end of the season, the farmers supply the crop to the output buyer and the output buyer deducts the loan amount from the sale proceeds and remits the loan to ICICI Bank in full settlement of the loan amount. The IASP receives a service fee for the loan processing and supervision services (1.5% on recovered loans). Loan default rates have been significantly lower with this integrated model that traps receivables and provides little actual cash to farmers. Transaction costs are reduced through more efficient loan processing by an agent close to the farmer and a de facto wholesale credit approval process at ICICI. This agency model allows ICICI to lend to farmers without a significant branch network and with almost no due-diligence costs.

The pilot will operate with one of these IASPs operated by Mahindra Shubhlabh (MSSL) which is headquartered in Mumbai. MSSL has 45 centres up and running, and plans to develop 180 agricultural service centres (ASCs) in India's major agro-climatic areas. MSSL offices operate on a franchise basis, financing around 4,000 farmers. The MSSL model uses "spokes" as agents, usually medium-sized but respected farmers who recommend borrowers. Sub-agents supervise borrowers through regular visits. Thanks to the close relationship between MSSL and the farmers, which includes backward linkages to output buyers, the default risk due to moral hazard is limited. Loan default rates are lower than those of comparable banks without these strong agency arrangements. Despite these close ties, covariate risk is still a major one for the existing loan portfolio as well as the expansion areas, and loan defaults (NPLs) are triggered mainly by monsoon failure or other calamities. Farmers find they are unable and to some extent unwilling to pay interest on their crop loans in a severe drought year and seek to reschedule principal repayments.

The crop loan insurance and risk management scheme would be a natural extension of the outlined MSSL–ICICI cooperation. MSSL acts effectively as ICICI's agent with farmers and would simply expand current ICICI services offered to farmers through

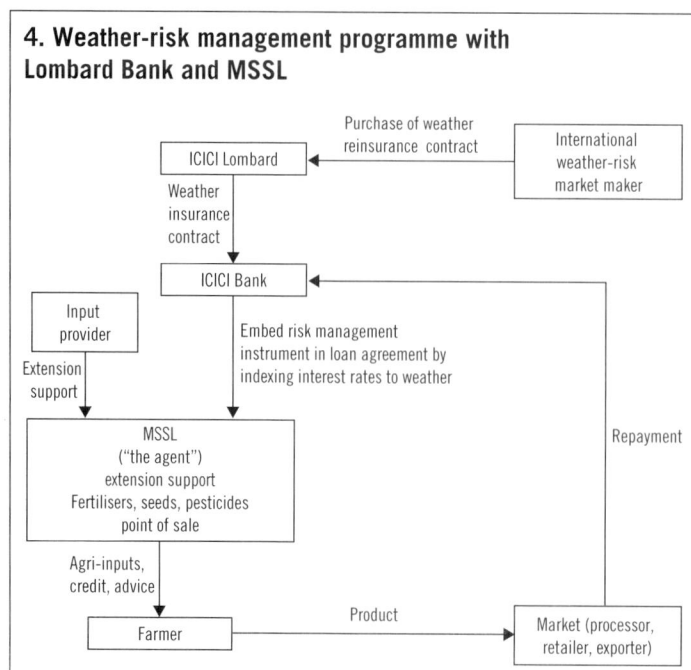

4. Weather-risk management programme with Lombard Bank and MSSL

this scheme. ICICI would incorporate a weather-risk management instrument into the lending that MSSL manages by indexing interest payments to rainfall measures. The borrower pays a higher interest rate in normal years, which comprises the weather-based index insurance premium, but, in case of a severe rainfall deficit and in one case excessive rainfall in critical periods, the borrower pays no or only partial interest on the loan. The desired effect is to keep the farmer bankable even throughout drought years.

For example, in Ujjain, Madhya Pradesh, crop loans of Rs2,000 with embedded weather insurance to soya farmers would attract an interest rate of 20.5% instead of 17.5%. While the overall rate goes up due to the weather insurance premium, the actual interest rate will be lowered with the cost of the weather-risk instrument stripped out. The insurance kicks in when cumulative weighted rainfall during the critical growing periods falls below 80% of the mean. The farmer receives interest payment relief of Rs10 per mm of rainfall index deficit. In the case of a 75% of the mean rainfall year, the interest payment would be Rs130 instead of Rs180. This interest payment relief is an important break for the farmer's strained budget after a failed harvest.

BASIX

The second pilot being implemented in India distributes weather insurance to farmers through BASIX, a well-established micro-finance organisation working throughout the region of Andhra Pradesh. BASIX was set up in 1996 as microfinance institution or rural livelihood promotion institution. The mission of BASIX is to promote a large number of sustainable livelihoods, including for the rural poor and women, through the provision of financial services and technical assistance in an integrated manner. BASIX is not a single institution but rather a combination of financial-service and technical-assistance companies. The two main partners in BASIX are the Bhartiya Samruddhi Finance Limited (Samruddhi), registered with the Reserve Bank of India as a non-banking finance company, which is the main operating entity through which credit is delivered, and Indian Grameen Services (IGS), an NGO involved in providing technical assistance and support services to Samruddhi borrowers and other rural producers and institutions. In February 2001, BASIX also got a licence from the Reserve Bank of India to open a local area bank. The Krishna Bhima Samruddhi Local Area Bank commenced operations in March 2001 in the districts of Mahaboobnagar in Andhra Pradesh and Raichur and Gulbarga in Karnataka (see BASIX, 2003).[28]

BASIX has gained significant experience with innovative crop insurance schemes. For dry-land agriculture, BASIX has developed a concept to mitigate yield risk based on self-insurance, mutual insurance and reinsurance with a role for the insured to participate in product administration. The concept has a built-in mechanism to minimise adverse selection and administration costs, and discourage settlement of false claims. BASIX also does seasonal pre-harvest financing, mainly to sunflower, cotton and groundnut farmers.

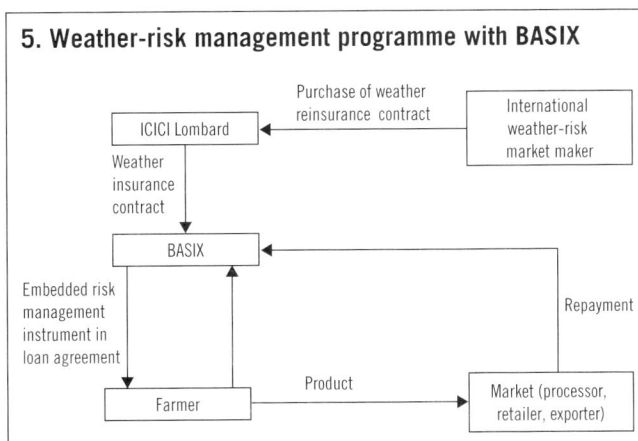

5. Weather-risk management programme with BASIX

100

INNOVATIVE
APPROACHES FOR
MANAGING
AGRICULTURAL
RISKS

Basix would implement an index-based weather-risk management scheme by embedding the weather-risk management in the loan agreement that they make with the farmer. They would purchase these weather-risk management instruments through ICICI Lombard, who would have, in turn, reinsured this risk on international markets. A payout from the insurance would go directly to BASIX to be credited towards the principal and interest owed by the borrowing farmer.

Other innovations[29]

Price- and weather-risk management improve the certainty of borrowers' cashflow and ensure that they will be able to repay the loan in cases of severe weather events and collapse in international prices for a commodity. If risk management contracts are endorsed to banks and rural financial institutions, then they can be a form of "liquid" collateral. Another form of liquid collateral that could improve the "creditworthiness" of farmers for banks and other financial institutions is the use of warehouse receipts. Warehouse receipts can prove to be good collateral after the goods are produced and deposited in a secure warehouse. Banks can lend using commodities in the warehouse as collateral because, in the case of loan default, banks have access to the goods that can sell and recover the loan. Security of the warehouse facilities and an appropriate legal and regulatory environment are usually needed for commodities to be safe collateral in warehouses. Currently, in the Mexican sugar sector, millers have begun relying on "reverse repurchase transactions" or *reportos* to obtain lending from there commercial banks. These millers, in a sector that supports 3 million people, are the primary source of financing for producers and require a certain amount of working capital to maintain their operations.

In this *reporto* scheme, millers deposit in a certified third-party warehouse an amount of sugar of equivalent value to the loan they wish to take out. The warehouse then issues certificates of deposit and bonds to the bank for the sugar for up to 80% of its value. While this looks like a typical warehouse receipts scheme, it is somewhat unique in that the bank takes complete ownership of the sugar when it is placed in the warehouse. Instead of just certifying the quantity of sugar in the warehouse, this *reporto* scheme gives the bank ownership of the sugar until the miller pays back the loan. The sugar is marked to the market and if the market moves and the value of the sugar diminishes by more then 5% the miller is required either to deposit more sugar in the warehouse (while at the same time selling it to the bank) or to return the part of the loan. If the sugar increases in value the miller will not necessarily receive an increased loan amount. Also, because millers typically borrow in groups, all considers a default by one miller a default.

Conclusions

Price- and weather-risk management instruments can both improve access to financing for entities exposed to price and weather risks. The effect of this combination would provide banks and other financial institutions the opportunity to take on far less risk when lending to farmers. As financial institutions look to expand their portfolio into agricultural markets, it must be determined how their financial services can be enhanced and expanded upon to make them suitable for use in the agricultural setting. Innovations such as market-based price-risk management and index-based yield/weather insurance are two innovations that can be used to improve the abilities of financial institutions to offer their services to accommodate agricultural producers. Furthermore, using commodity inventories as a collateral (and managing the price risk of stored commodities) rather than using fixed assets will provide a secure way to lend to producers and agribusinesses.

1 *The World Bank (2001).*
2 *Ibid.*

3 *The focus is on commodities with liquid international markets for risk management, mainly coffee, cocoa, rubber, cotton, grains, sugar and oilseeds.*

4 *The World Bank (1999) p. 5.*

5 *The World Bank (2001).*

6 *See Varangis, Larson and Yabuki (1998), and also Varangis, Larson and Anderson (2002) provide an extensive review of the literature about commodity price volatility and evolution of approaches and strategies to deal with it at both the micro and macro levels.*

7 *For an extensive review of income risks, coping strategies and safety nets, for rural households in developing countries see Dercon (2002).*

8 *See, for example, Quattara et al. (1990).*

9 *The World Bank (2002).*

10 *Bryla, Varangis, and Tiffen (2003).*

11 *Bryla, Varangis, and Tiffen (2003).*

12 *In addition, ongoing feasibility work is taking place in Cameroon, Costa Rica, Cote D'Ivoire, Dominican Republic, El Salvador, Honduras, Ghana, India, Kenya and Vietnam in the coffee, cocoa and cotton sectors, depending on the specific country.*

13 *This is not an issue if traders require an upfront payment of the premium, but it may be difficult for them to do so. Farmers also may lack confidence that the trader will deliver the price insurance if prices decline.*

14 *The World Bank (2002).*

15 *"Private-sector providers" here means the sellers of risk management instruments. They are generally international banks with commodity departments, but can also be commodity brokers or large multinational traders/processors.*

16 *This section draws heavily on Hess, Richter and Stoppa (2002).*

17 *See Skees et al. (2002).*

18 *See Hazell (1992).*

19 *See Skees, Hazell and Miranda (1999).*

20 *There are also cases where weather events affect the quality of the output more so than the yields.*

21 *In addition to weather events as the basis of the index, insurance can be written on area yields (eg, county yields). However, the use of area yields as an index requires adequate and reliable historical observations and the trust that future area yield estimates will not be manipulated.*

22 *Hess, Richter, and Stoppa (2002).*

23 *Ibid.*

24 *An example of such rules can be found in Mexico's Fund for Natural Disasters (FONDEN).*

25 *Survey of 500 farmers conducted by Indian Coffee Board in cooperation with Commodity Risk Management Group of the World Bank.*

26 *A Survey based on the Economic Census (1998), which covered over 30 million small-scale units across India.*

27 *The insurer can price the risk competitively by garnering the risk across districts and weather patterns in order to diversify his portfolio.*

28 *Basix website, URL: http://www.basixindia.com.*

29 *Information on Reportos was obtained from a presentation by Latin America Capital LLC. Berry, H., 2003, "Sugar Financing in Mexico", Day Robinson Sixth Global Meeting on Warehouse Receipt Finance and Collateral Control in Latin America, Miami, 25–26 February.*

102

INNOVATIVE
APPROACHES FOR
MANAGING
AGRICULTURAL
RISKS

BIBLIOGRAPHY

Bryla, E., P. Varangis, and P. Tiffen, 2003, "Couvrir les risque de prix des petits producteurs, quel intéret pour les banques et les marchés?", *Banquestratégie*, no 204 Mai 2003.

Hazell, P. B. R., 1992, "The Appropriate Role of Agricultural Insurance in Developing Countries", *Journal of International Development*, 4, 567–581.

Hess, U., K. Richter, and A. Stoppa, 2002, "Weather Risk Management for Agriculture and Agri-Business in Developing Countries", *Climate Risk and the Weather Market*, Risk Books, Risk Waters.

Mahajan, V., 2001, "Issues in Sustainability of Micro-finance Insitutions – A Practicioner's Viewpoint," Presented at the Workshop on 'Sustainable Micro Finance – Challenges Facing MFIs, Lucknow, January 15.

Parchure, R., 2002, "Varsha Bonds and Options: Capital Market Solutions for Crop Insurance Problems", National Insurance Academy Working Paper Balewadi, India. http://www.utiicm.com/rajaskparchure.html

Skees, J. R., P. B. R. Hazell, and M. Miranda, 1999, "New Approaches to Crop Yield Insurance in Developing Countries." International Food Policy Research Institute: Environment and Production Technology Division Discussion Paper No. 55.

Skees, J. R., P. Varangis, D. Larson, and P. Seigel, 2002, "Can Financial Markets be Tapped to Help Poor People Cope with Weather Risks?" Wider Press of the United Nations, Discussion paper.

Varangis, P., D. Larson, and N. Yabuki, "Commodity risk management and development", Policy Research Working Paper, The World Bank, Washington, DC.

The World Bank, 1999, "*Dealing with Commodity Price Volatility in Developing Countries, A Proposal for a Market Based Approach*", International Task Force on Commodity Risk Management, Washington, D.C., September.

The World Bank, 2001, "Delivering Price Insurance, Lessons Learned From Four Cases Studies", Commodity Risk Management Group, Washington, D.C. August.

The World Bank, 2002, "Delivering Price Insurance, Lessons Learned From Four Cases Studies", Commodity Risk Management Group, Washington, D.C. February.

SYSTEMS AND MANAGEMENT

10

Credit Risk Management in Agribusiness Markets

Benedict Roth*

WestLB AG

Introduction

Credit risk is the risk of financial loss as a result of a counterparty or a client or a trading partner failing to meet its contractual obligations.[1] For example, a borrower may fail to repay a loan, a supplier may fail to make delivery of raw materials or a client may fail to accept a shipment he has ordered.

Credit risk management is one of the oldest disciplines in the risk management handbook. But in recent years it has been revolutionised by the same derivative instruments, described in earlier chapters of this volume, which have had such a profound impact on the discipline of market risk management. Credit risk managers have developed new tools, and with these new tools have come new opportunities.

Why have derivative instruments had such an impact on credit risk management?

First and foremost, financial derivatives carry credit exposures of indeterminate size. This marks a fundamental change from traditional credit risk analysis, which was centred on lending. A lender's credit exposure is stable and well known, limited by the size of the loan. The credit exposure associated with a swap, in contrast, may be volatile and unpredictable and, under some circumstances, it may be unlimited. As a result, new risk exposure measures are needed. The purpose of this chapter is to provide an insight into these measures.

First, an orthodox credit risk measurement framework – which might apply to any industry – is introduced. Second, the peculiar and special features of agricultural business are introduced into the orthodox framework. Finally, some simple results from the orthodox model are used to calculate the economic costs and risks of real-world financing and risk management structures common in agribusiness today.

The orthodox model

An orthodox credit risk model would require four inputs.

1. *Exposure amount*: How much is at risk, or, in other words, what is the size of the potential credit loss? In the case of a swap or physical forward, calculation of this amount may not be straightforward because it depends on the future direction of market prices. Even for a vanilla loan, if it were secured on commodity inventory, market price changes could alter the amount at risk net of the value of the security.

2. *Loss or recovery rate*: In the event of default, what proportion of our net exposure might be recovered and what might be lost forever? Agribusiness borrowers often own nothing except physical inventory or production equipment related to raw materials. In this case the recovery rate is intimately connected with the market price risk on the materials concerned.

3. *Default risk*: What is the probability that a default takes place before the transaction matures? Default rates in agribusiness, like recovery rates, are closely connected to market prices.

---

* *Views expressed are those of the authors' and do not necessarily reflect those of WestLB AG.*

4. *Correlation risk:* To what extent are the default risks on my trading counterparties independent and to what extent might they all default together, over a short period? Because of the significance of commodity prices in agribusiness default rates and recovery rates, agribusiness default correlations may be higher than in other industries. In fact, agricultural lenders may have significant exposures to commodity price risk embedded in their credit profile. The only way to manage this lending risk is to help agricultural borrowers to hedge their economic market risk. Hence the dual focus on credit and market risk in this volume.

The orthodox model could produce, as its first and simplest output, the "expected" credit loss in the transaction, or in a group of transactions with a single counterparty. The expected credit loss is simply the product of the first three factors mentioned above and illustrated in Figure 1.

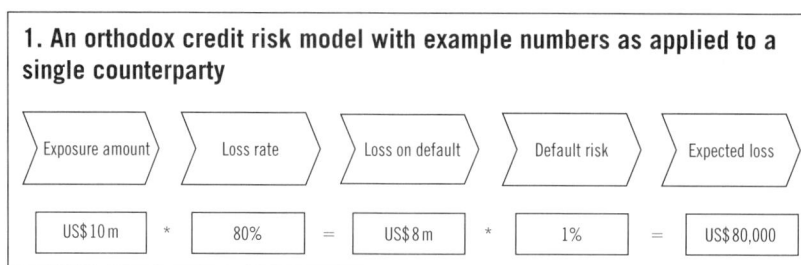

1. An orthodox credit risk model with example numbers as applied to a single counterparty

Exposure amount		Loss rate		Loss on default		Default risk		Expected loss
US$10m	*	80%	=	US$8m	*	1%	=	US$80,000

In the example above, which might describe a loan of US$10 million, the expected credit loss is US$80,000. This is a theoretical number, which might indicate that the lender should set aside US$80,000 on each completed transaction as a loss reserve. If he fails to make enough profit on the successful transactions to pay for this reserve, he will, on average, lose money.

In an efficient market, the margin over the risk-free rate at which the unsecured obligations of the counterparty trade will reflect the default and recovery rates that the market perceives as appropriate for that counterparty. Under these circumstances, if we discounted the contractual cashflows from the loan at this margin over the risk-free rate we would obtain a present value of US$10 million, exactly equal to the amount disbursed. A larger present value might indicate a better-than-market deal; a smaller present value would indicate a worse-than-market one.

In practice, the lender's real credit loss will be zero on very many transactions and up to US$10 million on a few. Assuming that he is sufficiently well-capitalised and profitable to withstand some of these losses, his eventual survival will depend to a large extent on whether he has an "unlucky" year when the failures all come within a short space of time or whether they are evenly distributed from year to year, with the total annual losses falling within the total annual loss reserves. These possible outcomes depend on the default correlation of the various counterparties, the fourth input to the orthodox model.

In practice, no one can adequately predict or manage recovery rates, default rates or default correlations. The material in this chapter therefore focuses on the first building block, the exposure amount. This is the key to active agribusiness credit risk management and the following sections show how to estimate exposure amounts, how to price them, and how to manage them.

Estimating the size of the credit exposure

Some lenders think of their exposure as the amount lent. In other words, if they lend US$1 million (to a counterparty who defaults) then their credit exposure is US$1 million. This number is usually near to correct in the case of a loan, but impossible to translate into non-lending situations such as fixed-price commodity sale contracts or options. For these transactions, a new concept is needed. That concept is *replacement cost.*

REPLACEMENT COST

Replacement cost is the cost to the non-defaulting counterparty of finding another entity, a new entity, to deliver the obligations of the entity who has failed. Without such a replacement, the non-defaulting entity is left holding a broken trade, as useless as a key without a lock.

In the case of a loan, the obligations to be delivered include interest and principal. In the case of a physical forward, they encompass the delivery of commodity against cash or vice versa. In the case of a swap, they require the payment or receipt of a cash amount related to the level of a market index.

No rational market participant would assume these obligations without requiring a fee equal to the present value of the obligations in question at prevailing market prices. Seen in these terms, replacement costs are variable: they can fluctuate in response to the state of the market.

Replacement costs can also fluctuate – albeit in a predictable fashion – according to the remaining term of the failed transaction: replacing a 10-year swap that still has nine years to run is very different from replacing it nine and a half years after trade date, when it has nearly expired.

Table 1. Replacement cost drivers for different transactions	
Transaction type	Replacement cost drivers
Loan	❑ Amount of principal and interest due ❑ Value of readily marketable collateral ❑ Cashflow due dates ❑ Market levels of risk-free interest rates ❑ Market levels of credit spread for borrowers of similar quality
Physical commodity forward or commodity swap	❑ Amount of physical or notional amount of swap ❑ Cash price/swap fixed price ❑ Settlement dates ❑ Market levels for the commodity in question on the relevant dates ❑ Market levels of risk-free interest rates
Commodity option	❑ For a sold option where premium has been received the replacement cost is zero because the market value, on the books of the seller, is always negative ❑ For a bought option, all the cost drivers for the commodity swap are relevant as well as, additionally, the market level of implied volatility
Commodity future	❑ Movement in contract price since most recent margin settlement date (usually previous business day)

Table 1 indicates which market prices determine replacement costs for common types of commodity trades.

By way of example, we will look at the replacement cost of a commodity swap with the following parameters:

❑ Index – Settlement price of New York Board of Trade Arabica coffee deliverable in December 2004.
❑ Fixed price – US$1,700/mt.
❑ Notional – 850 mt.
❑ Fixing – 1 December 2004 with settlement two days later.

The 850 mt underlying the example swap is worth about US$1.4 million at December 2004 prices. Let us suppose that the non-defaulting party, who initiated the trade, is a coffee processor. By the nature of his business he is exposed to price rises and wishes to insure against this possibility via the swap. He therefore contracts to receive US$850 for every US$ that the price of coffee on the New York Board of Trade rises over US$1,700/mt and to pay US$850 for every US$ that the price drops below US$1,700/mt. He is happy to pay when raw material prices fall because his product sells more or less at stable price levels from year to year. When raw material costs drop he becomes more profitable, and vice versa.

Figure 2 illustrates the market values and the replacement costs at various price levels of the commodity swap.

2a. Market values of a coffee swap at different price levels

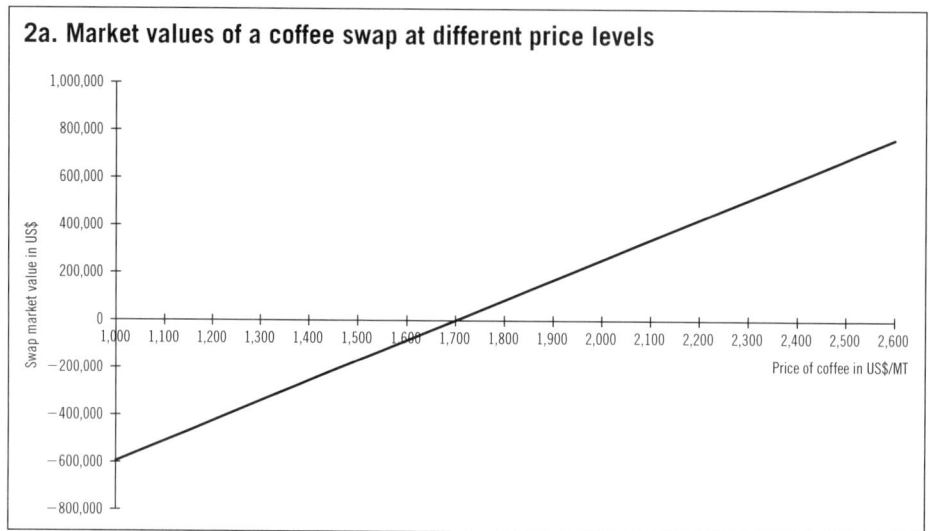

2b. Replacement costs of a coffee swap at different price levels

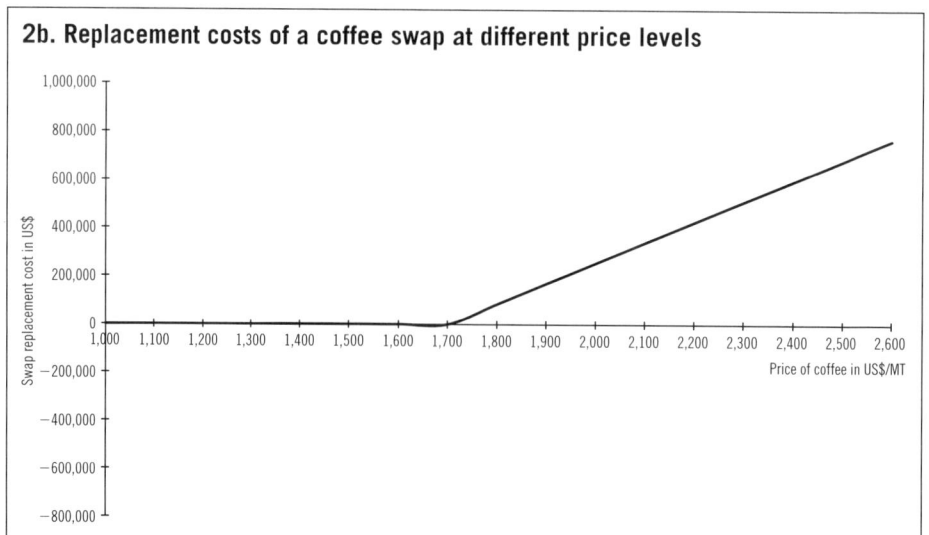

The market value, on Figure 2a, can be either positive or negative depending on the price of coffee: when the price is low the processor owes money to his counterparty (negative market value) and when the price is high he has a claim on his counterparty.

Given these market value profiles, how much would it cost to replace the transaction? Replacement cost is always positive because a bankrupt counterparty, while he cannot pay, can certainly receive. Or his liquidators will make arrangements to receive on his behalf. This replacement cost is illustrated on Figure 2b.

The practical obligations of two derivative counterparties during a bankruptcy are therefore asymmetric. And the asymmetry punishes the non-defaulting party who is damned if the market moves against him – for he must pay his contractual obligations – and damned if the market moves in his favour – for the market value of his transaction has risen but he will never receive this value. He will have to pay someone else in the market to assume the obligations of his defaulting counterparty. This "heads you win, tails I lose" situation lies at the heart of derivatives credit risk management.

A market-oriented reader will notice that the replacement cost profile illustrated on Figure 2b is the same shape as the pay-off profile of a vanilla call option. This is not a coincidence: in market terms we might say that the defaulter has a free option not to pay, which becomes more and more valuable as prices rise. We will return to this idea later in the chapter when we use the valuation of the call option to determine the correct market price for the credit risk concerned.

SIZING THE REPLACEMENT COST

How bad can the problem get? What level could the replacement value of the transaction attain? No one can answer this question with confidence because no one knows how high the price of coffee might rise over the term of the transaction.

Could we estimate an answer, based on previous highs, historic price volatility, or just "informed guess"? For short-dated transactions we might guess. For example, Arabica is currently trading in New York for delivery in September 2003 at US$1,330/mt; the market is well supplied; few observers would expect the price to exceed US$2,000/mt by September. The fact that an option to buy at US$2,000/mt in September is practically worthless shows that the option traders in the NYBOT agree.

But long-dated transactions, where most derivative credit risk resides, offer much greater forecasting problems. The example transaction above fixes in December 2004, eighteen months after the time of writing. Information about previous highs or previous volatility might not be relevant to developments in the future. An estimate considered prudent by one observer might be considered unreasonable or obsessionally cautious by another.

STATISTICAL ESTIMATES OF POTENTIAL EXPOSURE

If we can't forecast the future with accuracy – and it's clear from the material above that we can't measure credit exposure without forecasting – at least we could make some assumptions and consider critically their implications.

The most common assumptions used in potential exposure models are parallel to those used in Black–Scholes option pricing models:

❑ That prices move up and down in a unconstrained Brownian random walk motion.
❑ That the sizes of daily price changes are distributed lognormally. This makes upward and downward movements equally likely and the size of the absolute price changes proportional to the prevailing level of prices. As prices rise, price changes increase in size too and the potential eventual upward movement is, in theory, unlimited. Similarly, as prices fall, price changes reduce in size in proportion so that prices will approach zero but never touch zero.
❑ That price volatility is comparable to that of the recent past or that implied by the options market.

There are no fundamental economic reasons why these assumptions should be correct in agribusiness. In fact, agricultural markets have features known to be incompatible with Black–Scholes: non-zero economic price floors below which it is uneconomic to produce and finite economic price ceilings above which consumers substitute other commodities, demand drops and producers bring new capacity on stream.

Notwithstanding these features, the statistical models are widely used, for two reasons.

First, traders whose counterparties have each transacted a significant portfolio of trades, in different markets, at different maturities, and in different directions, need some objective measure of the total potential exposure on the counterparty portfolio as a whole. While the statistical technique for potential exposure looks little better than the "informed guess" technique for one trade in one market, it can also be extended to multiple trades under consistent assumptions in a way that the "informed guess" cannot.

Second, computation of potential future exposure is an inexact and imprecise science anyway, and the defective assumptions mentioned above probably don't degrade the results significantly. If they were felt to be crucial then the statistical model could be extended.

If we followed these standard assumptions we could build a probability distribution of future prices and then choose a confidence level large enough for comfort. For example, using the 97.5% confidence level price - ie, the price level that would be breached by only 2.5% of transactions - and plotting out the resulting upward and downward price paths, we would obtain a cone-shaped picture like the one in Figure 3. We have assumed annualised volatility of 35%, in line with the recent past.

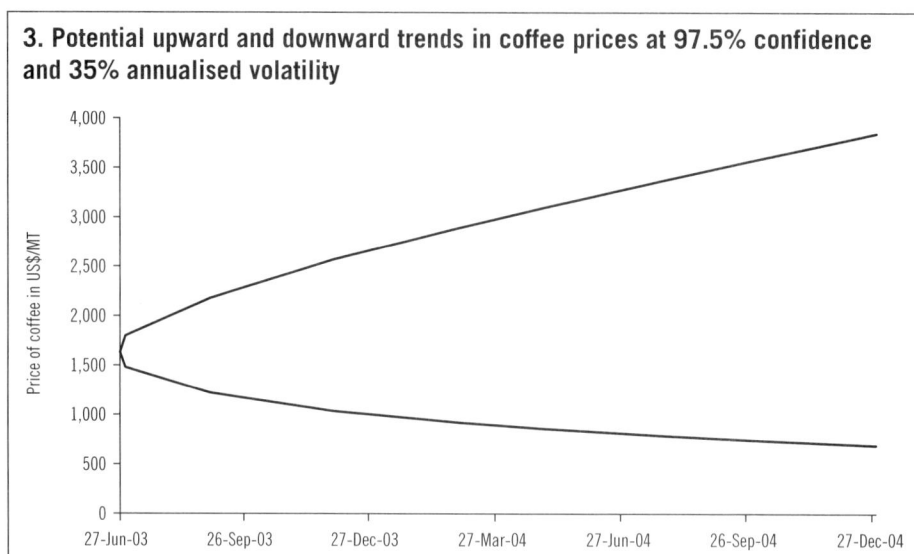

3. Potential upward and downward trends in coffee prices at 97.5% confidence and 35% annualised volatility

Note that the tip of the cone lies at US$1,630, which is the current price level of December 2004 coffee, and that the cone expands more slowly as time passes, in line with standard Brownian motion, where the distance to the eventual position of the moving object is proportional to the square root of the travel time.

In most derivative transactions only half the cone - either the top half or the bottom half - is needed. This is because most transactions carry credit exposure only one way. For example, in the coffee swap described above, the processor is paid when the price rises and incurs credit exposure only under those circumstances. He therefore cares only about the top portion of the cone. His counterparty has the opposite risk exposure: he would be paid when prices fell and would worry about the lower portion of the cone.

It should be noted that the credit exposure of someone who is paid when prices rise is always larger than his counterparty's, because the lower part of the cone cannot reach zero while the upper one is unconstrained.

Following the current example, after 18 months the 97.5 percentile price has risen to nearly US$4,000/mt. The positive market value (and the replacement cost) of the swap at that price would amount to US$1.8 million. For a trade that covered only a notional value of US$1.4 million of coffee at inception, this is a disturbingly large number.

The full exposure profile, at 97.5% confidence, is illustrated in Figure 4.

CREDIT EXPOSURE DEVELOPMENT AS TIME PASSES

Typical derivative transactions settle over a number of fixings, each fixing one or more months apart from the next. This has a major impact on the credit exposure profile.

For example, the hypothetical coffee processor described above who hedged 850 mt of coffee at December 2004 might have been more likely to hedge an ongoing production

4. Credit exposure profile for a single-period coffee swap based on US$1.4 million of coffee

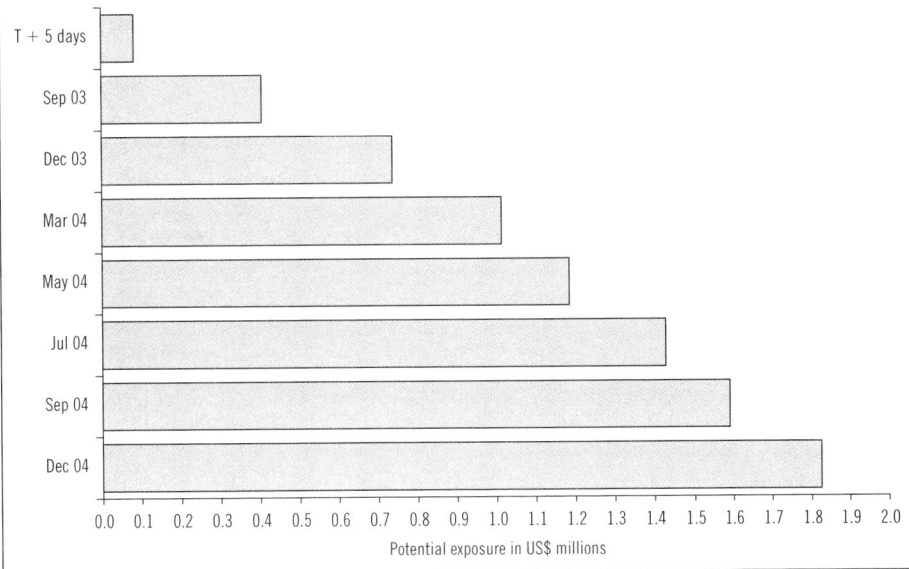

Potential exposure in US$ millions

schedule, for example 212.5 mt in each of the following four months: December 2004, March 2005, July 2005 and September 2005, in each case indexed to the relevant NYBOT coffee contract. In this case the potential future exposure would look like a camel's hump, as in Figure 5.

5. Credit exposure profile for a multi-period coffee swap based on US$1.4 million of coffee

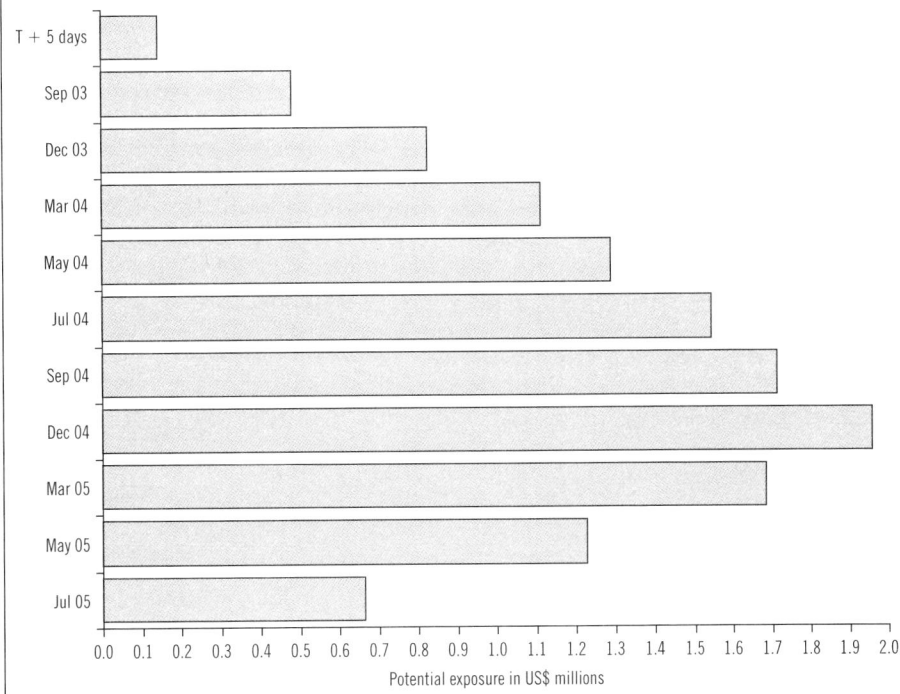

Potential exposure in US$ millions

At the beginning of the transaction the upward slope of the hump is driven by the assumption that increasingly large potential market prices drive the potential value of the transaction as a whole upward. But, as time passes, the transaction begins to settle. After two fixings, the replacement value to be calculated is no longer the replacement value of an 850 mt deal, but that of a 425 mt deal. By the time of the last fixing, although the potential price assumed is higher than any previous potential price, the amount of coffee concerned is only 212.5 mt and the impact on the overall credit risk profile is less important.

How to use the exposure estimate

I mentioned, while presenting the potential exposure measure, how rough and ready it was when applied to any time period greater than a few days:

❑ The statistical assumptions are very broad.
❑ The 97.5% confidence potential exposure is difficult to relate to actual loan exposure or to any other well-understood risk measure.
❑ The choice of 97.5% as a target confidence interval is purely arbitrary. Why not 90% or 99% or 100%?
❑ The use of current option-implied volatilities or previous historic volatilities as an estimate of future volatility has no theoretical justification. Both techniques may work much of the time in practice, because market indicators or past history often serve as a guide to the future, but they are bound to be significantly wrong some of the time.

Given these reservations, it may be surprising that potential exposure measures are so widely used. And they throw up such enormous numbers – the potential credit exposure on the coffee swap described above was much more than the total notional value of the transaction – that some agribusiness professionals may have trouble taking them seriously.

However, while these potential numbers are no more than rough estimates, they do provide insight into possible, feasible, market developments. The vast majority of commodity derivative transactions will never coincide with such extreme market movements. But a small number of transactions will see enormous price changes over their lifetimes and agribusinesses that fail to plan for these will suffer credit losses.

So, while the potential exposure mentioned above may never come to pass, it should be frightening enough to give a trader or processor undertaking such transactions pause for thought. If it does, some analysis might be initiated in one of the following three areas:

❑ More rigorous analysis of the counterparty, the documentation and the transaction.
❑ Exposure management strategies.
❑ Calculation of the fair market price for the risk concerned, and comparison with the profitability of the transaction overall.

Each subject is dealt with in turn in the following sections.

Counterparty and documentation analysis

Table 2 identifies key counterparty-related questions that should be answered before taking on any potential exposure, large or small. They fall short of formal counterparty credit analysis, which is outside the scope of this chapter, but they provide the key derivative-related questions, which would be required alongside that formal analysis.

After establishing the key facts related to the counterparty, it is necessary, for proper risk management, to establish the nature of the transaction documentation. No transaction can possibly be stronger than the agreement that documents it.

Most banking professionals now document derivative transactions with a standard agreement published by the International Swaps and Derivatives Association (ISDA). Both New York and English law versions of the ISDA document are commonly used. ISDA documentation is favoured by banks for three main reasons, which are relevant to agribusiness companies as well. These reasons are:

1. *Early transaction replacement.* Derivative transactions are typically long-dated. This means that a counterparty may go into administration or show other signs of

---

Table 2. Counterparty checklist

Counterparty questions

❑ Is the counterparty a bank, a broker, a trader, a processor or a producer?
❑ What is his credit rating?
❑ How strong is our relationship with the counterparty?
❑ How much money would we be happy to lend to him unsecured and how much would we charge to do so?
   ● Unsecured derivative exposure embedded in the market value of the swap carries all the risk of
     unsecured lending, but often with none of the rewards.
❑ How reputable is he and how sensitive is his business to the reputational risk that he would incur if he failed
   to honour a trade?
   ● For some counterparties, the possibility of reputational damage is a more potent contract enforcement tool
     than legal action is.
❑ To what extent is this transaction in the counterparty's normal course of business, in terms of amount,
   underlying commodity, direction and term?
❑ If the market moves against the counterparty on this transaction and he owes us money, what effect will that
   market movement have on the rest of his operations?
   ● If the counterparty is hedging an existing exposure then he should have cash irrespective of the direction
     of the market: if it moves one way his business improves and pays for losses on his hedge, and if it moves
     the other way his hedge profits pay for the shortfall in his business.
   ● But a counterparty who is speculating has no natural cashflow when the market goes against him and,
     like a gambler, may not be able to pay his obligations. In modelling terms we would describe this as
     unwelcome correlation between exposure size and probability of default.
❑ How much exposure to this counterparty do we already have?
❑ If our existing credit exposure is derivative-related, is it linked to the same market indices as the proposed
   new trade and is it the same way round?
   ● Trades in many different markets will tend to diversify the potential exposure profile (assuming
     appropriate documentation as discussed below) because, in all probability, not all markets will move
     unfavourably at the same time. Trades in the same market will either offset one another, if they are in
     different directions, or, if they are in the same direction, will double up each other's risks.

---

sickness months or even years before payments on the transaction are due. In this case the non-defaulting counterparty will wish to replace the trade as soon as possible – certainly before any failure to pay has taken place – in case adverse market movements begin to turn potential exposure into real market value.

ISDA documentation deals with the need to replace trades before failure to pay by defining "events of default", such as the appointment of administrators or the occurrence of a default on other, unrelated, obligations. Once an event of default has taken place, the non-defaulting party has the right to replace the trade immediately, at fair market value, and to recover any costs from the one who has failed. There is no need to wait for the counterparty's obligations to fall due according to the original payment schedule.

2. Netting. The fact that derivative transactions are long-dated means that two trading counterparties may possibly, at any one time, share a number of different open transactions. Some of these will probably have positive market values and some may have negative market values. The counterparty checklist above referred to this issue.

In the event of default, the ISDA document provides for the total fair market value of all relevant open transactions to be settled on a net basis. The enforceability of these netting provisions is well documented in many major jurisdictions. Without netting, a bankruptcy administrator or liquidator in some jurisdictions might have the right to "cherry-pick" transactions: putting in a claim to be paid on transactions where money is owed to him while refusing to pay on transactions where he owes.

Cherry-picking could have a explosive impact on credit exposures in situations where professional counterparties are trading multiple transactions in different directions. While the net exposure might be minimal, the number of cherry-pickable trades might be enormous. ISDA documentation, with netting, is the cleanest and safest protection against this possibility. It also paves the way for the counterparty's total net obligations to be supported by a single collateral account, as will be seen below.

3. *Standardisation and mastering.* ISDA is a standard, well-tested agreement that can be reviewed once and then executed with many counterparties. It is also a "master" agreement: once executed between two legal entities, it can cover many individual transactions. The individual transactions themselves require only a concise confirmation referencing the relevant ISDA master. Ideally – in order to take advantage of the netting provisions mentioned above – a single ISDA master would be used to cover all the derivative business of the two entities concerned.

Acceptance of a standard master agreement to be executed with many counterparties, each instance able to cover many transactions, makes for much more cost-effective derivative documentation overall. But with this standardisation comes the drawback that the resulting agreement is difficult for non-professionals to understand. Indeed, no agreement that is designed to cover multiple transactions in multiple markets can ever be simple.

Some agribusinesses, who decide that they do not require ISDA's netting provisions and do not trade frequently, may therefore decide that simpler, non-standard documentation is more appropriate for their purposes. And any entity attempting to force an ISDA agreement onto such an agribusiness should take great care (as noted in the documentation checklist below) that the business in question understands the agreement that it is signing.

Bearing in mind questions of netting and enforceability addressed by ISDA, and the fact that agribusinesses often trade in jurisdictions outside Europe, Japan and the Anglo-Saxon world, the table below identifies key documentation-related questions that should be asked when assessing a potential derivative exposure.

Table 3. Documentation checklist

Documentation questions

❑ How is the trade documented?
- Does the documentation provide for netting and, in the event of counterparty default, for early close-out?

❑ Was the documentation signed by an individual appropriately empowered by the counterparty?

❑ Do the officers of the company understand the documentation?
- If the agreement is so complex that the counterparty does not understand it enforcement could be problematic.

❑ Does the board of directors of the counterparty permit its businesses to engage in derivatives transactions of the kind proposed?
- If the transaction is held to be *ultra vires*, in other words that the counterparty's offices had no right to agree it, then the most watertight documentation, signed by the most senior individual, and the best enforcement capability, might not be adequate.

❑ In which jurisdiction does the counterparty reside?

❑ How will the provisions of the documentation be enforced in the event of default by the other party?

❑ Will it be necessary for the provisions of the documentation be enforced in the counterparty's home jurisdiction? Will this be possible?
- Some jurisdictions do not recognise derivative agreements, most notably Russia in the late 1990s. Other jurisdictions may have legal systems that are so slow and so unreliable that they offer little practical assistance in enforcing an agreement.

❑ Could a valid English or New York law agreement be overturned by a foreign court in the counterparty's home jurisdiction and an order served against the non-defaulting counterparty?
- This "nightmare" scenario is one that I have never seen in practice. But I have been warned of it by (prudent or obsessional?) legal colleagues.

Exposure management

Researching the counterparty, the transaction documentation and the cost of credit are analytical responses to concern about the size of a potential exposure number. Another response, more proactive than the others, might be to attempt to manage the exposure down. This is the subject of the current section.

Exposure management generally uses one of the following two strategies:

❏ Introducing a third party into the picture, who may be prepared to guarantee the obligations of the counterparty by intermediating in the trade, by providing insurance, or by selling a credit default swap.

❏ Taking cash or other collateral from the counterparty in order to support his obligations.

Each of these strategies will be discussed in turn.

THIRD-PARTY STRATEGIES

Intermediation. It is becoming increasingly common in the interest rate and foreign exchange markets for two counterparties who won't deal with one another directly to approach a third party and ask him, in exchange for a fee, to stand in the middle of a trade. Rather than deal with Beta directly, Argus chooses to deal with Consolidated, in turn who deals with Beta. Consolidated carries no market risk because his position is matched, but he does carry counterparty risk on both sides.

Why would Consolidated wish to carry out such a trade? First, it might suit his own trading position. The trade might offset an existing potential exposure that he already had with Argus or Beta. Second, he might have an existing banking relationship with Argus or Beta, perhaps with the ability to take collateral, which he could use to take the credit risk safely. Finally, he might simply have underpriced the relevant credit risk and thus be prepared to do the business at a fee acceptable to both of the other parties.

Intermediation is a growing field where some less sophisticated institutions may still be underpricing their services, and agribusiness clients, armed with correct pricing, may be lucky with their bankers. The subject of correct pricing for potential exposure is discussed later in this chapter.

Insurance. Traditionally, credit protection for agricultural contracts has been provided by insurance companies who guaranteed trade finance contracts. Insurance costs have been, historically, out of line with the market prices of credit in banking. This mismatch appears to result merely from differing levels of supply of and demand for credit protection in banking and insurance, rather than the result of some fundamental structural difference between the two markets. Agribusiness corporates, with access to both markets, are well placed to exploit these anomalies.

Credit default swaps. A credit default swap (CDS) is a financial derivative whose pay-off is contingent on the failure of a third party. It is normally purchased by paying a credit protection fee for a fixed notional amount. It is settled, in the event of a counterparty default, by exchanging cash for nearly worthless bonds issued by the defaulting entity.

The following example makes these steps clearer:

❏ The *protection purchaser* is concerned about its credit exposure to a certain *reference entity*.

❏ The *protection purchaser* agrees to pay the *protection seller* a fee of 1% per annum on a notional protection amount of US$10 million for a period of five years. The payments are made semi-annually in arrears, ie, US$50,000 per half-year.

❏ If an *event of default* occurs at the *reference entity* then the CDS is settled. The events of default will include all the usual ISDA events such as appointment of administrators or failure to pay, and may also include less well-defined events such as a debt restructuring that falls short of bankruptcy protection proceedings.

❏ When settlement takes place, the *protection purchaser* will receive from the *protection seller* US$10 million in cash, less any accrued fees to the time of default. It normally has to deliver, in exchange, US$10 million face value (not market value) of bonds issued by the reference entity.

The settlement procedures demonstrate how close the CDS market lies to the corporate bond market. Its most liquid maturity is five years, which is consistent with many new bond issues, and it trades around only those names with publicly traded debt. For these reasons it may be unsuitable for agribusinesses, who often require protection on smaller, less well-known names, whose contracts mature well within five years and who have no wish to go into the market and purchase defaulted bonds in order to settle their credit protection transactions. However, the CDS market is the only market that allows credit protection to be both bought and sold in small quantities and as such cannot escape a mention here.

"Digital" CDS's do exist, which give protection on the full notional amount without any requirement to deliver bonds in return, but these are less liquid.

REDUCING CREDIT EXPOSURE BY TAKING CASH OR OTHER COLLATERAL

Re-couponing. In the absence of a third party, the simplest way to reduce credit exposure is to agree to settle early in cash if the market value of a derivative transaction exceeds a predefined threshold. Under these circumstances the transaction will be terminated and replaced with a new one, identical to the old one but struck at up-to-date market levels. This process is known as "re-couponing".

Re-couponing is insensitive to the exact level of market rates used because any small positive error on the cash side of the process equates to an equal and opposite error on the mark-to-market of the new deal, and vice versa.

However, re-couponing is documentation-intensive, as transactions are cancelled and rebooked. This documentation burden may result in the agreement of market value thresholds that are higher than optimal. Finally, re-couponing is a device that works well on a single trade. If the credit exposure has been created by a large number of trades, perhaps in different markets, then documentation costs would make it prohibitively expensive.

For all these reasons, most professional counterparties prefer to manage their exposures by taking cash or near-cash collateral.

Collateral. Under a collateral agreement, cash or instruments with near-to-cash value, such as bonds, are put up by one of the parties to the transaction to support its obligations. The collateral is held by the other party in a segregated account or by a trusted third party, but remains the property of its original owner. As the market value of the owner's obligations changes, the amount of collateral is adjusted. Any failure to provide collateral when required constitutes an event of default and triggers the early termination/replacement of the transactions.

Most collateral agreements supporting financial derivatives are documented using the credit support annexe (CSA) to the ISDA document and thus take advantage of ISDA's netting provisions and early termination provisions.

Exchanging cash or near-cash collateral to adjust the level of a credit exposure has many advantages over other risk mitigation techniques:

❑ A single collateral account can support the net exposure over a number of transactions (assuming that the documentation supports netting).
❑ Cash and bonds can be transferred backwards and forwards in relatively small quantities as the market value of the transactions changes.
❑ The collateral agreement can protect both parties reciprocally if the market value of the transactions concerned moves up and down from positive to negative. Under these circumstances the party giving collateral simply takes back its cash and becomes the party receiving collateral, and vice versa.
❑ The value of the collateral is stable and easy to determine.

Once a CSA is in place and collateral has been taken, potential credit exposure is reduced to:

❑ the possible change in the market value of the portfolio between collateral adjustment dates;
❑ the possible change in its market value after a default while its trades are being replaced.

These time periods are normally matters of days, not weeks, and most of the uncertainty in the potential exposure calculations falls away. For example, assuming daily collateral top-up and a five-day portfolio liquidation period, the potential exposure on the hypothetical multi-period coffee deal pictured in Figure 5 above falls from nearly US$2.0 million to US$145,000. This figure was illustrated in the very first bar on Figure 5, labelled "T + 5 days".

Credit exposure can be reduced further by introducing what futures exchanges call "initial margin" and what the CSA refers to as the "independent amount". The independent amount is an amount of collateral that one party puts up to the other one to cover potential future exposure *in advance* of any movement in the market value of the transactions concerned. In other words, the independent amount is put up as soon as the transaction is initiated, when it has a market value of zero.

In the event of a later failure to provide daily collateral top-up, the party holding the independent amount can use it to support the other's obligations as the transactions are closed. By taking initial collateral of US$145,000 in this way, the credit risk in our hypothetical coffee trade could have been reduced to practically zero.

Given that our potential exposure figure started at US$2 million and has been reduced to an insignificant amount, this would seem a substantial achievement and it demonstrates most powerfully why professional banking counterparties like to exchange collateral under ISDA/CSA. Indeed, most banks have hundreds of millions of dollars of government bonds on their trading books all the time, which they put up as collateral (at practically zero cost to themselves) as required.

But the position in agribusiness is different: agribusinesses generally don't have large inventories of cash or bonds available to distribute to their counterparties. In fact, one common reason for trading over the counter rather than on futures exchanges is that they don't wish to put up collateral before the trade settles. Instead, they wish the cash-flows on their trading transactions to be deferred to match the natural future cashflows on the physical business, which those transactions are hedging.

Being forced to put up collateral early, before planned transaction settlement dates, could cause them major liquidity problems. In the famous case of Ashanti Gold Mines, the need to put up collateral pushed the business into bankruptcy.

Agribusinesses will prefer not to put up cash collateral even though banking counterparties will want to take it. What agribusinesses have available are raw materials. So any discussion of collateralisation in agribusiness must focus on the peculiar problems – and opportunities – of taking raw materials as collateral rather than cash.

Commodity collateral has special differences from cash.

❑ Exchanging small quantities to balance movements in transaction market values can be expensive.
❑ Monitoring and valuation are difficult because regular physical inspections of the warehouse are required.
❑ Even if the collateral is known to be in the warehouse, and has been valued, the local legal system may not allow the creditor to take control of it and sell it in the event of default.
❑ Commodity values can change as markets move.

The last of these problems is crucial because the credit risk exposure on a derivative collateralised with commodity will include not only potential exposure on the derivative but potential exposure on the collateral as well. This additional exposure would normally be detrimental to prudent risk management. But what if the two potential exposures could be made to cancel out? This is the subject of the next section.

HEDGING THE POTENTIAL CREDIT EXPOSURE WITH COMMODITY COLLATERAL
One of the key questions in the counterparty checklist above concerned the business objectives of the counterparty: is he hedging his exposure or is he speculating? If the counterparty is hedging then he should be immune to market movements because their

net impact on his business and on his trading transactions together should be small. Effectively, his business is immunised against unfavourable market movements.

This immunisation can be imported into the potential exposure calculation by taking as collateral against potential exposure the same commodity inventory that itself is hedged via the derivative.

For example, if the coffee swap that we have used throughout this chapter as a working example were collateralised in 850 mt of coffee, potential credit exposure would drop to zero. As prices rose, not only would the counterparty's obligations rise but the value of the collateral would rise too. The net impact would simply be that the processor (or whoever struck this particular trade) would have control over US$1.4 million of collateral with its market value fully immunised. In this case the processor could extend nearly US$1.4 million of credit – somewhat less in practice, allowing for valuation risk, ageing, transport to market etc – without running any economic credit risk.

This is a remarkable result. By themselves, the commodity financing and the commodity hedging programmes have significant market-price-related exposures that can be managed only via expensive third-party guarantees or via cash collateral that agribusiness players probably do not possess. Together, they constitute an unbreakable package, which could open up cheap, safe financing for anyone with the technical skills to control the legal and operational risk on the commodity and the market risk skills to transact the hedge.

Pricing the potential exposure

The potential exposure number, although superficially precise, is disturbingly vague when it comes to providing hard information to management.

❑ "Perhaps the counterparty exposure will reach US$1 million, but it may not."
❑ "With a probability of 2.5%, it may exceed US$2 million."

How can a credit officer decide whether to decline or authorise a trade based on this information? And how can the credit officer compare a derivative transaction whose potential exposure is US$2 million with a loan of US$2 million? What if the loan is collateralised with commodities? What if it is overcollateralised?

The first approach discussed above was to undertake qualitative analysis of the counterparty and the transaction documentation; the second was to attempt to structure the transaction in order to reduce risk. Both approaches have value.

But qualitative analysis and restructuring of the transaction is not sufficient. In considering whether to approve or decline a transaction, we must compute its economic cost, using the kind of model with which we introduced this chapter. We mentioned at that point that default and recovery rates are impossible to predict, but that the market price of an unsecured loan to the target counterparty should reflect the market's view of these parameters. Furthermore, the market price of unsecured credit indicates the opportunity cost to the credit officer of approving the transaction. If he doesn't approve the derivative he could, presumably, use an equal amount of risk capacity to approve a loan.

This section therefore shows how to use the market price of credit from the loan market to compute the credit cost of the derivative. Along the way, I show how to use the same technique on a loan secured with commodity inventory. We can therefore compare an unsecured loan both with a derivative and with a loan secured on commodity collateral.

In order to apply a discount rate from the credit market to a swap, where the exposure amount is indeterminate, we need to separate the respective payment obligations of the two parties to the trade. This separation is illustrated in Figure 6a describes the obligations of our hypothetical processor, who pays when market prices fall, and Figure 6b describes the obligations of his counterparty, from whom he receives when market prices rise. Cash received has a positive sign while cash paid away has a negative sign.

For convenience, I have used the simpler of the two example transactions described above, where the swap settles in its entirety on a single date in December 2004.

6a. The payment obligations of the processor at different coffee price levels

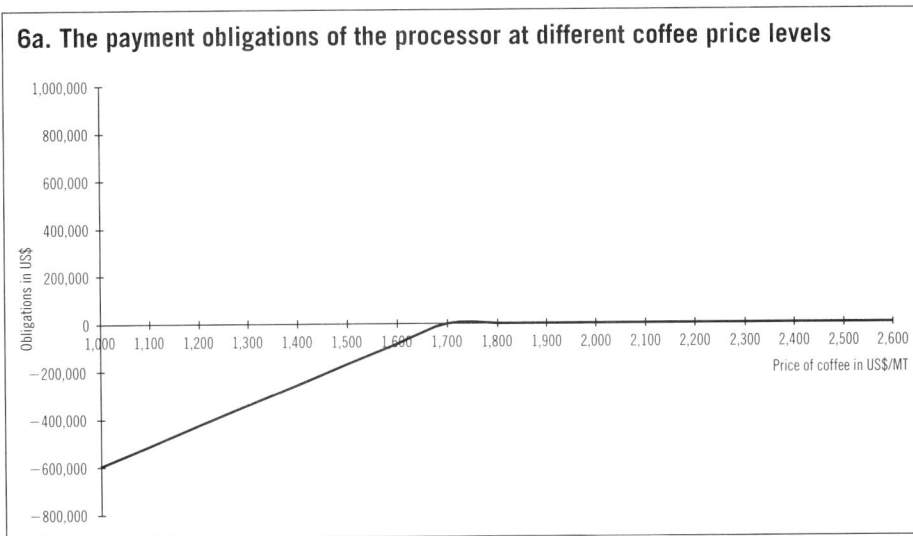

6b. The payment obligations of the counterparty at different coffee price levels

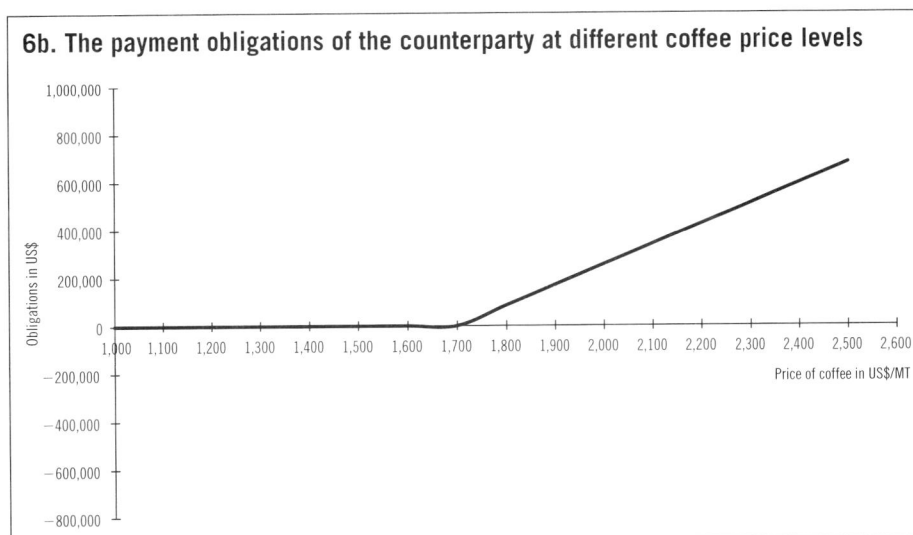

Added together, the Figures 6a and 6b represents the market value profile of the transaction as a whole, as originally illustrated in Figure 2. Separately, the two diagrams look like the payoff profiles of a short position in a put and a long position in a call. This is not surprising because a short put and long call, at the same strike, equate to a single-period swap.

Once the obligations of the two parties have been split up in this way, the forward value of each one can be computed using vanilla option models and discounted at an appropriate rate:

❑ risk-free for the processor, who has to make the payment under all circumstances;
❑ risky for his counterparty, who will not pay if he defaults.

All the statistical assumptions of the potential exposure model, in terms of lognormal distribution of changes in commodity prices or expected price volatility, are built into the option pricing algorithm and can be varied if desired.

Figure 7 shows the cost of credit, as a percentage of the transaction value, for our example swap, for counterparties with different costs of unsecured credit from 1% to 10% per annum. A price volatility of 35% has been used, as in the previous section. It shows that for a typical agribusiness counterparty, whose unsecured obligations might trade at 5% over risk-free, the annual cost of credit on our example 18-month swap is approximately 0.82% (82 basis points) of the notional value. This equates to US$16,700. A credit officer might want to see profits of at least this quantity reserved away until the transaction matured and, if the transaction did not generate sufficient income to justify such a reserve, he might recommend that the transaction should not go ahead.

7. The annual cost of credit in a commodity swap as a percentage of the notional value for counterparties with different market costs of credit risk

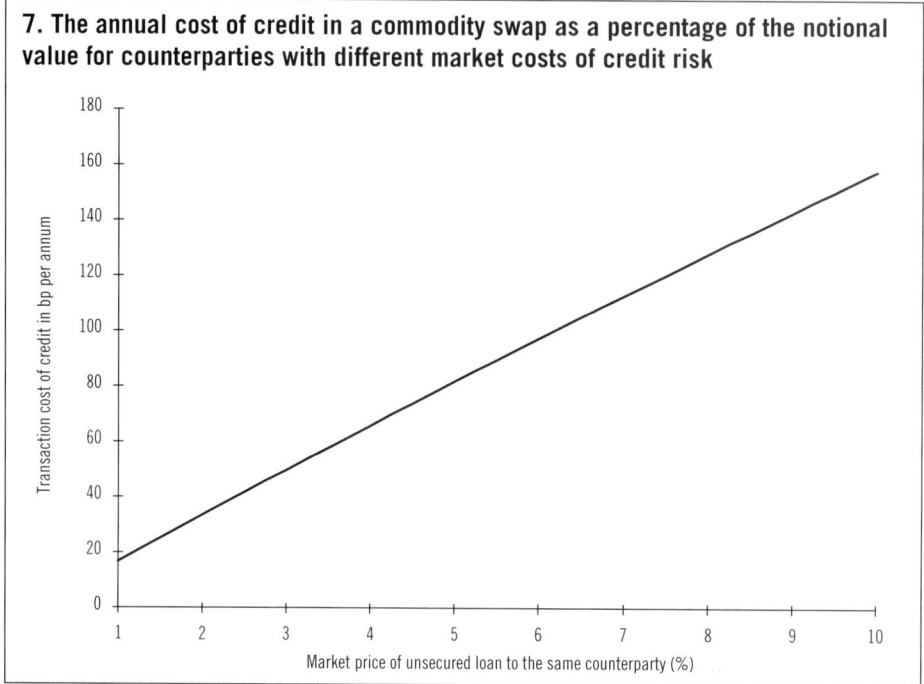

Figure 8 shows how the same annual cost of credit varies according to different assumptions about price volatility, assuming a constant counterparty cost of unsecured credit of 5%. It shows that as annualised volatilities rise from 35% to 100%, the cost of credit rises from 82 bp to around 220 bp. While we know – following the discussion at the start of the chapter – that predicting future volatility is impossible, with the benefit of a pricing model we can at least investigate the likely cost of any error in our predictions.

8. The annual cost of credit in a commodity swap as a percentage of the notional value for different commodity volatilities

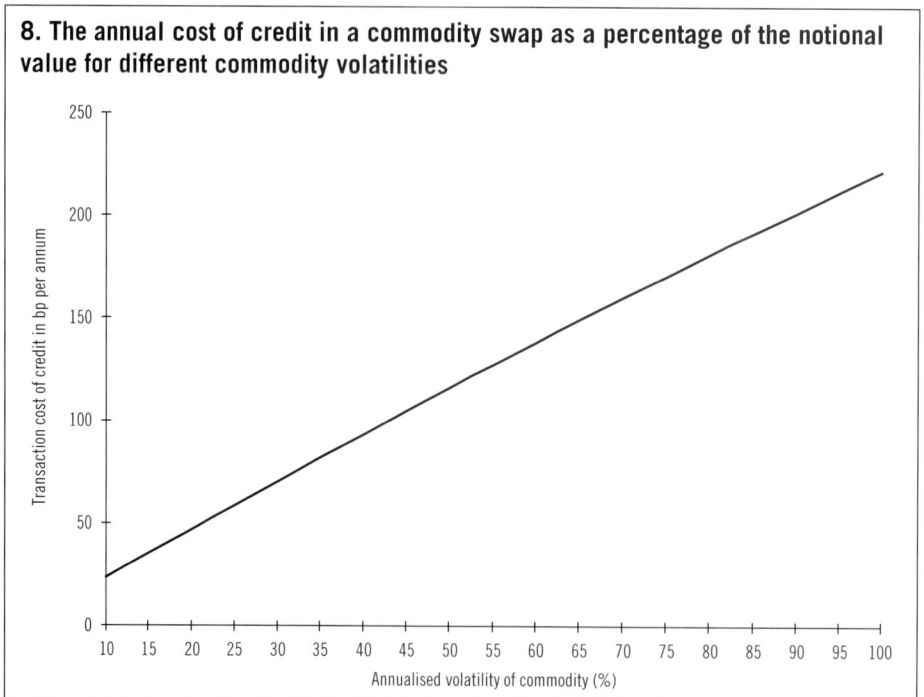

CALCULATING THE COST OF CREDIT IN A COLLATERALISED LOAN

A keen observer will notice that the commodity swap structure outlined here is identical to the structure of a collateralised loan:

❏ The lender is due to receive a fixed cash payment when the loan is repaid, analogous to the fixed side of the commodity swap;
❏ The same lender must return the commodity collateral, which has uncertain market value, just as if he were paying a market-related index.

In the case of a swap, settlement is made on a net basis while in the case of a loan settlement is made gross. But the credit exposure in both cases is calculated on a net basis.

The pricing model outlined above can therefore be used to assess the cost of credit in collateralised loan structures, allowing the user to adjust the collateralisation top-up frequency, the volatility of the collateral, the market cost of risk of the counterparty and the ratio between cash lent out and commodity taken in.

Because the model pulls together these four risk factors in a systematic way it allows the user to examine carefully the contribution of each factor to the overall economic risk in the loan. It can be used to compare the risks in different transactions on a consistent basis. It can be used to restructure transactions and minimise risk, or to calculate the economic cost of risk and the economic capital for commodity financing transactions.

For example, Figure 9 shows different costs of credit for different margin top-up frequencies. It makes the same assumption of 5% per annum cost of unsecured credit risk, which was made in the examples above and shows that with only monthly margining the economic cost of risk drops to as low as 25 basis points (0.25%).

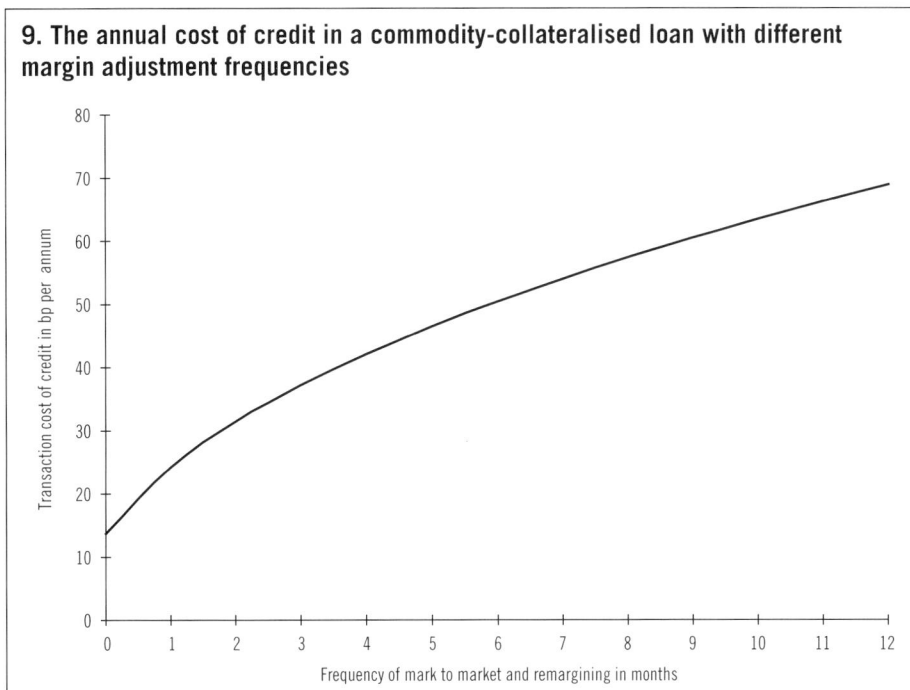

9. The annual cost of credit in a commodity-collateralised loan with different margin adjustment frequencies

Figure 10 shows the effect on the economic risk of variations in the loan-to-collateral ratio and shows, again, how rapidly the cost of risk drops even with a collateralisation ratio as high as 90%.

10. The annual cost of credit in a commodity-collateralised loan with different collateralisation levels

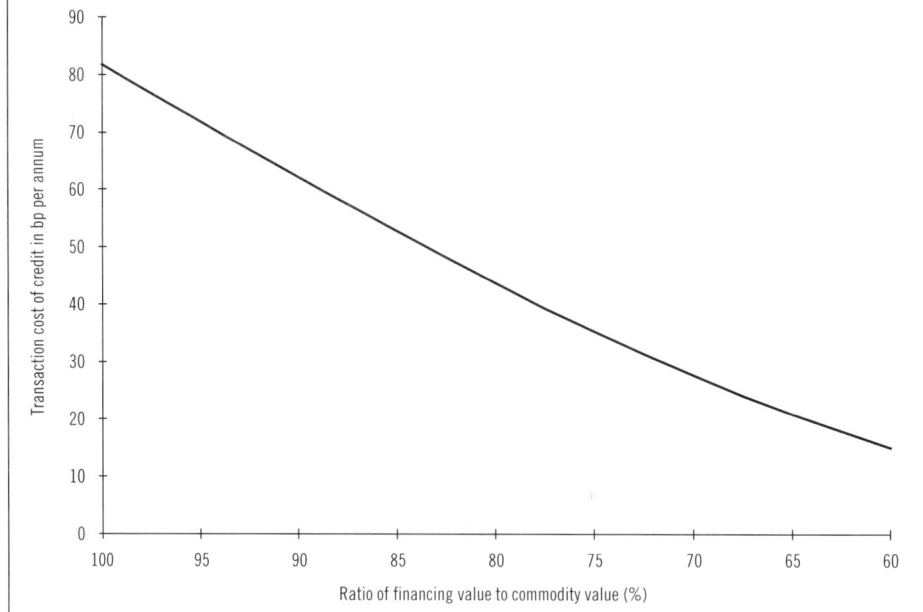

Transaction cost of credit in bp per annum (y-axis: 0, 10, 20, 30, 40, 50, 60, 70, 80, 90)

Ratio of financing value to commodity value (%) (x-axis: 100, 95, 90, 85, 80, 75, 70, 65, 60)

In summary, the model demonstrates that, in the commodity finance business, client-related risk factors such as credit quality are far outweighed by collateral-related ones.

This finding emphasises what many agribusiness professionals have known for a long time, namely that there is no substitute, in agricultural finance, for detailed knowledge of the markets and of the commodities traded. Indeed, it raises important questions about the emphasis in many banking credit departments and in regulatory capital calculations on ever more sophisticated counterparty risk-grading systems, perhaps at the expense of operational collateral-handling capabilities and market knowledge.

11

Price Risk Management Using Derivatives: Corporate Policy Creation and Management Control Guidelines

Tom James

Credit Agricole Indosuez

The relationship between risk and reward is at the heart of any business or industry. In any endeavour, the risk of heavy losses is seen as a justification for handsome returns, while lower-risk enterprises command more modest margins. All successful businesses must learn to assess and manage risk in ways that allow them to exploit opportunities while limiting their exposure to unpredictable factors in their operating environment. The more volatile the market, the more important this process of risk management becomes.

The agricultural industry and its associated markets certainly experience more than their fair share of volatility due to the many complex factors affecting prices, eg, crop success or failure through weather, soil problems or pollution; and then issues surrounding distribution of products. So it is no surprise at all, that forward (future) trading was first seen in agricultural products and has been established for many centuries, developing over the last 30 years into financial derivatives, allowing the protection of the price of crops and, if required, an outlet for physical delivery.

The main tools that have evolved for the agricultural industry are futures, swaps and options, generally grouped or referred to as "derivatives". These tools can be a "profit saver" for growers, traders and industry (processors), but, if not properly handled and controlled by management, can also create unwanted and unnecessary risk.

In this chapter I will focus on a practical approach to setting up a price risk management programme using derivatives within a company to help ensure that the use of derivatives does not cause any unwanted or unplanned difficulties.

Questions to ask when establishing a risk management or trading programme

These are some of the key questions to ask when collecting information that will help to create a policy for the usage of derivatives whether as a trader, speculator or hedger.

❑ What is your organisation? A consumer, a producer or a trader?
❑ What products does the organisation have price risk in?
❑ Which agricultural production?

    ,K
          ьING
       АTIVES:
     ,ГE POLICY
    ,REATION AND
    MANAGEMENT
CONTROL GUIDELINES

❑ If a grower (farmer), are you selling your production on fixed or floating price basis to the markets?

Is your organisation's aim hedging or trading? Which of these are you trying to do?

❑ mitigate a disaster risk scenario;
❑ protect budgeted levels;
❑ control overall price risk; or
❑ trade price risk as a speculator.

And you should ask yourself:

❑ Will you let traders (those responsible for executing derivatives trades) speculate or only hedge for your company?
❑ What is your total weight to hedge or how much do you wish to trade?
❑ As a hedger, how much do you want or need to hedge?

When hedging, look at up to 50% of exposure for general day-to-day hedging requirements. Any hedging over 50% of consumption or production volume is speculative and should be considered only as rare-case pre-emptive measures ahead of a "disaster scenario". This could be during protracted periods of extreme high prices (as a consumer) or extreme and extended low prices (as a grower). Or it could be as opportunistic hedging opportunities when historically high profitability can be ensured by locking in low prices as a consumer or high returns as a grower/producer.

Consider hedging around 30% of volumes around budget/target levels up to 12 months forward, leaving an additional 20–30% (up to 50% total) for "opportunistic hedging" if price levels achievable (as a buyer/seller) on the derivatives markets are better than budgeted levels.

Also, hedgers should generally look to have another policy for hedging in times of extreme price moves, allowing the trading/procurement department or the dedicated risk management departments to act quickly to protect the firm against extreme price moves that might be seen in times of bad weather, crop failures, etc.

Answering all these previous questions will help an organisation to look at the next step of putting together a risk management policy.

WHICH TYPES OF DERIVATIVES SHOULD BE USED?

❑ Futures.
❑ Options.
❑ Swaps.

Under "options" above, you might further ask:

❑ OTC? On exchange?
❑ Can traders only *buy* options or will they be allowed to sell options as well? (The selling of options can incur additional risk over and above the risk against which the option is supposed to be protecting the company (if not as part of a larger structure). Also, in some derivative disasters, the sale of options has been used to generate cash flow to cover up losses elsewhere in a portfolio.)

WHICH TENURES? AND HOW FAR FORWARD CAN THE ORGANISATION UTILISE THESE DERIVATIVES?
Normally, an organisation should state in its risk management policy (as a hedger) or derivatives usage document (as a speculator) which derivative types can be used, in which markets they can be used and also how far forward (length of tenure) each type of derivative contract (futures, options, swaps) in each market can be used.

WHICH DERIVATIVES MARKETS TO UTILISE?
For hedgers. This decision will be based on how well the available agriculture derivative markets correlate in terms of price (and also causation relationship) with the

125

**PRICE RISK
MANAGEMENT USING
DERIVATIVES:
CORPORATE POLICY
CREATION AND
MANAGEMENT
CONTROL GUIDELINES**

underlying agricultural market that is to be hedged and in which the organisation has price risk exposure. Then, once a list of possible commodity derivatives that match requirements are selected, an organisation must review this list with the contract liquidity in mind, (checking with brokers on the average daily volume, normal bid–offer spread price gap, and the number of active counterparts, and the types of counterparts (ie, are they all traders, all banks, all growers, all buyers, because ideally a good mix of participants should be seen in the market). If liquidity is bad, then an organisation may have to consider a "proxy" hedge.

A proxy hedge.   This is the use of a price-correlated financial derivatives (futures, options, swaps) instrument to hedge a particular agricultural product price risk when a direct hedge for that risk is not available. An example of this could be Vietnam Robusta coffee growers using the LIFFE Robusta coffee futures to hedge their price risk. In this example the two coffee prices may trend together but there is a risk that the London price may, in the short term, not move exactly in line with Vietnam prices, depending, of course, on how or if the grower is linking his sales on price formula with the LIFFE contract in London. Most "proxy hedges" are subject to some basis risk, which is the possibility of loss from imperfectly matched risk-offsetting positions in two related but not identical markets.

For traders/speculators.   This decision will be based upon liquidity of the agricultural derivatives markets (volume and number of counterparts trading the market) and also the level of price transparency that exists. For a trader/speculator the lack of price transparency can be an attraction, whereas for a hedger price transparency is more important than liquidity. Liquidity is more important for a trader because he/she will normally wish to trade out/close out a position ahead of its expiry/settlement. An organisation hedging will normally let derivatives contracts run their full term through to expiry, as it is hedging an underlying physical commodity price risk. So, for a hedger, the ability to trade out/close out a derivatives position may be less of a concern. The price linkage between the derivative and the commodity price risk being hedged may be more important to the hedger than the liquidity of the market (particularly if the derivative is cash-settled (using a money settlement) instead of settling on expiry via physical delivery (this occurs mainly in OTC markets).

HOW ARE OPERATIONS DEPARTMENTS GOING TO MANAGE THESE
DERIVATIVE POSITIONS?

Will the organisation require new IT infrastructure to process and manage these derivative positions? Does the organisation have the relevant skill sets or will training be required prior to the start of this activity? How will these derivative positions be valued? With they be:

❑ valued against the futures exchange settlement prices?
❑ valued against third-party forward-curve assessment data (if over-the-counter deal)?

How often will these derivative positions be valued? Daily, weekly, monthly or quarterly? If a trader/speculator how will the position limits be set?

❑ Weight/volumetric limits?
❑ Notional trade value limits?
❑ Will the limits be set by tenure and product?
❑ Which traders can trade which products and which types of derivatives can they trade?
❑ Who will be responsible for monitoring these positions and reporting any break in the organisation's policy for derivatives usage?
❑ What reports will be produced to assist risk monitoring/performance function? Will they be open-position reports, market-value reports, profit and loss reports, hedge-effectiveness reports (correlation analysis between the derivatives used for hedging and the underlying agriculture risk being hedged)? (NB: Hedge-effectiveness

126

**PRICE RISK
MANAGEMENT USING
DERIVATIVES:
CORPORATE POLICY
CREATION AND
MANAGEMENT
CONTROL GUIDELINES**

reports are now being required for new derivatives accounting standards, eg, FAS133 in the US).

❑ How often will these reports be produced?

❑ Who has to see these reports and sign them off as read?

❑ Prior to any activity, the organisation must assess the operational risk of this new business, as well as credit risk, market risks, legal risks, tax risks, etc. Who will be responsible for ensuring that there are ongoing regular reviews of these risks?

This is certainly not an exhaustive list but all of these questions can assist an organisation's management to start looking at policy decisions and to put together a short paper on what they propose to let their risk managers and traders do. Accounts departments can also get a good idea of what type of accounting for derivatives will have to be handled, either as hedges or speculative trades, which will aid them to make appropriate accounting report requirements and taxation checks.

All the information from this short paper and feedback on it from the relevant line managers in the organisation should then be put together for presentation to the board of directors/board of management, who should create a general policy and reporting structure for the organisation.

Line managers should then take this general policy and, with reference to the board's decision, fine-tune a more detailed risk management derivative usage guidebook for traders, operations and managers. This operational document should be submitted again for approval by the board of directors.

Creating a risk management or trading policy

The risk management and trading policy parameters for the usage of derivatives will vary from organisation to organisation, but here are some key guidelines and key stages that can help.

COMPONENT 1: BOARD-LEVEL APPROVAL

The board of directors should establish and approve an effective policy on the use of derivatives that is consistent with the strategy, commercial objectives and risk appetite of the underlying business and should approve the instruments to be used and how they are to be used.

The board of directors should:

❑ review the proposed purpose and use of derivatives;

❑ ensure this is consistent with management capabilities, financial position and commercial objectives, including any legal restraints;

❑ approve a list of derivatives and agree the reason for using them;

❑ ensure the appropriate policies and control procedures are in place;

❑ implement an independent review of risks and rewards;

❑ nominate two or more board members to be responsible for derivatives;

❑ frequently review actual derivative usage;

❑ ensure that management reports are fit for purpose; and

❑ ensure ongoing training of key personnel.

COMPONENT 2: POLICIES AND PROCEDURES

Senior managers should establish clear written procedures for implementing the derivatives policy set by the board. These should cover:

❑ trading authority – who can trade and what they can trade;

❑ management reporting lines;

❑ position limits in derivatives markets;

❑ counterparty approvals;

❑ documentation approvals; and

❑ valuation procedures.

127

PRICE RISK
MANAGEMENT USING
DERIVATIVES:
CORPORATE POLICY
CREATION AND
MANAGEMENT
CONTROL GUIDELINES

Here is a checklist:

1. Appoint a senior manager to be responsible for policies and procedures.
2. Design and document limits for market and credit risk.
3. Design and document procedures for when limits are passed.
4. Design and document procedures for approving brokers or counterparties to be used.
5. Ensure that accounting policies have been established.
6. Ensure that all taxation implications have been considered.

COMPONENT 3: CONTROL AND SUPERVISION

Senior management should ensure derivative activities are properly supervised and are subject to a clear framework of internal controls and audits to ensure that derivative usage is in compliance with corporate policy (and external regulation in the case of a financially regulated institution).

Here is a checklist:

1. Frequently review the level of expertise in the organisation.
2. Perform an independent review of the internal controls.
3. Ensure that management reports are fit for the purpose.
4. Examine computer systems and check they are robust and cannot be amended by unauthorised personnel.
5. Ensure regular internal audit checks.

COMPONENT 4: ORGANISATION, ROLES AND RESPONSIBILITY

Senior management should establish a sound risk management function, providing an independent framework for reporting, monitoring and controlling all aspects of the risk matrix.

The risk matrix

The risk matrix illustrates how all the risks shown interrelate and affect each other and makes it clear that relationships between them are never two-dimensional. It also makes the point that it is impossible to manage price risk effectively without reviewing all the other risks that an organisation may face.

As the matrix shows, the key risks to be managed in an organisation when using derivatives for trading or price risk management purposes are: credit risk, liquidity risk, cash flow risk, basis risk, legal risk, tax risk and operational risk. All these risks will have a direct bearing on which derivatives are employed and the choice of trading partner. They will also affect decisions on where trading takes place (which is dependent on jurisdiction and tax risk), and how much is traded (which will depend on operational risks).

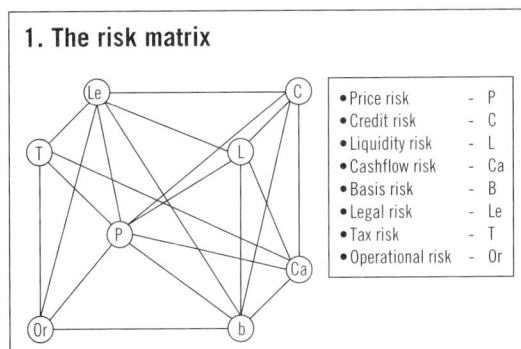

1. The risk matrix

- Price risk   - P
- Credit risk   - C
- Liquidity risk   - L
- Cashflow risk   - Ca
- Basis risk   - B
- Legal risk   - Le
- Tax risk   - T
- Operational risk - Or

Here is a checklist:

1. Allocate very clear responsibilities to individuals using organisation charts and clear job descriptions.

128

PRICE RISK
MANAGEMENT USING
DERIVATIVES:
CORPORATE POLICY
CREATION AND
MANAGEMENT
CONTROL GUIDELINES

2. Use appropriate market risk and valuation techniques.
3. Ensure all significant limit excesses are reported to the board of directors (in exception reports).
4. Perform price-movement stress testing to assess the effect of abnormal market movements on positions.

COMPONENT 5: CREDIT PROCEDURES

All credit risks to which the organisation will be exposed should be measured and analysed, and these risks should be minimised through the use of effective credit management (eg, collateralisation of positions with credit-weak counterparts, credit defaults derivatives, credit insurance).

Here is a checklist:

1. Analyse the risks inherent in both exchange-traded and OTC derivatives.
2. Minimise credit risk through netting agreements and other techniques.
3. Establish credit risk limits in derivatives markets (overall limits) and counterpart by counterpart limits.
4. Establish procedures for authorising credit limit excesses. Decide on the person responsible for giving approvals and the person who will deputise in his or her absence.
5. Establish policies and procedures in the event that a counterparty or broker becomes insolvent. If positions are held in futures markets with a broker, the organisation's funds should be segregated from the operating capital of the broker. This is the regulatory norm these days, but it is worth checking the agreements with the broker, since it means that the funds are protected if the broker goes bankrupt.

COMPONENT 6: LEGAL AND DOCUMENTARY

Procedures should be in place for monitoring legal risk, covering legal capacity, authority, compliance and the need for the appropriate documentation.

Here is a checklist:

1. Establish that the organisation has the power (internally and externally) to use derivatives in the manner envisaged.
2. Ensure that the authority to deal in derivatives is delegated to the appropriate staff.
3. Complete a list of authorised existing and potential brokers and counterparties. Note any restrictions.
4. Obtain a warranty from each broker or counterparty as to its power to deal in derivatives.
5. Review documentation.
6. Use master trading agreements for OTC derivatives. The use of standard ISDA agreements for cash-settled OTC deals will mean an organisation will have access to lots of legal and other expertise on matters relating to their derivatives deals. This can help keep up-front legal costs down as well as create greater legal assurance and certainty in situations of default or disputes.
7. Ensure margin or credit arrangements are well documented.

All of the guidelines and information compiled from these components of the management control matrix will help an organisation to produce a risk management policy document (sometimes referred to as a risk management or derivatives usage procedure manual). This should be distributed to all heads of business units in the organisation and to all front office and back office staff. The policy document will enable staff to effectively conduct their day-to-day activities referring to the document as required to ensure they are operating in line with their organisation's operating procedures. A section on management reporting lines in the policy document should clearly inform staff whom they should report to for special approval if they need to take any action involving derivatives contracts that is outside the normal boundaries set by the risk management policy document.

Corporate derivatives risk management policy and procedures document

The primary components of a sound risk management process are:

- ❏ a comprehensive risk measurement approach, eg, VAR;
- ❏ a detailed structure of position limits;
- ❏ guidelines and other parameters used to control the usage of derivatives (either for hedging or speculative purposes); and
- ❏ a strong management information system for controlling, monitoring and reporting risks.

Expanding on these primary components, we can illustrate the key contents of a typical derivatives policy or manual.

Example of key contents in policy document

1. What is the organisation's purpose in using derivatives?
- ❏ speculation, to take advantage of risk opportunities;
- ❏ hedging, to reduce price risk exposures; or
- ❏ both.

2. What type of derivative instruments is the organisation willing to utilise?
- ❏ on-exchange futures;
- ❏ on-exchange options (traded options);
- ❏ OTC swaps; or
- ❏ OTC options (exotics).

3. Which markets can the organisation's traders utilise?
- ❏ what are the position limits of the derivative markets used?
- ❏ overall company-wide position limits; or
- ❏ individual trader limits;
- ❏ position limits for each of the agriculture derivatives markets which traders have access to, in order to control liquidity risk.

4. What percentage of the agriculture exposure should be hedged?
- ❏ the minimum amount to be hedged; or
- ❏ the extra volume allowed for opportunistic hedging if prices are within budgets.

5. What are the limits on the tenure of derivatives utilised?
- ❏ This may be listed by agriculture derivatives market. The decision on how far forward traders can trade in a particular market will depend on counterpart creditworthiness and the general liquidity in the market.

6. Which counterparts are used for OTC?
- ❏ A list of authorised counterparts regularly updated and passed to traders (front office and back office) to prevent accidental unauthorised trades;
- ❏ For trader guidance a clear policy should be set on credit quality required for counterparts in OTC markets;
- ❏ Credit policy should also include what tenures of deals can be executed with different credit quality entities.

7. Policy on types of legal documentation that must be in place prior to any derivatives trading commencing with new counterparts.

130

PRICE RISK
MANAGEMENT USING
DERIVATIVES:
CORPORATE POLICY
CREATION AND
MANAGEMENT
CONTROL GUIDELINES

8. Management reporting lines.
❑ A clear diagram showing reporting lines will help front and back office staff and management handle problems quickly and efficiently.

9. Reports to be generated daily.
❑ A list of reports and who is to produce them on a daily basis, eg, exception reports, position reports, profit and loss reports.

10. Exception reports
❑ Clear policy on who is to see these reports and who must sign off and be responsible for taking action to resolve matters.

Back office systems

An organisation may succeed in putting in place a clear management and reporting structure, with a written risk management policy that all staff are familiar with, but all this effort will have been wasted if an appropriate back office system is not in place. The back office is key for protecting an organisation, as it is where all data on trades are collected, where positions are valued each day and where core management information reports are generated (eg, exception reports).

Any back office or control system is only as good as the quality of the data that have been input. These inputs can be summarised as follows:

❑ new transactions;
❑ exercises (options that expire and create a new swap/futures position or even exercise into physical delivery of a commodity);
❑ market price data;
❑ close-outs and settlements;
❑ deliveries;
❑ receipts and payments; and
❑ data on any documentary credits/guarantees from trading counterparts – values, expiry, type.

Controls of input data

Whether a reporting/control system is manual or computerised, the proper control and validation (double checking) of input is essential. Responsibility for particular input tasks should be clearly allocated, with password control used for screen operators. Input routines should require a standard format containing all relevant detail for a new transaction (eg, date, counterparty and full transaction data – volume, settlement and price). Source documents (trading tickets from trading desk) should be time-stamped, or otherwise marked to indicate the time of execution, and then also marked by the back office to indicate that they have been input. All input should be subject to validation routines (eg, computer proof listings of new transactions entered requiring confirmation or validation prior to updating the main transaction records). A unique reference number should also be assigned within the system to each item of validated input – on most occasions this number is the actual ticket number written out and time-stamped by the trader on the trading desk.

Straight-through processing

Some companies are already moving towards what is known as straight-through processing (STP). Futures markets are very close to this already with trades from the exchanges going into clearing house systems and clearing broker member systems automatically. The OTC market is slowly moving this way, too, with several organisations starting e-confirms for OTC derivatives transactions. These allow confirmations of deals done on and off electronic trading platforms to go straight into counterpart back office and risk management systems. OTC is generally still recapped by postal confirmations

131

**PRICE RISK
MANAGEMENT USING
DERIVATIVES:
CORPORATE POLICY
CREATION AND
MANAGEMENT
CONTROL GUIDELINES**

and faxes. By reducing the human involvement in the trade processing and back office management, companies are already trying to reduce the risk of human error in inputting deal data.

According to the International Swaps and Derivatives Association (ISDA), many organisations are now well on the way to implementing STP as a key part of their back office systems. The association's 2002 operational benchmarking survey summary was based on responses from 65 firms around the world and reported that:

❏ front office trade data are available for same-day processing as follows: 100% for forward rate agreements; 98% for plain vanilla swaps; and

❏ errors in front office trade data, which most commonly occur in dates, are more common for credit derivatives (21%) than for FRAs (10%) and plain vanilla swaps (17%).

It appears that plain vanilla swaps are more automated than credit and equity derivatives. It is also interesting that the most common results are either zero automation of processes or totally the opposite with substantial automation of operational processes, suggesting an all-or-nothing approach: that is, once a firm institutes some automation for STP, it applies it across the company. Functions with a high degree of automation include the transfer of data from the front office to the back office operations systems, transfer of trade data from the operations system to the general ledger and addition of data to the front office trade record.

Reports and records

TRANSACTION RECORDS

A back office system should create and maintain complete records of all transactions and should be able to break up reports between trader, counterparty (for OTC products), the product traded, trade/executed date, volume, time traded, and broker used where appropriate.

POSITION RECORDS

With open positions, it is essential that each input transaction settlement be accurately reflected in statements of position.

MARGINS AND EQUITY

Exception reports assist effective monitoring by highlighting potential risk situations, such as:

❏ position limits being broken;

❏ counterparty's equity falling below a certain level; and

❏ contracts nearing delivery date (futures) or expiry (options), or pricing out (swaps).

COUNTERPARTY DOCUMENTATION

Appropriate counterparty documentation should be generated for the confirmation (on a daily basis) of contract settlement account, to advise the counterparty of details of contracts closed out (netted off) or priced out and the profit or loss agreed and then settled between counterparties.

MANAGEMENT INFORMATION/RISK MANAGER

❏ Exception reports and positions close to expiry.

❏ Critical area (knowledge of different delivery processes for on-exchange derivatives such as futures is vital).

❏ Position reports.

❏ Profitability reports presented in various ways, eg, by department/individual trader; by market/product; by period – showing performance trends; value at risk for the firm – calculations.

PRICE RISK
MANAGEMENT USING
DERIVATIVES:
CORPORATE POLICY
CREATION AND
MANAGEMENT
CONTROL GUIDELINES

WHO SHOULD LOOK AT THE REPORT AND RECORDS?

In most medium to large organisations, a corporate treasurer or risk manager is responsible for identifying and managing risk. Where the scale of the trading or risk management activity is not sufficient to justify a separate independent risk management function, responsibility for monitoring risk is usually allocated to members of management who are not directly involved in the day-to-day management of risk (eg, traders).

Derivative back office management

It is essential to have tight security on back office systems. A company should not rely on just one risk manager or person to monitor or pick up errors. It should also have a system that prevents people who are active in the risk management and trading areas from altering records.

To check for irregularities, some banks and brokers have asked their employees to take at least five consecutive business days as holiday at short notice. The person who takes over has a good chance of picking up on mistakes that have been made through operational error, losing positions that have been concealed or, indeed, fraud.

This should certainly allow the organisation to expose its skill shortages and perhaps target staff for further training so that the organisation is not overreliant on any particular individual.

Internal controls and the back office

The basic framework of internal controls that any back office system should be able to support is as follows.

❑ Risks (business risks, position risks, human and operational risks, credit risks).
❑ Fundamental controls (authority levels and limit-setting features, automatic exception reporting and monitoring of position limits, profitability reporting).
❑ Organisational controls (legal considerations, policy monitoring, segregation of duties and the operation of internal checking).
❑ Position risk (trading, types of derivatives, limits in markets, limits with counterparties (OTC swaps), monitoring and reporting against limits, hedge reporting).
❑ Counterparty authorisation. The back office system should preferably be integrated with the trading desk in order to stop trades being finalised with counterparties who have already exceeded credit limits or position limits. Remember that, when your traders agree the deal, it doesn't matter whether it is a futures trade or OTC swaps trade on the telephone: your firm is committed!
❑ Counterparty set-up. Credit departments and risk managers should be the only people able to set up new counterparts on the system; they should also be the only ones with access to setting trader and counterpart position limits.

Ideally, the back office system should be able to automatically produce an alert or printout of exception reports (eg, loss limits, counterpart credit limits breaches, internal trader position limit breaches).

Operational risk and the back office

It is difficult to talk about internal control systems without looking at the structure of back offices. Operational risk then comes into play when designing the back office. One definition of operational risk is the risk of loss caused by failures in operational processes or the systems that support them, including those adversely affecting reputation, legal enforcement of contracts and claims.

So, it is important to structure the back office system in such a way as to help prevent underlying causes of operational risk and, in turn, to keep internal controls and risk management processes operating effectively.

PRICE RISK
MANAGEMENT USING
DERIVATIVES:
CORPORATE POLICY
CREATION AND
MANAGEMENT
CONTROL GUIDELINES

Role of external or internal audit and compliance

Derivative operations should be subject to periodic reviews (eg, quarterly, half-yearly) by the company's internal audit function or external auditors if in-house expertise for this is not available.

It should be the responsibility of the board of directors to ensure that internal audit and compliance department (if applicable) are staffed with personnel with sufficient skill and expertise to undertake reviews of the company's derivative operations. The exact role of external auditors and the processes that they use will vary from country to country. However, auditors should check that financial statements are free from material misstatements, and check the derivative transactions and records supporting financial statements and balances and disclosures. An external auditor should assess the accounting principles used for derivatives, and also comment on the scope, adequacy and effectiveness of a company's internal control system, and derivative-pricing methodologies (if any) including any internal audit approach/system that exists.

A risk management review

A risk management review is something that should be done on an annual basis at the very least. Its purpose is to gather guidance for management on ways to improve existing operational procedures and controls, or to highlight lack of controls in specific areas where regulations may have changed since the last time risk management policies were reviewed.

This review is usually carried out by an independent external consultant or, if available, risk management staff from another office could take up this task if you operate in a large international organisation and as long as those conducting the review are considered independent of the operation they are reviewing.

Risk management reviews, unlike audits, focus on providing valuable feedback to management so that they can improve processes and controls to keep up with the latest industry and (where appropriate) financial regulatory guidelines. They tend to rely more on oral representations from staff than an audit.

Most large accounting firms, when auditing companies, look at trading controls and reporting structures and quite often auditors will make comments or notes in their annual accounting reports.

BIBLIOGRAPHY

James, T., 2003, *Energy Price Risk* (London: Palgrave Macmillan).

IMPACT OF RISK ON FINANCING

12

Consequences of the New Basel II Regime for Food and Agri Companies

Geert Embrechts*

Rabobank International

Introduction

It is widely acknowledged that banks need capital for the risks they run. Bank capital is a buffer to cover unexpected losses. Since 1988, the Basel Committee has determined what are now called 'BIS I' guidelines on how banks should calculate the minimum capital requirements to cover for these unexpected losses in their portfolio. The impetus behind this move was widespread concern about declining levels of capital held generally and the increased level of risk banks were assuming. Since that time the BIS I Accord has been adopted by more than 100 countries. These BIS I rules will be replaced by new guidelines in at the end of 2006.

As with the Basel I rules, the new Basel II principles will have a major impact on how banks run their business and in particular on decisions of banks to extend credit to clients and at what interest rate level.[1] Since banks are currently preparing for BIS II, the expected developments are already casting their shadow on the current bank environment and the access that companies have to funding from banks.

If not adequately addressed, these changes will impact the often leveraged commodity companies (with exposure to commodity price risk) to a larger than average extent. This is also the reason why the Basel Committee has decided to allow for a "specialised" treatment of commodity finance (CF) in the BIS II regulations.

In this chapter, the BIS II regulations will be discussed in a nutshell. The regulations are generally seen as quite complex and unfortunately a good understanding of these is key to getting a good overview of the impact of BIS II on commodity companies. The impact on corporates and food and agri companies in particular will be discussed in more detail. Finally, options to solve to the restricted access to funding will be given.

BIS I rules: the (in)famous 8%

Since 1988, banks are required – as a general rule – to set aside 8% of the exposure they have on corporates.[2] If, for example, a bank supplies funding to a trading company for the amount of US$100 million, the bank is required to reserve US$8 million of its capital to cover the unexpected event that the loan will not be repaid (default risk). In the BIS I regulations, it does not matter whether this corporate had an AAA-rating, or was rated B−. Moreover, no distinction is made between an unsecured loan and a senior loan, although the rules allow certain low-risk products or strong collateral agreements

*The opinions do not necessarily express those of the Rabobank. The author would like to thank Arie Endendijk for comments on an earlier version.

(eg with cash or guarantees) to be rewarded. Loans to OECD banks are generally seen as of lower risk as well, and are therefore weighted for 20%. This means that a €100 million loan to another bank attracts only €1.6 million (€100 m × 8% × 20%) of solvency (ie, capital). The same holds for loans to non-OECD banks with a maturity up to one year. Finally, a letter of credit has a lower weighting (generally 10–20% as well).

The imposition the 8% requirement has led to a rationalisation of credit, in particular in emerging markets.[3]

BIS II regulation in a nutshell: three pillars, three risks, three approaches

The new Basel II framework will replace the old Basel I (credit risk) rules dating from 1988.[4] During the last four years, proposals for these regulations have been submitted for comments of the industry. The final version of the Basel II Accord is expected at the end of 2003. The new rules will come into force in 2007, but banks must have already implemented them in 2006.

Major change with the capital requirements is that BIS II will allow for a better discrimination of risk in a specific transaction. Where BIS I does not distinguish between an AAA-rated and a B-rated company, BIS II will. This will mean that less capital will have to be put aside for the higher-rated corporate for a similar transaction.

Basel II distinguishes three determinants (pillars) of supervision by the central bank (see Figure 1): (1) *capital adequacy* (2) *supervisory review* and (3) *market discipline*. Capital adequacy is the major determinant of the minimum capital requirements for banks and therefore the major focus of this chapter. This Pillar I gives detailed minimum capital requirements for (a) credit risk, (b) market risk and (c) operational risk.

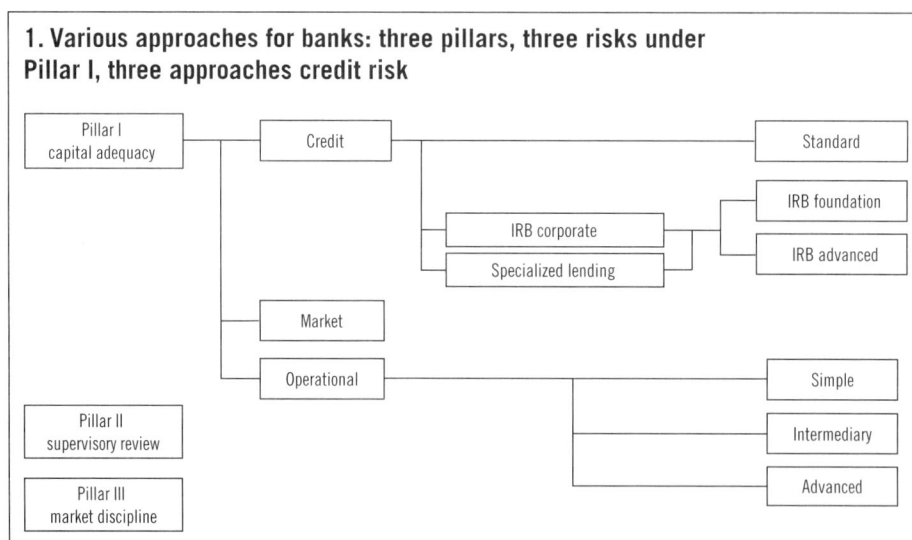

1. Various approaches for banks: three pillars, three risks under Pillar I, three approaches credit risk

Of these three types of risk, credit risk has always been the most important risk that banks in the F&A sector are facing. Credit risk can be defined as the risk of a loss for the bank resulting from a potential failure of its client to honour the financial obligations vis-à-vis the bank.

The new BIS II credit-risk rules allow banks to use three approaches: (i) the standardised approach, (ii) the internal-ratings-based (IRB) foundation approach and (iii) the IRB advanced approach.

THE STANDARDISED APPROACH

The standardised approach can be compared to the BIS I rules, with the major difference being that the standardised approach under BIS II puts greater emphasis on the role of external ratings as provided by the rating agencies. Under BIS I, there was a distinction only between OECD and non-OECD banks and governments. No distinction was made between quality of corporate credit risk.

Table 1. BIS II weightings for corporates under the standard approach					
	AAA to AA−	A+ to A−	BBB+ to BB−	Below BB−	Unrated
BIS I	100%	100%	100%	100%	100%
BIS II	20%	50%	100%	150%	100%

Table 1 summarises the effects. Where an AAA-rated company would receive a 100% weighting under BIS I, the weighting under BIS II would be only 20%, saving a bank 80% in capital. Banks are required to hold more capital than under BIS I, for corporates rated lower than BB−. Unrated corporates will be treated the same under BIS II as under BIS I, leaving unrated companies with a low credit quality slightly better off than companies with a rating below BB−.

THE INTERNAL-RATINGS-BASED APPROACH

BIS II also increases the scope for financial institutions to use their internal risk ratings under the internal-ratings-based approach (IRB). For a correct understanding of the IRB approach it is important to distinguish the loss drivers for a bank: *probability of default* (PD), *loss-given default* (LGD) and *exposure at default* (EAD). These are discussed in Panel 1.

PANEL 1

EXPECTED AND UNEXPECTED LOSSES

A bank can calculate its average, statistically anticipated level of loss over time. This credit loss is called *expected loss* (EL), which must be treated as the cost of doing business. If losses always equal their expected levels, there would be no uncertainty and no economic rationale to hold capital against risk. The risk arises from variations in loss levels, which are due to *unexpected loss* (UL). For example, after the attacks on the World Trade Center, the airline sector suffered from serious problems and some airline companies went into bankruptcy. Banks that, for example, lent to Swiss Air and Sabena experienced losses that were substantially higher than their long-run-expected losses on the two companies or on the airline industry in general or over a longer period of time. This is the unexpected loss. It can be defined as the (unforeseen) risk that more than average of the expected losses occur at the same time interval. Unexpected losses require capital to be set aside to absorb shocks, so that the bank will not experience financial stress by their occurrence.[5]

Four factors are used to determine the expected and unexpected losses:

1. Probability of default (PD): What is the probability of a customer going into default?
2. Loss-given default (LGD): How large will the loss rate be in the event of default?
3. Exposure at default (EAD): How large will exposure be in the event of default?
4. Maturity/tenor.

The expected loss (EL) is defined as:

$$EL = PD_{tenor} \times EAD \times LGD$$

with *probability of default* (PD) linked to ratings and *loss-given default* (LGD) based on the type of transaction/product and collateral. LGD is defined as the total loss incurred by the bank (including the cost of carry and the work out costs), as a percentage of the deal exposure at the time of default.

> The calculation of the unexpected loss is driven by the volatility of the expected loss. Quite complex rules for these guidelines are laid down in the BIS II document. Banks often use their own (more strict) models to calculate the maximum unexpected loss at a certain confidence interval. This is called ECONOMIC CAPITAL. This is the basis for the calculation of the risk-adjusted return on capital (RAROC), a minimum hurdle rate that has to be met.

What drives credit ratings?

As explained in Panel 1, the credit rating will be an important driver of capital in BIS II. Rating agencies and banks have all developed their credit models to determine the credit ratings of their clients. Although these models vary and are confidential, it is fair to say that all the quantitative parts of these models pay most attention to the following risk drivers:[6]

❏ a high leverage;
❏ high-volatility assets (eg commodities);
❏ high-earnings volatility (eg because of commodity-price volatility);
❏ higher-risk activities; and
❏ emerging-markets risk (country risk).

The higher the risk associated with these drivers, the higher the PD and the more capital a bank needs to set aside to cover for its potential losses.

In addition, valuation of collateral backing the security of the loan will play an important role, but in the BIS II models this will be included in the LGD models and not in the rating (ie, PD) models. The losses in case of a default (LGD) by the client are of often determined by:

❏ the level of seniority;
❏ the collateral title;
❏ the collateral management; and
❏ the covenants.

IRB foundation versus advanced approach

To determine the default probability of a client, banks generally use rating models, in the same way that Standard & Poor's and Moody's assign ratings on the basis of a model and expert judgment. If banks can convince the regulators that their rating models provide a sound and unbiased estimate of the default probability of their portfolio of loans, banks are allowed to use their own estimates for the PDs. In order to qualify, a proven track record of five years is needed. In the IRB foundation approach the regulators will still provide estimates for the LGD. For example, the LGD for a mortgage loan is set at 11% and the LGD for corporate unsecured loans is set at 45%. Certain collateral is recognised as eligible for a lower-than-45% LGD. Eligible financial collateral (cash, gold, investment-grade debt securities), receivables and real estate are all recognised as having a lower-than-average LGD. For other, not recognised, collateral, the minimum LGD is 40%, which represents only a minor improvement compared with LGD for unsecured loans (45%). Requirements in order to qualify for the 40% LGD are quite tight: for receivables and other collateral, an overcollateralisation of 125% and 140% respectively is required. Overall, it can be concluded that the LGD weights as imposed by the regulator in the IRB foundation approach appear to be very conservative.

In the advanced approach, banks are allowed to use their own estimates for LGD, Banks can qualify for the IRB advanced approach only if they can prove that their loss models along with their own estimates for PDs have been extensively tested and unbiased predictors of losses in the last seven years. In general it is expected that the outcome of LGD models of banks will generally be substantially lower than the aforementioned LGD estimates, as set by the regulators.

Impact on pricing and the client relationship

Banks are currently preparing for BIS II. Models are built and (back-)tested and exposure-measurement systems are made compliant with BIS II. On the basis of new MIS, it is possible to calculate the minimum returns to cover for the capital the needs to be put aside for covering the unexpected loss on a transaction. Tables 2 and 3 display the minimum margin to be required, setting a standard of 20% return on capital.

Table 2. Minimum pricing hurdles for a senior unsecured loan to an AA/AAA-rated counterpart

	BIS I	Standard	Foundation IRB	Advanced IRB
Loss-given default			45%	35%
Risk-weighted assets	1,000,000	200,000	147,664	68,910
Risk-weighted assets as %	100%	20%	15%	7%
Regulatory capital	80,000	16,000	11,813	5,513
Pricing, for target RoC* (20%)	1.60%	0.32%	0.24%	0.11%

*Excluding origination costs.

Table 2 shows that, under the current regime of BIS I for an AAA-rated company, a bank needs to make 160 bps in order to get a gross return on capital (RoC) of 20%. In practice, however, no bank will charge an AAA-rated company 160 bps for its funding, since internal risk-measurement systems and competitive pressure from other banks force banks to quote substantially lower margins to their AAA-rated clients.

Under the BIS II standardised approach, this will decrease to 32 bps, while if a bank is allowed to apply the IRB Foundation – or, even better, the advanced approach – the required margin will be much lower (24 bps and 11 bps).[7] Note that there is a direct relation between the required RoC and the minimum pricing hurdle.

Table 3. Minimum pricing hurdles for a senior unsecured loan to a B+-rated counterpart

	BIS I	Standard	Foundation IRB	Advanced IRB
LGD			45%	35%
RWA	1,000,000	1,500,000	1,360,022	1,057,795
RWA as %	100%	150%	136%	106%
Reg cap.	80,000	120,000	108,802	84,624
Pricing, for target RoC* (20%)	1.60%	2.40%	2.18%	1.69%

*Excluding origination costs.

The story is quite different for a B+-rated entity. Here, the pricing minimum rises from 160 bps under BIS I to 169 bps under the BIS II advanced approach to 240 bps under the BIS II standardised approach.[8]

Along with the BIS II changes, banks have introduced new internal performance benchmarks that directly link income made on a transaction with the required capital. The best-known benchmark is RAROC, the "risk-adjusted return on capital" (see Panel 1). Although even for this benchmark, different definitions exists, it can be defined as follows:

$$RAROC = \frac{Income - Cost}{Economic\ capital} \times 100$$

In the numerator, income minus costs should be seen as the additional income, on top of the cover for operational costs and expected loss.[9] As explained in Panel 1, the denominator, Economic Capital, is the capital required to cover for unexpected losses. Economic Capital will often be higher than the required capital for BIS II.[10] The consequence is that margins to be made on transactions will be much higher than calculated in Tables 2 and 3.

Banks want to ensure that on a client level they meet the minimum hurdle rate. The conclusion from Tables 2 and 3 – that, for clients with a lower rating (and thus a high PD), unsecured loans will become much more expensive while for higher-rated entities funding costs may decline – still holds.[11] The return made on unsecured loans to lower-rated clients will often not be sufficient to meet the internal hurdle rate and cover for the unexpected losses. Banks will therefore ask clients to give them more profitable business, such as M&A transactions, leads in syndications etc, to improve the income made on client level. If the minimum hurdler ate across all products will not be met, the bank may decide to exit the client relationship.

Commodity finance

Banks will evaluate their portfolio of commodity clients using the same principle. A commodity company's balance sheet looks very different from the balance sheet of a manufacturing or service company. On the liability side, commodity players typically tend to have a low level of fixed assets, large amounts of current assets, mainly inventories and receivables. The commodity business is based on small margins, with profits often linked to the commodity "boom–bust cycle". Large trade volumes have to be generated to cover operating costs and make the required return. This results in a relative high gearing and a high portion of short-term debt on the asset side of the balance sheet.

How will the BIS II complaint-rating models then evaluate the credit quality of the commodity traders? The large traders are all well capitalised and will therefore probably stand the test. BIS II may impact them substantially through the back door, since these traders often approach banks to take over country and counterparty bank risk in emerging markets. As explained before, certain low-rated OECD countries (eg, Turkey) and consequently their banking systems will probably be punished substantially.

If the standardised or IRB foundation approach is applied to the smaller commodity players, it is almost certain that they would loose from BIS II. Recalling the aforementioned drivers of credit risk and default probabilities, most F&A companies are highly leveraged and have volatile assets and income. The smaller commodity houses are often specialised in one or a few commodities, leaving them exposed to large-sector and commodity price risk.

Assets and earnings are often volatile and correlated with commodity prices. On top of that, these companies are often situated in an emerging market or have direct or indirect emerging market-risk exposure.

In addition to the aforementioned problems commodity finance also has a specific risk that is not covered in the standard rating and LGD models. A basic assumption of BIS II modelling requirements is that PD and LGD are uncorrelated. In commodity-finance practice, this is often not the case, since both PD and LGD often will correlated to commodity-price returns. If commodity prices go up, the value of (unhedged) collateral will go up, but residual value of liquidation will be returned to the client. If commodity prices go down, a collateral shortfall may exist, which is to be borne by the bank. Basel requires banks to take this explicitly into account when dealing with commodity finance.

The typical risk-mitigating structures in commodity finance in the corporate models have been the reason why the Basel II introduced a specialised approach to commodity finance.

Specialised lending

Given their high leverage, these commodity companies are generally not financed on their balance sheet but on the basis of cash-flow-generating assets that are – in one form or the other – pledged to the bank as collateral. The borrowing capacity of the company is often linked to the value of the underlying assets (eg a borrowing base structure).

The Basel Committee has recognised that the corporate approach punishes these companies disproportionally and has therefore proposed a *Specialised Lending* (SL) approach for commodity finance.[12]

The SL approach for commodity finance (CF) once again distinguishes three approaches: the CF basic approach (comparable to the standardised approach), the CF IRB foundation and the CF IRB advanced approach.

COMMODITY FINANCE BASIC APPROACH

Although many items are yet open for debate, the guidelines for the CF basic approach shed a light on what regulators require to be covered by the models. The models will asses six important parts of a commodity-finance transaction:

1. financial strength (including a degree of overcollateralisation of the trade);
2. country risk;
3. market liquidity of the commodity collateral (quotation) and susceptibility to damage from external causes;
4. strength of the sponsor;
5. asset-control measures embedded in the financing facility; and
6. insurance against loss or damage.

On the basis of the outcome, the transaction is qualified "strong", "good", "satisfactory", "weak" or "default", with the last being not relevant for the purpose of this article.

As with the aforementioned standardised approach, regulators provide guidelines for the capital to be put aside. Table 4 provides five possible transactions. Transaction I shows an ideal commodity-finance transaction: an investment-grade counterparty has a transaction outside the emerging markets (no country risk) and the underlying commodity is quoted on an exchange, with hedges in place. This transaction will still require a pricing minimum of 80–120 bps.[13] Note, however, that providing collateral is beneficial only to companies with a rating BBB. For companies with a higher rating, the corporate standard approach will require less capital. Example II is slightly more realistic, since it concerns a BB-rated company. The required pricing would be between 120 and 160 bps. The most realistic examples are IV and V, where the financial strength of the counterparty is low, country risk is high and the commodity is liquid but often not quoted. Here, the required RoC would rise to 240–560 bps. Once again, the CF basic approach compares unfavourably with the corporate standardised approach (see Table 3). In general, it is fair to conclude that CF basic approach is not very beneficial to banks (in particular if they have a substantial commodity-finance portfolio) or to clients that are engaged in the commodity finance business and are dependent on funding as provided by the bank.

Table 4. The risk-slotting method to commodity finance

Examples	I	II	III	IV	V
	Strong	Good	Satisfactory	Satisfactory	Satisfactory
Counterparty rating	BBB− or better	BB+ or BB	B+	B+	B to C−
Risk slot	50–75%	75–100%	150%	150%	350%
Required return (RoC = 20%)	0.8–1.2%	1.2–1.6%	2.4%	2.4%	5.6%
Country risk	None	Low	Medium to high	High	High
Commodity characteristics	Quoted	Quoted	Liquid	Liquid	Liquid
Strength of sponsor	Excellent	Good	Good	Sufficient	Sufficient
Trading controls and hedging policy	Strong	Good	Good	Good	Sufficient
Security Package	Strong	Strong	Good	Good	Sufficient
Rating Grade	Strong	Good	Satisfactory	Weak	Weak
Realistic case?	Very low	Low	Medium	High	High

CF IRB foundation approach

Banks that meet the aforementioned "foundation" requirements for the estimation of PD are allowed to use the general foundation approach for the corporate asset class to derive risk weights for SL risk classes. This will not accommodate these banks and their clients, since commodity clients will often receive a comparably low rating and thus a high PD. The LGD will generally be set at 40%, which is typically too high for a well-structured commodity finance transaction.

CF IRB ADVANCED APPROACH

Banks that meet the aforementioned "advanced" requirements for the estimation of both PD and LGD can use their counterparty rating model and their commodity-finance model to determine PD and LGD. Here is where the risk-mitigating effect of a tight structure will feed through a low LGD into a low capital requirement, enabling the bank to charge a relatively low margin on the funding the bank provides. The low charge matches the tight structure of the transaction.

THE SL APPROACHES COMPARED

Table 5 summarises the findings for a commodity-finance transaction (140% overcollateralisation) for a counterparty rated B. Interestingly, the SL treatment to commodity finance pays off only in the SL advanced approach.

Table 5. Minimum pricing hurdles for a commodity-finance transaction for a B-rated counterparty					
	BIS I	Standard	Specialised lending (basic approach)	SL Foundation	SL Advanced
LGD – CP3				40%	25%
RWA	1,000,000	1,500,000	1,500,000	906,681	377,784
RWA as %	100.00%	150%	150.00%	120.89%	75.56%
Reg cap.	80,000	120,000	120,000	72,534	30,223
Pricing, for target RoC* (20%)	1.60%	2.40%	2.40%	1.45%	0.60%
*Excluding origination costs and costs of handling collateral.					

From this example it is fair to conclude that only banks that apply the advanced approach to SL will be able to accommodate the smaller commodity traders. It therefore pays off to see what are the exact requirements that banks should meet with regard to collateral, (in particular with regard to commodity collateral).

Emphasis on tight and well-documented collateral management

The Basel II workforce has laid down a lot of strict requirements for collateral to be eligible as risk mitigants in the LGD. Apart from the obvious requirement of having clear and effective procedures in place, the Basel Committee sets high standards for collateral management and control. In a nutshell, these requirements can be summarised in three:

1. The structure must give banks *clear rights over the collateral*, including the possibility to liquidate it and take possession in case of default. This capacity should be well documented and supported by legal opinions.
2. The bank should have *effective control* over exposure to guarantors and collateral-management service providers. Banks should monitor the quality of the guarantors and collateral-management companies and in addition should actively manage the concentration risk to certain companies.[14]
3. Collateral value should not be greater than the current fair *market value*. The collateral should be marketable to liquid markets. It should be marked to market frequently. In addition to statistical revaluation, it should be revalued by professional appraisers as well. The periodic revaluation process must include physical inspection of the collateral.

The good news regarding these tight regulations is that banks that do not yet have these policies in place will certainly improve their risk-management standards and consequently reduce their (unexpected) losses. The bad news is that the administrative burden on banks and their commodity clients will rise as well. Another consequence is that countries that have companies operating in weak legal jurisdictions will have more difficulty with meeting the aforementioned standards, and therefore have more difficult access to commodity-finance funding.

Integrating internal risk management to finance

Another important way of improving companies access to funding at reasonable rates in times of commodity price volatility is to integrate their commodity finance with their hedging policies and risk management. Funding requirements of traders depend on the volume of the business and the commodity price: in the event of rising commodity prices, more working capital. Commodity companies that use commodity futures to hedge their commodity price exposure are sometimes faced with liquidity shortages (higher-margin requirements) in these events, since the profit on the commodity collateral can be exploited only later on. To avoid these problems, an integrated commodity-finance and price-risk management product will above all reduce the default risk borne by the bank and allow banks to accommodate further needs of working capital finance.

Trade-off between credit risk and operational risk

Apart from setting capital aside for credit-risk losses, banks will also have to reserve capital to cover operational risk. This is a new requirement, because it was not covered by BIS I regulations at all. More complex structures will often result in a reduction of credit risk, but a rise in operational risk. For example, in a borrowing base structure, the credit risk is mitigated by the pledge of collateral, but the administrative burden and required collateral checks will raise the probability that mistakes will be made, resulting in losses, to be borne by the bank. BIS II regulators require banks to put capital aside for that. It is yet uncertain how this will affect clients.

Small and medium-sized enterprises

As mentioned before, smaller, undiversified commodity companies (in particular if domiciled in an emerging market) may suffer from the BIS II regulations. At the request of the German banks (who have a substantial "*Mittelstand*" portfolio), the Basel Committee has set out compensating measures to offset part of the negative impact on small and medium-sized enterprises.[15] The more favourable treatment regulations are quite complex but, as a rule of thumb, this will help small F&A companies with a reduction of required capital of about 20%.

Conclusion

In this jungle of regulations and approaches to risk, it is important to explore ways how F&A companies can ensure good access to financing from banks. In commodity finance, preparation of the bank and its clients is needed for a fair access to bank funding under the BIS II regime. In a nutshell, three groups of factors can be distinguished that will drive the capital requirements of banks:

1. the risk-management standard of the bank and its qualification for the BIS advanced approach;
2. the structure of the transaction and how the models of the bank award the risk-mitigating features of the structures; and
3. the internal risk-management policy of the client.

Banks are currently ensuring that their models will be compliant with BIS II. For banks with a substantial commodity-finance portfolio, qualification for the IRB advanced is required to keep offering clients financing at competitive rates. Given the substantial costs of developing models and building the infrastructure, banks will need a long-term commitment to finance commodity companies. The flip side of this is that clients need to pick those banks that are best positioned to use the IRB advanced approach for commodity finance. Other approaches will require too much capital to be put aside for commodity-finance transactions, and will – in the absence of cross-selling – require banks to charge higher premiums to their clients.

As discussed at length in this article, the BIS II regulations require a lot from banks in terms of documentation. Banks will, for example, have to ensure that their legal title on the collateral is strong and supported by legal opinions. This will increase business costs and will also require more information from the client regarding its security position. Banks will move away from being light on documentation and heavy on local knowledge. The same will hold for F&A companies. Effective management of internal processes (including their MIS) and their asset types will be essential in the selection of useful assets that qualify for eligible collateral.

Requirements for doing structured transactions in emerging markets will be set higher. Soft indicators, such as long-standing experience and local representation of the client, will remain important but will have to be supported by more objective, hard evidence (eg, a clear legal title). It is important for banks to ensure that these soft but important factors be adequately taken into account, since these may be the difference between a default and a profitable deal for the bank and the client. The "blue eyes" principle, if still existent, will disappear.

1 *The third consultative document can be found on the BIS website: http:// www.bis.org/ bcbs/bcbscp3.htm.*
2 *Note that, to a limited extent, a distinction was made for low-risk products and low(er)-risk counterparts, such as government and banks.*
3 *Griffith-Jones and Spratt (2001), p. 7. In particular, the pro-cyclicality of the current BIS I and the future BIS II regulations is highlighted, as discussed by numerous other authors as well.*
4 *The 1996 Amendment for market risk will be included as well.*
5 *See Caouette et al (1998), p. 242.*
6 *See Saunders (2000), Chapter 11, for an overview of credit models.*
7 *Assuming an LGD of 35%.*
8 *Assuming an LGD of 35%.*
9 *A so-called economic capital benefit (because of higher-than-needed rating) may be added as well.*
10 *The reason for this is twofold. First, banks face capital scarcity and therefore business units have to compete with each other for capital allocated, driving up the minimum hurdle rate. Second, banks often have a higher rating than the regulators strictly require. In order to ascertain this rating, capital to be reserved to guard the rating (ie the economic capital) is larger than the capital required by BIS II.*
11 *In practice the latter has already happened, with the former being less often the case.*
12 *Along with an SL approach for project finance, income-producing real estate and object finance. See http://www.bis.org/publ/bcbs_wp9.pdf for the full document.*
13 *Depending on the policy of the local central bank.*
14 *For a more extensive discussion on the role of collateral management companies, see Budd (2003).*
15 *With a total sales volume between €5 million and €50 million.*

BIBLIOGRAPHY

BIS, 2001, Basel Committee on Banking Supervision, "Working Paper on the Internal Ratings-Based Approach to Specialised Lending Exposures", October, URL: http://www.bis.org/publ/bcbs_wp9.pdf.

BIS, 2003, Basel Committee on Banking Supervision, "The New Basel Capital Accord, Consultative Document", April, URL: http://www.bis.org/bcbs/bcbscp3.htm.

Budd, N., 2003, "Treatment of structural and operational risk in commodity-financing transactions under Basel II", *Trade and Forfaiting Review*, April, pp. 34–40.

Caouette, J. B., E. I. Altman and P. Narayanan, 1998, *Managing Credit Risk: The Next Great Financial Challenge*, John Wiley and Sons, New York.

Griffith-Jones, S., and S. Spratt, 2001, "Will the proposed new Basel Capital Accord have a net negative effect on developing countries?", unpublished paper for the Institute of Development Studies, University of Sussex.

Saunders, A., 2000, *Financial Institutions Management; a Modern Perspective*, McGraw Hill, Boston.

13

Collateral Management

Rodolfo Barros

Daimler Chrysler Capital Services

Introduction

This paper is written from the perspective of an asset-based lender who provides financing secured by movable goods (ie, collateral). These goods move as they are being bought, held/converted and sold onwards along a supply chain. This paper seeks to provide the reader with a framework of principles and methods to systematically manage his or her collateral.

Collateral management is a constant search for detail (monitoring requirements) and for protection (control requirements) against often conflicting legal and economic ownership interests. Collateral management is a subset of the monitoring and control process.

Monitoring is the ongoing review of the assets given as collateral and of the other commitments/undertakings between all parties to the credit. Control is the ongoing decision-making capability with respect to movability and saleability of the asset given as collateral. Therefore, monitoring and control processes consist of a multiplicity of events that are time-bound and that mark a requirement for decision making.

The monitoring and control processes of movable assets and their financing is a discipline supported by principles and methods. The principles are based on definitions. The methods are based on processes.

The definitions are embedded in the documents that arise from transactions along a supply chain and within the confines of a legal framework. These documents form the basis for a (monetary) settlement.

The methods can be found in the processes used to assume credit risks. These processes include the structuring process (*planning* to buy a risk), the underwriting process (*deciding* to buy a risk), the documentation process (*documenting* a risk to be bought), the execution process (*buying* the risk), the distribution process (*selling* the risk that was bought), and the monitoring and control process itself (*verifying* that the risk that was bought was assumed according to plan). The decision to buy a risk is granted according to each institution's credit standards, including the comfort level with its monitoring and control. It is important to note that time is the most important monitoring and control factor throughout these event-driven lending processes.

To standardise the monitoring and control process of the lending, one has to follow the documents that are the instruments used to assume the risks (*loan documentation*) and to protect against the occurrence of such risks (*collateral documents*). Portfolio collateral management and collateral management are related, but are dynamic processes in their own right, which can be planned, executed and controlled.

A key success factor in collateral management is, "Say what you do and do what you say." Weigh each word in its meaning and in its operational implementation. The more detail the better. Anticipate on all possible direct/indirect risks and formalise them through the establishment of limits (expressed in terms of money and time) for each stage of the supply chain. Verify the faithful execution and ongoing performance of these risks against their limits. The objective of good collateral management is to make true on the deliverable: *to guarantee the sufficiency of protection for the assumed risk.*

A monitoring and control system (MCS) standardises collateral tracking in order (a) to greatly reduce input time by the administrator in daily posting of collateral; (b) to have the ability to quickly generate exception reports on any upcoming agreement (eg, trust receipt expiration, and or deficiencies in collateral pools caused by sudden drops in market prices); (c) to reduce capital requirements (BIS II); and (d) to increase transparency to shareholders. It greatly reduces overall risk to the lender by providing up-to-the-minute information on collateral value and detailed exception reporting.

The definitions

LEGAL FRAMEWORKS

Legal frameworks provide tools for the creation, perfection and enforcement of security interests.

Creation

The laws of security interests in all goods, which are financed, as well as in the accounts receivable that are created when such goods are sold, are governed for their *creation* by the legal frameworks, which are particular to each jurisdiction. In most jurisdictions, possession of the goods, which represent collateral for a loan, is not necessarily required to create a security interest in such goods. Also, in many jurisdictions it is possible to limit the lender's security interest to specific transactions financed by limiting the security agreement to such transactions.

Perfection

Generally, filing of the security interest in public registers is required for the *perfection* of the security interest. The filing has the effect that the interests of the lender are well protected (priority) and also that the lender's security interest is known to third parties.

Enforcement

The *enforcement* of the rights is subject to the judges' or courts' own evaluation. The holder of a security interest has rights in the collateral, which can be enforceable against both the borrower and the borrower's other creditors. In the event of a default, the secured party may have the right to take possession of the collateral, regardless of who then has possession, and even by self-help as long as the required authorisation from the judge has been obtained.

If taking possession of the collateral is not feasible, the secured party ordinarily commences a judicial action for possession. Once it has possession the secured party has to sell or otherwise dispose of the goods through public auctions in order to satisfy the borrower's obligations.

CREATION/PERFECTION OF COLLATERAL TYPES

These legal frameworks provide broad categories for the creation, perfection and enforcement of different collateral types. The lender has to establish proper structural documentation in order to create a perfectible and enforceable security interest.

Collateral types – creation and structural documentation

Two separate ways by which security interests in goods (as well as in receivables) may be created without possession of the goods is through (a) the creation of an asset-specific security interest that continues throughout the relationship of the borrower with the lender (*revolving security interest* or *floating charge*), and (b) the taking of possession of, or rights in, the documents of title that represent the goods or receivables in question (*transactional security interest* or *fixed charge*).

Each type of security interest to a large extent duplicates the other, or they complement one another. A secured lender should ordinarily maintain an asset-specific security interest with each borrower at all times and also seek to maintain a security interest in the documents of title.

Revolving security interest or floating charge

In many jurisdictions it is not possible to create a general lien on all of the company's current assets, such as cash, receivables and inventories (otherwise known in the US as a general security interest). However, it is possible to create (asset-) specific liens in each individual transaction financed by the lender (otherwise known in the US as a specific security interest).

All that is required is: a duly executed written specific security agreement; that the borrower have rights in the collateral; and that a notice of the security interest be filed in the appropriate state/country in the form of a public deed.

A separate security agreement is required to obtain a security interest in all of the proceeds of the sale of such goods.

Transactional security or fixed charge

Security interest in documents of title: Movable goods are normally represented by negotiable documents of title (eg, warehouse warrants, bills of lading). In some countries, it is possible to create valid security interests in goods represented by documents of title without having a specific security agreement in place. Generally, possession of a negotiable document of title represents possession itself of the goods which are covered by the document. A security interest in a negotiable document of title can be perfected in two ways: by possession of the document itself, or by the creation of an (asset-) specific security interest.

Possession of documents of title: Some legal systems are not very practical in that they do not recognise that there may be reasons why a lender may not be able to maintain continuous possession of documents of title in which it has a security interest. In this situation, some legal systems do not provide for continuation of a lender's security interest, since the lender does not have possession of the document of title. If the goods are sold, the lender would retain a perfected security interest in the proceeds of the sale only if it has a valid revolving security agreement or a specific assignment of the receivable in question. Thereafter, the lender must rely on its specific security interest to cover the cash proceeds of the sale.

Security interest in documents of creditor rights: Receivables are normally represented by negotiable documents of credits, typically in the form of contracts, promissory notes, acceptances and cheques. Under the law, possession of a negotiable (properly endorsed/assigned) document of credit represents ownership of the rights emanating from the document. A security interest in a negotiable document of credit can be perfected in two ways: by endorsement/assignment and possession of the document itself, or by the creation of a (asset-) specific security interest.

The underlying structural documentation to create an asset-specific security interest usually takes the form of a pledge agreement (if no separate security agreement is in place). The pledge agreement creates a security interest in the goods and is granted to finance inventories in warehouses. Possession of a warrant and/or a warehouse receipt creates this security interest and the collateral is released only against repayment of the outstanding loan. The goods do not even have to move and may be held by third parties for and on behalf of the lender.

In a collateral trustee agreement backed by a pledge agreement, an employee of the borrower (often the CEO/owner) undertakes to monitor and segregate the collateral on behalf of and for the lender. It must be understood that, as long as the lender has not taken possession of the collateral, his security interest is imperfect.

In case a borrower has lodged with the lender documents of title as security, the documents will normally be released to the borrower in order to facilitate the sale of the underlying goods. The trust receipt reconfirms the security interest of the lender in such goods and sale proceeds. The assignment agreement transfers the rights and (not necessarily) the obligations of the owner in the proceeds emanating from the sale of goods and is used to finance receivables.

Filings – priority through perfection
The filings are public declarations of a lender's interests in certain assets of the borrower, either fixed or floating. The general rule is that a secured party must file in the state/country where the last event required to perfect a security interest takes place. The filing is done in the same jurisdiction as the lender, in the same jurisdiction as the borrower, and in any jurisdictions where there is significant inventory and/or accounts receivable.

Depending on the country/state/province, the filings have to be done at the state/province/county levels and the country level, or at both levels. The filing is an acceptable form for perfecting a security interest in all countries and requires several documents to be filed. The general rule for the priority between conflicting perfected security interests about the same collateral is that such security interests rank according to the time of filing or perfection, whichever is earlier. Possession of documents of title will always give first priority.

Key to the efficacy and the trustworthiness of this system is the soundness of the registries system itself to help prevent duplications and other weaknesses.

Transactional documentation
Transactional documentation (eg, a transaction and collateral report) is not needed to establish or perfect a security interest, as is the structural documentation. However, it is essential in order to identify the transactions financed and to monitor the collateral on a timely basis periodically. It is helpful in ascertaining the existence of the collateral, in confirming the lender's security interest in such collateral and in determining the value of the collateral (loan-to-value).

Having briefly reviewed the legal framework and the collateral types, we can now discuss two very important monitoring and control instruments the secured lender has to protect his interests: the *lending arrangement* (which determines the monitoring and control intensity) and the *advance margins* (which determines the level of protection sought against the undertaken risk).

TYPES OF LENDING ARRANGEMENT (MONITORING AND CONTROL INTENSITY)
Lending arrangements are the "degrees of freedom" the lender is prepared to grant the borrower. It is the freedom from time limits and constraints that dictate the intensity of monitoring and control the lender is willing to apply.

The simplest type of lending arrangement is unsecured lending and not the subject of this chapter, but interesting nonetheless because of the derived monitoring and control features that may also be applied to the secured borrowers (eg, reporting covenants and financial covenants). Conversely, unsecured lending could use many of the secured borrowing techniques to determine adequacy of exposures, liquidity and leverage.

Secured lending arrangements have different methods of creating, perfecting and monitoring security interests that present varying risks to the lending institution. The three primary types of secured lending arrangements are:

❑ borrowing base financing;
❑ collateral pool financing; and
❑ transactional financing.

In order to evaluate the individual risks and to institute adequate collateral controls, the following subsection will briefly describe the above types of secured lending arrangements and their individual risks. We will then review the various specific credit/collateral criteria and standard procedures for all secured lending.

Borrowing base financing

Borrowing base financing is a secured lending arrangement whereby the lenders are lending against a defined pool of assets, based on a periodic report from the borrower, and typically does not have actual title documents or specific collateral held by or delivered to the lender or any independent third party on behalf of the lender. All lenders share *pro rata* in all of the pledged assets. When taken to its extreme, the key characteristic of borrowing base financing is that the lender never controls or holds any collateral. It encompasses a number of risks: lack of physical control or evidence of collateral; more subject to MIS/accounting error; slow-moving or obsolete inventory not easily recognisable; and inventory valuations are not always verifiable; finally, problems with A/R can be hidden.

All of these risks can be mitigated with proper collateral controls, more stringent credit standards for this type of lending, and periodic outside independent audits of both collateral and accounting controls/procedures.

It should also be noted that borrowing base financing does provide some additional protection in that secured creditors share equally in all of the collateral, avoiding possible disputes over security interests in specific collateral and lessening the risk of a specific transaction collateral default (ie, an account-receivable default due to bankruptcy).

Collateral pool financing

Collateral pool financing is a secured lending arrangement whereby each financier lends against a specific individual pool of assets and the title documents are delivered to the specific lender or an independent third party (typically another lender) acting as collateral agent. The title documents are released against a trust receipt and the monitoring thereafter is provided by a periodic collateral pool report that lists the inventory and outstanding account-receivable relating to sold-inventory. The lender does not follow and approve individual sales and account-receivable, but the collateral pool report does enable the lender to review and follow account-receivable flows and quality.

The primary risks here are: not individually approving A/R; not controlling each transaction and the specific repayment cycle.

Transactional financing

The financing commences with the opening of an L/C secured by a pledged cash deposit, continues with the receipt of negotiable title documents and the documents are not released until full satisfactory details of the sales terms and A/R acceptability are approved. Each transactional borrower will vary in the type and form of sales and account-receivable information required. In the tightest form of transactional financing, the actual payments are coming directly to and from the lender and the buyer confirms that he will pay the lender at the due date.

Depending on the tightness of control on the A/R side of the transaction, the principal risk here is default of the A/R. This is controlled by the approval of A/R quality.

Lenders and the collateral control departments regularly have to update required collateral margins per good/commodity according to market developments.

ADVANCE COLLATERAL MARGINS

Regulatory bodies have established certain advance margins for collaterals. For instance, rules on concentration of credit prescribe that when the collateral is government bonds the ratio debt/collateral may be 100%, but if the collateral comprises mortgages, pledges, securities instruments, assignment of credits due to government entities or credit card issuers, then, at a minimum, the collateral may have to represent 125% of the debt. The advance margins are often fixed in time without paying proper consideration to the variability of the value of the underlying good (price volatility).

Advance collateral margins on goods

One of the instruments available to the lender as protection against price fluctuations and liquidation is the use of collateral margins at the onset of the loan (loan-to-value).

On and above the above regulatory minimum, it is advisable to publish on a regular basis a margin table per good/commodity, which will account not only for the price risk of the asset but also for the quality, the location and the nature of the asset (sold/unsold, and if sold, to counterparty/futures markets). The price risk can be computed by using statistical methods to determine the price volatility of the asset with a 90% degree of certainty. The advance margin must also take into account the location of the asset and the related transport costs to the consuming markets.

Collateral margins on receivables

Financing of receivables is like providing unsecured credit to a buyer of goods. Determination of the advance rate will depend on the quality of the buyer and on third-party support to his commitments (eg, letters of credit). As a rule of thumb, the overall receivable of the seller should not exceed 10% of its capital base.

Management process: measures to prevent, detect and correct (monitoring and control)

Management implies active monitoring and control of the created and perfected security interest. Monitoring and control procedures establish measures to *prevent*, to *detect* and to *correct* the potential occurrence of the approved and undertaken risks. The aim is to ensure sufficient protection in the eventual occurrence of the risk.

MEASURES TO PREVENT – COLLATERAL PROCEDURES/REPORTS TO
MONITOR AND CONTROL
Standards for all secured lending

Even though there are technical, collateral and monitoring differences between the various types of lending arrangements, the majority of the procedures and standards for prudent risk management are identical. The following standard procedures should apply to every borrower. For ease of understanding and to follow a normal transaction flow, the standards are listed in the order that they normally occur.

Standard procedures before credit approval and prior to booking any engagements

Anticipate the needs and all possible risks. Establish measures to prevent, detect and correct situations that may impair the repayment of the loan. All documents and their dates have to be recorded in the credit file. The originals must be placed in vault documentation files. In addition to security documents, one should obtain copies of acceptable insurance policy(s) and the appropriate loss-payee endorsement.

Standard procedure at the time of booking any engagement

Check all title documents for proper endorsements, and the quantity and price of the goods. One has to verify compliance with all parameters of the approval, particularly total credit limit, advance rates against inventory and receivables, duration of transaction, and any sublimits for collateral (ie, unsold inventory limit).

Standard procedure for inventory in storage (warehouse receipt/warrant monitoring)

Goods have to be stored in approved warehouses (guidelines and approval procedures have to be in place) and their value has to be verified on a daily basis. If any margin short-fall exists, the borrower has to correct the deficiency. Quarterly written confirmations have to be sent to all warehouses. Also, one should confirm quarterly with all borrowers all inventory locations to recheck the completeness of the filings. Copies have to be placed in both the documentation and the credit files and any new locations will require immediate filings.

Standard procedure for inventory in transit (bill of lading/truck receipt)

Goods have to be transported by approved transporters (guidelines and approval procedures per transporting company/vessel should be in place) and their value has to be verified on a daily basis. If any margin shortfall exists, the borrower has to correct the deficiency.

Copies have to be placed in both the documentation and the credit files. No filings are required when the vessel is on international waters. Filings may be required in each state when transported by inland.

Standard procedure for A/R and trust receipt (T/R) monitoring
Upon request for a release of title documents against a T/R, one has to ensure compliance with all limits (dollar limit for T/R, maximum allowable maturity etc).

If it is in compliance, the trust receipt release may be authorised. In those cases where transactional approval is required for each specific A/R, one must review the A/R (the maximum total A/R exposure to any one counterparty has to be limited to 10% of the borrower's capital funds unless backed by an acceptable letter of credit). The borrower has to be contacted to review the status of the trust receipt. If the trust receipt proceeds are paid to the lender, the loan is repaid and the collateral records have to be reduced accordingly.

Standard procedure regarding foreign domiciled collateral, either inventory or A/R
Legal counsel must always confirm that the security documents are sufficient for enforcement in that country. For goods in non-OECD countries, the country risk has to be covered by an acceptable counterparty or be specifically approved as an exception in the credit proposal. Once an A/R is approved, the monitoring would follow all the same parameters as in standard procedure for A/R and trust receipt (T/R) monitoring.

Additional collateral procedures/reports for borrowing base financing
In addition to all of the standards for all secured lending, the following are required for all borrowing base borrowers:

❏ Procedural audit prior to inception of borrowing to ensure proper MIS/accounting systems.
❏ Borrowing base report at least once per month. This report must at least list all approved collateral and margins, and individual and total exposures of lenders as specified in the original credit proposal. Subject to individual negotiation, position reports and details of trade debt and other liabilities should be requested.

Collateral procedures/reports for collateral pool financing
All of the standard policies and procedures in the previous section apply to collateral pool financing. In addition, the borrower has to provide, at least once a month (preferably weekly), a collateral pool report listing the assets being financed.

Collateral procedures/reports for transactional financing
In addition to all of the standard policies and procedures in the previous section the following are required for transactional financing:

❏ All A/R (unless specifically approved in the credit proposal) must be approved prior to T/R release.
❏ It is important to receive in advance a transaction report, which outlines the details of the transaction to be financed and acknowledges a specific security interest in the collateral by referring to the signed security agreement, and warranting that no other borrowings are outstanding against such specific transaction.

MEASURES TO DETECT – EXCEPTION REPORTS AND APPROVAL
Documentation exceptions are not acceptable without the written approval from senior management or legal counsel.

There are many types of collateral exceptions. Not all of them are quantifiable. The principal types of collateral exceptions are:

❑ margin deficits – collateral: Deficits in collateral margin, where the credit engagement is still 100% covered.

❑ margin deficits – principal: Deficits in collateral margin and insufficient collateral at 100% to cover engagements.

❑ trust receipt maturity expiration without repayment: Trust receipts that are not paid within the approved maximum expiration period. This can mean that the A/R is in default or there can be a reasonable explanation and evidence for the delay.

❑ credit line or sublimit excess.

❑ A/R problems: excess concentrations, questions regarding quality, and large past due A/R; and

❑ other: eg, outside audit discrepancies that question collateral values or accuracy.

These collateral exceptions should require approval as indicated below, under "Measures to correct – internal and external controls". Any other problem that can be calculated to a dollar collateral deficit basis would then follow the same exception matrix as "margin deficits – collateral" or "margin deficits – principal", described above. If the deficiency is questionable in nature and difficult to put in dollar terms, it should be reviewed and approved by senior management.

Technical exceptions

Technical exceptions are varied in nature and importance and consequently it is much more difficult to design rigid standards. It is the responsibility of the experts in the industry to be aware of both the borrower's financial capacity and the market environment, and to determine when a technical exception is a pure accounting, operational delay or when it is possibly due to more serious financial problems.

Despite the aforementioned caveats, reasonable reminders and standards to ensure the correction of technical exceptions have to be set up as follows

❑ Receipt of required collateral reports, financials, covenant compliance certificates and any other regularly generated reports has to be monitored. If they are not received on time, the lender must contact the borrower to ascertain the status. If any of these reports are not received on time, an exception report has to be issued. The borrower is contacted and the reason for non-delivery has to be noted on the exception report. Any exceptions that appear to be extraordinary have to be reported to senior management. The borrower stays on the exception reports until the required information has been provided.

❑ A copy of insurance renewal is also kept on a scheduling system and followed exactly the same as way as a trust receipt, and, if it is not received on time, an exception report is provided to the senior management.

❑ The system has to have a control feature to pick this up daily as an exception and it is double-checked each quarter through the confirmation to the borrower of warehouse locations. Upon discovery of the deficiency, filings are immediately done in the appropriate states/country.

❑ One has to track each transaction maturity to ensure that it does not exceed the approved maximum duration. An excess report has to be generated the day the maturity is reached, the borrower contacted, and, if it is not immediately corrected, the excess is reported to management (if the excess exceeds a certain amount or is deemed to be a serious problem).

MEASURES TO CORRECT – INTERNAL AND EXTERNAL CONTROLS
Internal controls (exception approval procedures)
In addition to stringent collateral-monitoring standards, any collateral system, to be effective, has to have specifically spelled-out collateral exception reporting and approval

procedures. Therefore, one should establish an exception approval matrix, which specifically exhibits the dollar approval authority required for all collateral deficiencies and the required approvals for any documentary or other technical exceptions. All collateral exceptions have to be layered into reports and require sign-off at various executive levels according to degree of exception. This is the final link in proper collateral monitoring that ensures the lender both the strongest possible controls and appropriate approvals/communication.

External controls
Outside audits have to be utilised to provide additional comfort regarding a borrower's accounting/collateral controls and to verify the actual physical existence of the collateral. Another key advantage of specialised auditors is that, in addition to checking controls and verifying physical collateral, they can also do sampling and quality checks to ensure the ascribed collateral value is appropriate. Any shortfalls have to be reported immediately to senior management and to a credit committee, if deemed necessary.

Systemising the monitoring and control process through standardisation of prevention, detection and correction
Although at first glance these standards and procedures might appear to be very complex and costly to implement, the majority of the controls and procedures can be easily automated and are fairly standard for each borrower. The main variables are the due dates (scheduling/reminder system) and the exposures against their limits.

ORGANISATIONAL REQUIREMENTS

❑ Proper training on the contents of a collateral policy has to be provided. The standards and procedures become automatic and perfectly understood by all levels of the organisation (marketing and sales, operations, risk management).
❑ A standard "transaction flow chart" for each borrower should be a required part of all credit proposals. It must detail all key collateral criteria, the transaction flow and the audit controls.
❑ The approved credit proposal with the approved "transaction flow chart" must be discussed and reviewed with the administrator of the monitoring and control system (MCS).
❑ Segregation of the collateral-monitoring function from the account manager has to be achieved to ensure their independence and impartiality. Both should have crossed dual reporting lines (hierarchical/functional) to risk management and to marketing.

FUNDAMENTAL IT PRINCIPLES

❑ Identify and define each asset to be monitored and controlled according to its descriptors.
❑ Identify and define each collateral document that the organisation is prepared to accept in each legal framework.
❑ Associate each identified asset with each acceptable collateral document to form a unique type of security interest that the organisation is prepared to accept.
❑ Define all lending arrangements on the basis of the security interests that would be required.

STANDARDISING PREVENTION

❑ All details of the approved credit and transaction chart (to include line amount, sub-limits, collateral margins, trust receipt parameters etc) must be entered into the MCS and then verified by both an MCS administrator and the account executive to verify the accuracy of the input.

❑ A transaction report is to be provided by the customer prior to entering into a transaction, and there should be a regular collateral report (if applicable).

❑ PC-based scheduling system should be provided to monitor both the maturity and the proper location (jurisdiction) for all of filings.

❑ All documents and their dates have to be recorded.

❑ Periodic reviews of all legal documentation (in addition to the legal department's review at inception) should be carried out to ensure its completeness and accuracy. This has to be done at least annually at the time of each annual revision of existing credit facilities.

❑ There should be appropriate maturity reminders for all transactions with a particular borrower.

At maturity, MCS will generate advices to the account executive and exception reports for all of the above listed required data.

STANDARDISING DETECTION

❑ The scheduling system maintains control over the timely receipt of the report from the borrower and the subsequent review by officers. Exception and maturity reports for most of the above listed items has to go to the marketing units and other members of senior management, when appropriate.

❑ Closely related to the collateral item, each credit transaction has to tie into the various pieces of collateral and the borrowing bases to the individual loans, BAs or L/Cs, as well as track totals outstanding against facility limits and sublimits; and, in the case of L/Cs, follow amendments to expiration and/or amounts.

❑ As an added control to any borrowing base debtor, multi-period collateral numbers have to be reviewed to determine trends and large changes in asset composition etc.

❑ All filing information is logged into the system and daily reminders and exception reports are provided to maintain the integrity of the filings.

❑ There should be monitoring of all collateral/facility sublimits (particularly since most sublimits are collateral-related).

❑ If the title document is a warehouse receipt, confirm that filings exist in that location (often overlooked).

TIME-SENSITIVE DETECTION

❑ There should be quarterly confirmation (by the lender's collateral staff) of all physically held collateral directly with the independent warehouses.

❑ The maturity of all trust receipts (physical collateral that has been released to allow for delivery to a warehouse or for final sale) should be verified regularly to ensure that repayment takes place when expected, that repayment terms are the industry norm and within the parameters of the credit approval, and that the receivable quality and concentration is acceptable (if applicable).

❑ Reminder system should be in place to ensure that total transaction duration does not exceed the approved credit proposal, typically 180 days.

❑ Where collateral insurance policies are endorsed to the lender, a reminder should ensure that one monitors and receives appropriate annual extensions.

PRICE-SENSITIVE DETECTION

❑ Daily marking to market of all collateral, where applicable. Information such as the type and quantity of the good, date of initial shipment, date of the trust receipt, date of warehouse receipt, name of warehouse and location, age of crop, corresponding loan, L/C or BA with dates opened, receivables information, margin percentages, share percentages with other lenders and excess or deficit amounts have to be held against available credit facilities and outstandings under such facilities.

PORTFOLIO LEVEL

❑ Market prices (including pricing differentials) have to be used to re-evaluate the collateral portfolio at any given moment with the rise and fall of the various markets.

STANDARDISING CORRECTION

All of these standards must be adhered to and no exceptions can be made without the approval of a duly appointed senior manager, specifically approved within exception approval procedures described under "Internal controls (exception approval procedures)" above.

On the agricultural goods

The adoption of the above monitoring and control processes simplifies the specific evaluation and definition of the agricultural goods that have to be tracked. Tenor, geography/location, quality, quantity and price can define any (agricultural) good. Key differentiators among goods are their descriptors. Cotton, for example, has several descriptors (eg, staple length, fibre strength, colour, etc). To remain truthful to the teachings of the above definitions and methods, each good should be monitored and controlled according to all its descriptors. Such level of detail has been made increasingly possible as a result of ongoing technological developments in biometrics and telemetrics, which are providing large quantities of data relative to each good. Collateral management departments should be prepared to capture, absorb and comprehend these data to satisfy the more demanding regulatory environments and shareholders.

Conclusion

Any lender seeking to do secured financing has to avail himself of a collateral management policy. For this he needs to review the legal framework in which he seeks to operate and assess the collateral types provided by that jurisdiction in their creation, perfection and enforcement. Having determined the suitability of the environment for secured financing, the secured lender can then determine the desired level of monitoring and control intensity for the different types of targeted customers and their respective lending arrangements. The intensity of the monitoring and control triggers the reporting and financial events necessary to prevent, detect and correct possible situations of loss. Standardising these events sets the stage for the development of information systems to capture increased levels of information (especially in agricultural goods) to better protect the secured lender.

Contrary to popular belief, the administrative costs of portfolio collateral management are manageable through the application of standards and new technologies. Regulatory pressures (BIS II) and shareholders' demands for transparency have now made this into a requirement.

14

The Challenges of Introducing a Warehouse Receipts System in Developing Countries

Rolf W. Boehnke

Common Fund for Commodities

Prior to the liberalisation of the economies in many developing countries, the marketing of major agricultural commodities and provision of related services were managed by the state through parastatal organisations such as Commodity Marketing Boards. The governments were directly involved in domestic purchasing, transport, marketing and storage of commodities and financing of inputs.

Under this system all producers could be paid fixed prices for the season (derived from a percentage of world prices adjusted for costs of transportation, marketing and support services). As the boards were the sole institutions responsible for purchase and marketing, they could also supply inputs and recover the cost of such inputs from the sale of proceeds. The governments, through these interventions, effectively insulated farmers against intraseasonal price fluctuations, provided inputs for production and collected export taxes.

Liberalisation of trade – impact on producers and trade

The role of the parastatals was substantially modified during the implementation of the Structural Adjustment Programmes. Their involvement in purchase and marketing of products and financing and delivery of inputs was severely curtailed. Their withdrawal drastically changed the procurement and marketing structures, and altered the pattern of distribution of inputs. The parastatals had extensive networks of buying posts for procurement. Through these buying posts they aggregated the produce.

Their withdrawal saw an emergence of a number of buyers – either working on their own account or as agents of larger companies. As there was no agency to consolidate the small parcels produced, each producer was forced to fend for himself and find buyers. On account of the small quantity offered for sale, absence of warehouses and little competition among buyers, producers were not in a strong position to negotiate prices. The producers consequently became dependent on a few buyers for the sale of their produce. With lack of resources to hold on to their produce and the need to receive payments at delivery to clear debts and finance inputs, they frequently sold their produce to the first buyer at the offered price.

The liberalisation of trade coupled with a general lack of financing in the rural areas and absence of interseasonal durable warehouse facilities for agricultural commodities created serious constraints in the marketing chain. Marketing Boards used to enjoy privileged access to bank funds and international capital markets. Now producers and traders had to approach banks individually to meet their financing needs. In the absence of previous credit history, they were often unable to obtain credit.

Commodity financing

In the majority of African countries, commodity financing is not readily available. What can be made available is financing of stocks of commodities entering the export or import trade that are backed by:

❑ security of goods of known quantity and quality deposited in secure warehouses;
❑ goods held in custody of independent operators;
❑ confirmed exports and import orders for the commodity backed by letters of credit issued by reputable banks.

In developing countries, investment finance and working capital are serious bottlenecks for smallholder farmers because of the general absence of viable and sustainable rural financial systems. Freely tradable stocks of commodities could be used as collateral for a loan either by producers or on their behalf by cooperatives or by traders. Financial institutions could be willing to lend against such a collateral if they are assured of both the security and quality of goods, which they can access and dispose of with relative ease in case of default.

What is a warehouse receipts system (WRS)

Warehouse receipts are documents of title to goods. Warehouse receipts can be issued against goods located in a warehouse as long as independent control is exercised. These receipts, sometimes known as warrants, when backed by legal and regulatory mechanisms that guarantee quality and delivery of specified quantities, provide a secure system whereby stored agricultural commodities can serve as collateral, be sold, traded or used for delivery against financial instruments, including futures contracts. These receipts are documents that state the ownership of a specific quantity of products with specific characteristics that are stored in a specified (and approved) warehouse.

Such schemes have been in operation in many countries of the developed world and exist in two basic variations: a one-part receipt in common-law countries (ie, the UK, US model); and two-part receipts in civil-law countries (most of Europe and Latin America). The basic difference between the two is that full ownership documentation is provided for with either one or two documents. A typical warehouse-receipt scheme involving a two-part receipt contains the following steps:

1. After harvest the farmer deposits his produce in a licensed warehouse and receives a Certificate of Title (CT) and a Certificate of Pledge (CP). The warehouse will release the produce only to the owner of both documents.
2. The farmer approaches the bank for a loan and in exchange for the monies lent he gives the bank the CP as security (and the CT for safekeeping so that the bank knows who is the owner of the produce).
3. Before the loan matures (typically up to three to six months), the farmer sells his produce to a processor or trader by selling the CT (on consulting the bank).
4. When the loan matures, or when he needs the produce, the processor or trader repays the loan to the bank and in exchange receives the CP.
5. The processor, now owning both the CT (from the farmer) and the CP (from the bank), can collect the produce from the warehouse.

The key to successful mobilisation of credit for commodity financing through a warehouse receipts system is how such an operation is structured and the reliability of the operators. Warehouse receipts must be functionally equivalent to stored commodities. They must specify the quality and quantity of the goods stored. The rights, liabilities and duties of each party to a warehouse receipt (producer, bank, warehouse and so on) must be clearly defined. Ideally, receipts should be freely transferable by delivery and endorsement.

163

THE CHALLENGES
OF INTRODUCING
A WAREHOUSE
RECEIPTS SYSTEM
IN DEVELOPING
COUNTRIES

The essential features of a warehouse operation are:

1. WAREHOUSE

Quality of warehouses is determined by their management, reputation, methods of operation and financial strength. Physical characteristics of a warehouse are very important. Some of the essential features of a reliable warehouse are:

❑ physical structure suitable for storage;
❑ competency in conducting warehouse business, including grading and weighing of goods, safety and care of goods during storage, maintenance of integrity and identification of goods in storage;
❑ reputation of the warehouse operator;
❑ sufficiency of net assets of the warehouse operator – security for payments of any indebtedness arising out of the conduct of the warehouse business;
❑ mechanism of delivery of goods.

2. PERFORMANCE GUARANTEES

For warehouse receipts to be accepted by traders and banks, there must be a performance guarantee for warehouses. These guarantees provide for compensation if stored goods do not match what is specified by the receipt, either due to negligence or fraud by the warehouse. Without such guarantees, farmers and traders are reluctant to store crops and banks are unwilling to accept receipts as collateral for financing. Performance guarantees are usually in the form of insurance bonds. Holders of receipts must have the right to receive stored goods or their fungible equivalent if the warehouse defaults or its business is liquidated.

3. INSURANCE

Insurance is a risk-transfer mechanism only, which neither eliminates nor reduces the occurrence of a loss. The value of the collateral needs to be protected against theft and other operational problems and against natural disasters (drought, flooding, fire, sabotage). Carrying adequate insurance by the warehouse company is important both for the depositor and to the financing bank. Insurance should preferably be covered by all-risks policies.

4. COSTS OF STORAGE

Returns to storing commodities should be market-determined. The costs of storage should be reasonable so that the farmers and traders can meet the cost of storage through additional income derived from the sale in lean season.

Licensing and inspection of warehouses

In many developing countries the legal and policy framework for commodity trade is not in place. Operators rely on established business and legal codes and policies that are not specifically targeted to agricultural product markets and trade. The existing legal and policy framework needs to be consolidated and improved to respond more adequately to the needs of operators in the agricultural sector. The legal framework should be built in consultation with all stakeholders, including producers, processors, traders, transporters, freight forwarders, bankers, insurance companies and governments.

A system of warehouse licensing and inspection of warehouse facilities is essential to ensure that they meet basic standards, both financial and physical. If such procedures are not in place, warehouse receipts will not have credibility and will not be treated as a reliable liquid asset. Governments should set up an independent body to license the warehouses, and should also license inspectors. The inspection of warehouses and stored commodities needs to be conducted by approved inspectors or inspection agencies. Normally, such functions are performed by the approved agents under a licence (usually issued by the ministry of agriculture or commerce).

164

THE CHALLENGES
OF INTRODUCING
A WAREHOUSE
RECEIPTS SYSTEM
IN DEVELOPING
COUNTRIES

Alternatively, the function of licensing and inspection could be performed by a commodity exchange, a group of banks or a trade association. Such a private-industry arrangement would be more limited in scope but could be more cost-effective.

Inspections need to ensure that warehouses are:

❏ financially viable and administratively reliable so as to be trusted by banks;
❏ technically able to maintain quality standards during storage;
❏ capable of preserving identity of goods, if required.

Collateral managers

Collateral managers do not trade in commodities, but simply hold the stocks as security for the lender or the lending bank. The collateral manager:

❏ guarantees to deliver the goods to the final customer and states the company is acting only as lender's trustee;
❏ remits the proceeds from sale of commodities to the lender in payment of the loan;
❏ keeps commodities fully insured against all risks.

Quality assurance (grades and standards)

Quality standards and grades need to be specific enough to give a clear description of the quality of the goods stored without the need for the goods to be physically examined. In addition, there needs to be a system in place to resolve conflicts if the quality stated in the receipt turns out to be different from the crop in storage. Although some crops can be stored ungraded, on an identity-preserved basis, the existence of appropriate quality standards and grades is necessary to allow more efficient use of storage space and the standardisation of commodities stored and to ensure that the quality deposited is the same as that withdrawn.

Financial institutions

The role of the local banks is central to the success of the WRS. The banks may need to invest in training their staff to appraise commodity transactions fully and establish clear internal procedures, including a system for monitoring the prices of commodities being used as collateral. Banks should be able to determine, before granting a loan, whether there is a competing claim.

Information system

Good and timely market information, especially on prices and crop forecasting, is essential for effective decision making. Such information allows farmers to assess when is the best time to sell; financial institutions to assess and monitor changes in the market value of the security; and processors to be able to assess the value of buying the crop at a particular time and quality.

Role of public authorities

Public authorities need to shift their role from directly intervening in prices through manipulating supply and demand towards creating a necessary institutional framework. The key steps required of the government in this respect are:

❏ to pass and implement legislation on warehouse-receipt law and standards and conditions for licensed warehouses;
❏ to set up a licensing and inspection system for licensed warehouses;
❏ to set up a performance-guarantee system;
❏ to work with the private sector to establish viable quality and phytosanitary standards.

Benefits and constraints of a warehouse receipts system

A warehouse receipts system has the benefits of:

❏ creating a secure collateral for the farmer, processor, and trader for mobilisation of credit;

❏ improving access to credit in rural areas, reducing risk of lending in rural areas;
❏ smoothing market prices by facilitating sales throughout the year rather than immediately after harvest;
❏ increasing market power of smallholders by enabling them, mainly through their cooperatives, to choose at what point in the price cycle to sell their crops;
❏ lowering transaction costs by guaranteeing quantity and quality;
❏ increasing quality awareness (value of product being determined by its quality);
❏ helping to upgrade the standards and transparency of the warehousing and storage industry since it requires better regulation and inspection;
❏ contributing to lower post-harvest losses due to better storage conditions;
❏ helping to create commodity markets that enhance competition and market information;
❏ increasing confidence and comfort level of banks by pledging goods as security that are backed by warehouse receipts, under the control of independent and approved operators.

The major constraints affecting the development of a viable warehouse receipts system are:

❏ government intervention in market prices, which can reduce incentives for private warehouses and crowd out private investment and participation;
❏ distrust or absence of the legal and regulatory mechanisms necessary to ensure confidence in local warehouses;
❏ the high cost of intraseasonal financing, which can make it unattractive for farmers, traders, and speculators to store;
❏ inadequate or low-quality infrastructure, which makes warehouses unreliable in maintaining the value of a crop;
❏ warehouses that are often not spread throughout the producing areas, so transportation costs become excessively high for most distant producers.

The Common Fund's experience

Several risks have been identified in the commodity marketing chain. The principal ones include defaults on credit faced by financiers, price risks faced by all market operators, risks of poor contract performance faced by traders and quality and other technical risks faced by both producers and traders. The current concentration of market share in a few companies and the tendency for the full cycle of operations to be undertaken by a limited number of traders are indicative of market imperfections and contribute to the practice of discounting prices at primary levels. The Common Fund's projects are addressing the above issues through the development of a system of commodity-trade finance based on inventory collateralisation and warehouse receipts.

The Common Fund's warehouse receipts projects

The Common Fund for Commodities is funding the implementation of the following projects involving warehouse receipts:

❏ Improvement of Cotton Marketing and Trade Systems in Eastern and Southern Africa (Uganda and Tanzania);
❏ Coffee Market Development and Trade Promotion in Eastern and Southern Africa (Uganda, Tanzania and Zimbabwe);
❏ Improvement of Cocoa Marketing and Trade in Liberalising Cocoa-Producing Countries (Côte d'Ivoire, Nigeria and Cameroon);
❏ Development of Grains-Marketing Systems Using Warehouse Receipts and Inventory Credit in Africa (Ethiopia, Ghana and Zambia – covering grains);
❏ Development of a Pilot System of Warehouse Receipts in the Grain Sector in the Russian Federation.

The aim of the projects is to facilitate the flow of more affordable credit to smaller producers and traders who thus far had little or no access to credit.

THE CHALLENGES
OF INTRODUCING
A WAREHOUSE
RECEIPTS SYSTEM
IN DEVELOPING
COUNTRIES

PROJECT COMPONENTS

The following are the main components of the projects:

❏ development of a system of commodity trade finance based on inventory collaterali-sation and warehouse receipts system; and testing the system through pilot trade financing;

❏ promotion of privately run warehouses;

❏ development of a basic market information system;

❏ development of quality-assurance and certification system;

❏ dissemination of project results.

IDENTIFICATION OF WAREHOUSES

As a first step in the implementation of the projects, a survey of all warehouses was carried out to identify existing warehouses and to assess their quality. The intention of the survey was to initiate the necessary improvements in the privately owned warehouses and to enable their participation in a warehouse-receipts-based system of financing.

The warehouses were classified into 'A', 'B' and 'C' according to the following criteria:

❏ soundness of construction;

❏ ease of accessibility at all times;

❏ quality-control facilities;

❏ experience of the manager;

❏ availability of means of communication such as telephone, fax etc;

❏ security.

Based on the surveys and inspections, a listing of the warehouse standards was made. Warehouses in a satisfactory state (parchment warehouses, ginning factories and export warehouses) were classified as Grade A while those in an unsatisfactory state were classified as Grades B (stores and buying posts) and C. The survey also assessed the skills levels of staff of the warehouse operators and identified skills that needed to be upgraded, which is being addressed through development of a warehous-ing guide.

In the cotton sector, it was noted that the ginneries acting as warehouses have the distinctive advantage of providing maximum security for banks and do not neces-sarily require the involvement of a separate collateral manager. In the coffee sector the curing factories have realised that, by providing collateral management services free of charge, they could develop a distinctive competitive edge, and consequently have taken over a large portion of the coffee storing against which pre-finance is being obtained.

Banks insist on having collateral-management companies involved in financial trans-actions. The latter have adopted their interventions to prevailing circumstances, and their services either cover full collateral management with all its concomitant responsi-bilities or may restrict themselves to stock-monitoring exercises on a regular basis in a certain area. Considering the costs of storage and the costs for full collateral manage-ment, the restriction of responsibilities of collateral managers to stock-monitoring exer-cises may be considered acceptable and is certainly more economical for primary stakeholders. It has been experienced that banks, too, seem to favour an environment that does not require full collateral-management services because of the associated costs involved.

COLLATERAL MANAGEMENT

There are only a few established collateral-management companies operating. Their operations are mainly limited to warehouses located at ports or in capital cities. Collateral managers have not yet penetrated the hinterland to provide services at a field-warehouse level. When they do provide services at a field level they are more inclined to offer systematic stock controls than full collateral-management services.

167

THE CHALLENGES
OF INTRODUCING
A WAREHOUSE
RECEIPTS SYSTEM
IN DEVELOPING
COUNTRIES

In the case of pre-financing primary societies, banks look towards hiring a collateral firm that would be responsible for simple stock-monitoring exercises in order to lower the cost. This approach has proved to be quite successful, as borrowers have rarely defaulted and have repaid their loans promptly in the few transactions piloted.

QUALITY-ASSURANCE AND CERTIFICATION SYSTEM

In many countries, standards have not been adopted by the national governments. What prevail are the generally accepted trade standards. First, with the help of national standard-setting institutions, farmer associations, processors, traders, exporters and commodity-development authorities, the appropriate standards were set. Thereafter, to lend credibility to the quality-assessment system, third-party certification systems were subsequently introduced.

Quality is one of the most important aspects in price determination. It was noted that little or no equipment was available at the field level to assess or control quality. To overcome this deficiency, moisture meters and basic quality-control equipment were provided to primary societies, equipment for the liquoring rooms, dehumidifiers for cotton quality-assurance and certification systems and establishment of a high-volume instrument to speed up testing of cotton.

In coffee, the capacity for quality assurance and certification at buying posts and at the curing factories was strengthened through provision of equipment and training of operators. Primary societies were provided with quality-testing equipment to ascertain and monitor quality at the field level. At the pilot sites where quality equipment was provided there was an improvement in quality. Farmers are now observing quality procedures as the moisture meters and the HVI machine take the necessary measurements. This has increased comfort to the farmers and quality classifiers in the primary society stores. It has also enabled farmers to respond well to the requirements as they are now in a position to see for themselves what they need to do better and thus avoid penalties, eg, reduced income.

A mechanism has now to be put in place to spread this positive experience to other primary societies, which appears to be far more effective than training sessions on a large scale.

MARKET INFORMATION SYSTEM (MIS)

Information needs vary according to the user and the proposed purpose of use. Information needs of smallholder farmers, growers associations, extension agents, research stations, marketing boards and coffee mills were determined. The steps involved in development of MIS were:

❏ determination of data to be collected;
❏ points of collection;
❏ selection of appropriate software and hardware;
❏ linkage of the information system to the auction systems and pilot station;
❏ training of data clerks;
❏ collection, analysis and dissemination of information.

The major issues that emerged during the discussions with the stakeholders were:

❏ business rules (eligibility of members);
❏ sustainability (payment on joining, membership fees and income from advertisements);
❏ data-collection training;
❏ housing of the database.

The connectivity of data-collection centres to the data-processing point is difficult on account of the poor telecommunication network. An effective system of exchange and dissemination of information is yet to be fully established. The concerns on sustainability through imposition of user charges are being addressed. Satisfactory resolution of the above issues will determine the subsequent sustainability of the system.

168

THE CHALLENGES
OF INTRODUCING
A WAREHOUSE
RECEIPTS SYSTEM
IN DEVELOPING
COUNTRIES

WAREHOUSE RECEIPTS SYSTEM AND THE FINANCIAL INSTITUTIONS

The banks, in general, are reluctant to lend to the agricultural sector because it is still viewed as a relatively high-risk area. The banks have sufficient liquidity and funds but, owing to the availability of alternative (and more remunerative) avenues of investment such as high-yielding treasury bills (risk-free investment), they are content to limit their operations to lending to established clients. They are also constrained by their limited branch networks, which restrict their outreach and increase the cost of assessment and monitoring of loans to the agricultural sector. With the sensitisation of management and staff of banks to the WRS, their initial reluctance has been partially overcome. Banks are now more willing to evaluate the risk-mitigating structure of lending against the WRS.

Some banks have volunteered to participate and are providing trade finance under the warehouse receipts system. The results have been satisfactory. The knowledge of the system is spreading, primarily thanks to some pioneering banks and the positive results achieved in lending based on the WRS.

The local banks and other financing institutions should be strengthened to carry out trade finance. The staff of banks should be trained in issues such as exposure to commodity transaction cycles; the identification and management of market risks (technical, financial, counter-party and price risks); the evaluation of trade credit proposals and management of credit; and appropriate hedging operations.

Mobilising credit to support a warehouse-receipt-based commodity-financing system

TRADE FINANCE

Access to offshore finance facilities is limited and credit from the local banking sector is expensive, owing to the inherent risks perceived and associated problems in the participating countries. In these circumstances, access to trade finance is an effective barrier to entry into international markets. There is a real need to ease the trade finance problems by addressing the constraints holding back both local and international banks from providing trade finance.

Foreign buyers are very selective regarding quality, delivery schedules of the produce and price, including any credit terms. The pre-export, commodity-linked, hedging and warehouse-warrant-receipt financing facility has an essential role to play in enabling exporters to offer competitive services and assure their abilities to meet these increasingly strict contract terms and conditions.

LEGAL AND REGULATORY FRAMEWORK

Draft legal documents covering warehouse receipts systems, in consultation with the stakeholders, have been developed in most of the pilot countries. The legislation proposed such matters as a cover licensing system, warehouse bonds, delivery of goods, grading and weighing of goods, inspection, safety of goods and care of records, warehouse charges, identification of goods stored, care in storage of goods, procedure for handling deteriorated goods, liability for nonreceipt or misdescription, negotiation and transfer of warehouse receipts – all essential features of a reliable WRS.

The drafts were circulated to all stakeholders and discussed before presentation to the national authorities. In many countries the appropriate cabinet or parliamentary papers have already been prepared and are likely to be enacted by respective parliaments soon. After the passage of the legal draft into law the regulations for operations – including the design of appropriate accounting and reporting rules, supporting documentation and format for warehouse receipts, insurance bonding and indemnity guidelines, and monitoring and supervision arrangements shall be prepared.

Conclusion

The experience of piloting a warehouse receipts system in certain developing countries and countries with economies in transition has been extremely challenging. The steps towards the creation of competition in markets and for performance of contracts have

THE CHALLENGES
OF INTRODUCING
A WAREHOUSE
RECEIPTS SYSTEM
IN DEVELOPING
COUNTRIES

been initiated. Competition in markets is being facilitated by the promotion of increased participation of producers and local traders and exporters in the domestic commodity market through training and improved access to more affordable credit. The projects are linking the different categories of traders to undertake a complete cycle of market transactions. Contract performance is being enhanced by a clear definition of the legal, policy, regulatory and procedural framework within which market operators engage in trade, according to the terms and conditions of contracts, including specifications of quality, price and delivery etc. The project is encouraging the publication of regulations and a code of practice for each sector.

The projects faced some resistance from dominant players in each part of the trade chain who prefer to maintain the status quo. Banks have also been sometimes reluctant to get involved in the development of the warehouse receipts system.

In most of the countries the governments have acted proactively and are convinced of the merits of the system. They are keen on this reform, because it will improve the whole commodity-trading cycle.

The introduction of warehouse receipts will provide an instrument to obtain credit at competitive rates for producers and national traders, which so far had no or only limited access to finance. The WRS will also give comfort to the banking system and other lenders, as the risks of providing loans are substantially reduced. In this way, the warehouse receipts system will contribute to making the commodity sector more efficient.

APPENDICES: DEBATES

15

Managing Commodity Price Risks in Developing Countries: A Debate

Henny Gerner and Ineke Duijvestijn

European Commission; Dutch Ministry of Foreign Affairs

Market reforms of the last decade did not only provide farmers in developing countries with the opportunities of a liberal market system, but also exposed them to the risks of the private market structure. This risk exposure is partly due to the reduced protection by governments following the dismantling of marketing boards and the collapse of the stabilisation funds. It is also due to the increased price volatility at international markets since the 1970s.

During the 1990s one realised that volatility was not a transitory phenomenon, but a lasting element of the world market. Farmers, traders and local processors in developing countries have difficulties coping with this situation, which demands other skills, institutions and support services. As a result of the remaining exposure to volatility, commodity producers and traders, exporters and financial institutions tend to be more risk-averse, invest less and produce less. It has negatively affected credit availability, rural employment and income. Producers invest in low-input, low-yield technologies, they tend to overdiversify their household income and make a sub-optimal allocation of their assets.

At the macro/country level, governments of some of the poorest commodity-dependent countries face problems in their balance of payments, their government's budget and social expenditures, and volatility has often led to increased social vulnerability and poverty. Putting price-risk-management instruments at the disposal of developing countries may contribute to reducing poverty.

Hedging is a well-known and often used market-based technique to mitigate price risks in developed countries and international business. Until recently it was not used in developing countries, due to underdevelopments of markets, lack of transparency, a regulatory environment etc. Thanks to the commodity risk management initiative of the World Bank, introduction of price risk management in developing countries can count on growing international attention and support.[1]

This initiative focuses on the facilitation of markets for risk management instruments to developing countries. Following extensive studies and pilots in the last three years, the Commodity Risk Management Group (CRMG) of the World Bank confirmed the feasibility and need for market-based price risk instruments for commodities in developing countries.[2] Under the pilots, farmer cooperatives purchased hedging instruments (put options) from international banks/brokers. As such they were able to offer minimum prices to their supplying farmers and contribute to more income security (see the case of Tanzania in Panel 1). The simplicity of the instrument used (put-option) seems to be decisive for success.

Although the pilots in Tanzania and Uganda have shown that market-based risk instruments can be brought at farmers' level in even least developed countries, the delivery costs are still too high to make it a commercially viable instrument. The sustainability of success will depend on some critical elements and include "leveraging" the benefits, the creation of regular and sufficient effective demand, developing competitive multi-supply channels for hedging instruments and sustaining international support and cooperation for awareness raising, training and capacity building. The different elements of the sustainable introduction are the focus of this debate. The case of Tanzania is used as an illustration.

Leveraging the benefits of hedging instruments

By using hedging instruments, the buyer is able to mitigate directly the price risks and predict its income better. Although this is the most important reason to hedge, in reality hedging provides all kind of important additional benefits, such as access to credit, lower interest rates, better financial management and investment decisions. Furthermore hedging can lead to better selling strategies and lower marketing margins for the benefit of the farmers. Because the cooperative can offer minimum prices to its members, the farmer can improve his or her investment decisions, leading in general to more investment, to higher quality, profitability and food security. Because the cooperative hedged its price risk, banks became interested again to lend money at a lower interest rate with the put-option as guarantee. Improved creditworthiness of the cooperative and access to credit at better terms is one of the most important side effects of risk management. Establishing the link between risk management and finance (liquidity) seems pivotal. Triggering and leveraging these additional effects is a real challenge to the initiative and may contribute to profitability in the long-term.

Creating a regular and effective demand for hedging instruments in developing countries

The pilot transactions stimulated the interest and enthusiasm for price-risk insurance in these countries. The demand extended from coffee to other commodities, such as cotton. The hedging for cotton can be arranged at the ginnery level, at which there are usually sufficient volumes to make hedging commercially viable. Because of high initial transaction costs, these have to be brought down to attract banks, international financial institutions and international traders to provide these services. Currently, the key question is how to create a regular and critical effective demand that will trigger the interest of several international providers.

Another challenge is the ability to keep pace with the growing need for training and capacity building as demand for these hedging instruments increases. Possibilities to increase effective demand might be found by concentrating on regions instead of individual countries. East Africa is such a region, where there seems to be an effective demand.[3] Demand could be stimulated further by mainstreaming price hedging in other ongoing commodity reform programmes, rural development programmes, agricultural and financial sector programmes. Risk management could also be incorporated in the curricula of agricultural and financial training institutions. The final goal should be integration in poverty-reduction strategies, which is critical for political support.

At the moment, price risk management is the core business of the CRMG. The inclusion of other risks, such as weather, would render the market for risk management more attractive to the provider. In addition, there is still another potential field where risk management could be used: governments of developing countries could use hedging instruments to cope with their budget and balance-of-payments problems caused by the volatility of export as well as import prices. If the instruments are properly designed and used, governments of especially least developed countries (LDCs) and heavily indebted poor countries (HIPCs) may well be able to insure (parts of) their budget revenues and foreign exchange. In so doing, they would be better able to manage their macroeconomic situation and become a more predictable partner for international financial institutions. The use of hedging in budget support is a new and challenging area for not only the Bretton Woods institutions, but also for the European Commission and bilateral donors.

Developing competitive multi-supply channels for hedging instruments

In most pilot transactions, the CRMG facilitated a direct relation between a cooperative and an international bank. This is a necessary but time-consuming investment because partners don't know each other, there is no track record and a lot of preparatory work has to be done before such an international financial transaction can take place (anti-money-laundering requirements). These make initial transactions both at the demand and the supply sides costly and often cumbersome. Only the larger cooperatives and exporters will be able to bear these costs and invest in building up a track record. It prevents most international banks and financial institutions from doing business with other types of entrepreneurs in developing countries. In the pilot of Nicaragua, for instance, the cooperative could not become a counterpart to international banks. Instead, an international trade house offered put options to small farmers. It is important that other channels for making hedging instruments available to clients in developing countries be explored, such as via traders and/or local banks. Traders prefer providing put options over futures contracts, because of the difficulties with enforcing contracts in many developing countries. Another promising channel with synergies to hedging instruments is the local financial sector. The CRMG concluded recently, that the local bank could combine hedging with lending in three main ways: (a) hedging the exposure of their overall portfolio to commodity prices; (b) hedging on behalf of their borrowers; and (c) requiring that borrowers provide evidence of price protection.[4] It is clear that local banks need to build relations with an international bank or brokerage house in order to do any of these.

Sustaining international support and cooperation

In line with the further development of risk-management markets in developing countries, there is a need for sustained international support and cooperation. The assistance of the CRMG will not remain the same as in the last three years, when it focused on case studies and the direct facilitation of pilot transactions. The CRMG as such will never be able (in terms of neither human resources nor money) to deliver all the necessary support, training and capacity building, once the demand for risk-management instruments increases. Building sufficient local capacity and ownership in a timely manner is a prerequisite for sustainability of the initial success. This is to increase effectiveness of training, particularly to farmers, at significantly less cost. Local ownership will also contribute to sustainability of efforts while reducing help from outside. The CRMG is already setting the basis for such local capacity in Uganda and Tanzania, where it has hired local coordinators to work on farmer training and education. Furthermore, in the case of Uganda CRMG is working with SUFFICE (a joint Government of Uganda–EU programme) to deliver training and education to farmers.

The CRMG will also have to collaborate more closely with other international agencies that undertake related work, such as FAO, UNCTAD and the Common Fund for Commodities. A division of work seems necessary to exploit comparative advantages and to avoid the duplication of efforts. The International Task Force on CRM is an excellent platform to promote this. The task force is an informal network of public institutions, private companies, NGOs and international organisations interested in making market-based risk instruments available to developing countries. Each year the International Task Force on CRM discusses progress of the initiative and gives advice on further work.

International donors have set up an informal donor consultation and a multi-donor trust fund for CRM with the World Bank. Currently, the initiative receives support from the World Bank, the Netherlands, the European Commission and Switzerland. The Common Fund for Commodities also has resources dedicated to the promotion of market-based risk instruments in developing countries. However, these funds will cover only initial pilots and capacity building: they will never be enough to cover all the necessary training costs and capacity building, once demand increases. Available money and human resources should be tapped from ongoing programmes and projects that are willing to integrate risk management in their development strategy.

PANEL 1

EXPERIENCE OF THE HEDGING PILOT IN TANZANIA

The first pilots with price-risk instruments for coffee farmers in low-income countries took place in 2002 in Uganda, Nicaragua and Tanzania. In Tanzania, coffee farmers of a local cooperative benefited from the initiative of the cooperative to buy put options on the international market. Following extensive capacity building and technical assistance from the Commodity Risk Management Group of the World Bank, the Kilimanjaro Native Cooperative Union (KNCU) purchased its first international "put option" from an international bank (Rabobank) in October 2002. The KNCU received technical assistance and training to meet the intense international due-diligence requirements, which include, among other things, the need to provide detailed information about ownership, structure, financial status and trading history of the cooperative union. With anti-money-laundering laws getting particularly stringent, this part of process took a lot of energy and time. Without the technical assistance provided by the CRMG, providers would not be willing and able to transact with such new clients in developing countries. The training with the KNCU focused on four primary areas: (1) global markets, activities and risk-management products for producers; (2) risk assessment and design of a price-risk management programme; (3) membership awareness and adoption of the programme; (4) account opening and mechanics of trading. The KNCU opted for buying put-options, the simplest risk-management instrument, just to protect themselves (and the farmers) against falling prices and to be able to set a minimum price for the farmers in advance. The KNCU can exercise the put-option at the end or during an agreed time period. The price quotation on the international commodity exchange is used as the reference. If the price on the day of execution is lower than the insured price, the KNCU will receive the difference from the international bank. If the price is higher, the KNCU will receive nothing from the provider, but can be satisfied with the higher-than-expected price.

The first transaction was followed by four other transactions, increasing in volumes, in the same season, equivalent to 40% of the total sales of KNCU and 4% of the national production. The KNCU activity included reselling options, when it no longer had exposure, and purchasing new option to cover upcoming months. The last of five transactions in March 2003 was effected in just two days and without the assistance of the CRMG. The premium paid for the put options averaged 3–5% of the insured price. Sometimes the put options paid and sometimes not – but in that case farmers got the higher than insured price.

The main benefit for hedging in the case of KNCU was that a local bank, CRDB, not only provided the KNCU with a loan for paying the premium, but was also willing to provide additional loans at a lower interest rate than usual. The put-option served as a guarantee. The additional loans at lower interest rates are considered by the KNCU as an important unexpected benefit. It has improved their performance considerably.

Not only were they able to pay a first payment at delivery, but they also managed to make a second and third payments. Several thousand coffee farmers benefited from the scheme. At the same time, the KNCU became a much more trustworthy partner for the CRDB. During the season, the union improved its overall financial status and was able to monitor it carefully throughout the season, without having to worry about the impact of price falls. Two larger cooperatives (KCU and KDCU) have expressed interest in the initiative. Also, the CRDB requested technical assistance in order to be able to provide complementary finance to the coops. It can be concluded that banks now seem to go out aggressively: they have become the advocates for hedging and are considering to hedge their own portfolio.

Source:
World Bank, 2001, *Tanzania Coffee Price Risk Management, URL: http://www.itf-commrisk.org; and personal communication during the ITF-meeting on 4–5 June 2003.*

1 *See declarations G8 (June 2003), Monterrey (2002), Johannesburg (2002), LDC-III (2001), etc.*
2 *The CRMG has undertaken multiple-country studies at the global level and facilitated several pilots on market-based price-risk instruments. Pilots concentrated on simple put options for coffee and cocoa. From June 2002 to April 2003, the CRMG facilitated seven pilot transactions with three companies in three countries: Uganda, Tanzania and Nicaragua.*
3 *Other key regions for the CRMG are Central America and West Africa.*
4 *CRMG, 2003, "Innovative approaches for improving access to agricultural lending: the use of price and weather risk management instruments", the World Bank.*

16

Government Policy and World Trade Organisation Agreements – Crop Insurance Reforms and Market-oriented Legislation

Pierre Bascou

European Commission*

Introduction

This chapter provides an overview of the reasons, objectives and modalities of government intervention concerning risk management, and discusses the future of the policy instruments implemented in various countries and regions in the framework of the World Trade Organisation (WTO) agreements. It first briefly recalls the different types of risk that agriculture faces, the tools available to manage these risks and the lessons that can be learned from existing public involvement in agricultural risk management. These elements will form the basis for reflections concerning the development potential of risk management policies.

The framework of the WTO Uruguay Round Agreement on Agriculture, and in particular the disciplines on domestic support it introduced, will then be presented. Considerations regarding future perspectives in the current agricultural trade negotiations will eventually be given.

Agricultural policy and risk management

The risks faced by farmers typically include price risks and production risks. Whereas the former are likely to increase due to further potential trade liberalisation, the latter might increasingly be influenced by rising quality requirements, the growing movement of animals and plants and climate change. Various risk management tools are at the disposal of farmers. In this respect, several types of risk management strategy may be distinguished: (1) on-farm strategies that concern farm management (eg, rotation) and include selecting products with low-risk exposure (eg, products benefiting from public intervention), choosing products with short production cycles, holding sufficient liquidity or diversifying production programmes; (2) risk-sharing strategies that include concluding marketing and production contracts, vertical integration, hedging on futures markets, participation in mutual funds and insurance; (3) diversification through increasing the share of income from sources outside agriculture and/or merely relying on public assistance (disaster aid).

* The views expressed in this presentation are those of the author and do not necessarily reflect those of the European Commission.

180

GOVERNMENT POLICY
AND WORLD TRADE
ORGANISATION
AGREEMENTS – CROP
INSURANCE REFORMS
AND MARKET-
ORIENTED
LEGISLATION

Ideally, markets should provide a wide range of risk management tools. The most important markets for risk coverage are futures markets and insurance markets. The development of futures markets in the world is uneven, with European futures markets being hampered by CAP-induced price stability. As price volatility on the European markets is likely to increase with possible further trade liberalisation, the conditions for the development of futures markets and other market-based risk management tools are expected to improve. Insurance markets may cover production risks when the latter are as little correlated as possible across insured individuals (independence of risks) and if farmers and insurance companies have similar information concerning the effective risks involved (symmetry of information). The classical example of such an insurable risk is hail. Mutual funds are a special case of insurance. Mutual funds are owned by the participants and cover losses of members through money already available in the fund and/or through an additional collection among participants.

However, incomplete and/or missing markets for risk management tools have in the past led to public intervention. The main reasons for incomplete or missing markets lie on both the supply and the demand sides. On the demand side, the lack and high costs of acquiring know-how to make use of certain risk management tools (eg, futures and options markets), the underestimation of risks faced by farmers ("cognitive failure"), may all result in low demand for risk management tools. Even if farmers do not under-estimate the risks they face, they might count on other safety nets, including off-farm income, and therefore might not use available risk management tools. On the supply side, the reasons may vary from product to product, with a lack of offer of insurance products linked to insufficient conditions for insurability (such as independence of risk, symmetry of information), limited agricultural reinsurance markets, inappropriate conditions for a successful establishment of futures and options markets.

Public policy intervention may take place at various levels. The establishment of the necessary legal framework for risk reduction (eg, sanitary and phytosanitary legislation) and/or for the creation of markets for risk management tools may constitute a potential field of action. Public policy may also favour the development of such markets by encouraging training in the use of risk management tools (market facilitation) and/or by lowering the costs of such tools (for instance through the provision of subsidies for insurance premiums). Governments can also provide risk coverage themselves (eg, by providing reinsurance, disaster payment aid, public insurance or a specific safety net).

Various systems of agricultural insurance may be found in the world. They generally differ in terms of coverage, public-sector involvement and uptake. Although the development of agricultural insurance in the European Union remains rather limited, there exist comprehensive systems of crop insurance in the USA and Canada. In the latter, a subsidised savings programme for farmers and an anti-cyclical income safety net that secures individual whole-farm income also exist.

From these insurance schemes, it appears that even for well-developed agricultural insurance systems the coverage in terms of products and participation rates remains limited. This is true even for products that are specifically designed to provide basic safety-net coverage for every farmer and are provided at very low cost. In Spain, 30% of the farmers participate in the system, resulting in 30% of crop production and 10% of animal production covered. In the USA, 20% of farmers participated in the system at the turn of the decade, while two-thirds of the country's total eligible acreage was covered. Furthermore, covering a wide range of perils at a level of protection that is interesting to the farmer seems to require considerable state involvement (USA, Spain), which may call into question the efficiency of these insurance programmes as well as social and regional equity.

Impact on production and trade – WTO issues

Government interventions have become more disciplined within the framework of the Uruguay Round Agreement on Agriculture (URAA), which was concluded in 1994 and

181

GOVERNMENT POLICY
AND WORLD TRADE
ORGANISATION
AGREEMENTS – CROP
INSURANCE REFORMS
AND MARKET-
ORIENTED
LEGISLATION

brought agricultural trade more fully under international trade rules and obligations. Reform commitments were differentiated between three major groups: market access, export competition and domestic support. For that purpose, policy instruments for domestic support were classified under three categories: the "amber box" (instruments that have an impact on production and trade, as given in the aggregate measure of support), the "blue box" (direct payments under "production-limiting" programmes) and the "green box" (support that has no, or at most minimal, trade-distorting impact). The level of support for the measures included in the "amber box" had to be reduced under the URAA by 20% in six equal annual instalments starting from 1995, as compared to the base period 1986–8. The two other categories of support (green and blue boxes) were exempted from the reduction commitments.

To be classified under the green box, support measures have to fulfil certain conditions as specified in Annex 2 of the Agreement. A number of conditions relate to all green-box measures (no price support, no or at most minimal trade-distorting effects, no effects on production) (Point 1 of Annex 2). Additional conditions relate to specific types of support. Among others, specific conditions relate to (1) income insurance and income safety nets and (2) disaster aids.

(1) Subsidies for insurance and government participation in income safety-nets (Point 7, headed "Government financial participation in income insurance and income safety-net programmes")

Government financial participation in insurance is classified as green-box-compatible in the following circumstances:

❑ If the insurance relates to *income* shortfall based on a reference period. The payments may *not* relate to the type or volume of production (including livestock units) or the prices (domestic or international) applying to such production or to the factors of production employed.
❑ If the income loss is more than 30% and the amount of payments compensates for less than 70% of the producer's income loss.

The same conditions apply for government participation in income safety nets.

(2) Disaster aids (Point 8, under the heading "Payments made (either directly or by way of government financial participation in crop insurance schemes) for relief from natural disasters")

Government payments for relief from natural disaster (made available either directly or by way of governmental financial participation in crop insurance schemes) have basically to fulfil the same conditions. There are, however, a number of differences. Payments can be triggered only by a production loss resulting from a disaster that is specifically recognised as such by the government. Payments can relate, besides income, also to losses of livestock, land or other production factors and can compensate up to 100% of the total cost of replacing losses. Where producers receive payments under income insurance/safety-net programmes *and* payments for relief for natural disaster, the total of such payments must be less than 100% of the producer's total loss.

Future perspectives

For more than ten years, major producing and exporting countries/regions have embarked on a process of agricultural policy reform towards a reduction in the overall support and protection of the agricultural sector, while addressing legitimate domestic concerns relating to environmental sustainability, food safety, food security and rural development in ways that do not unnecessarily distort production and trade. In the European Union, this process has notably led to a substantial reduction in market price support and the introduction of a more decoupled form of farm payment (the so-called single farm payment).

The future development of risk management tools should clearly be seen within this broad policy framework. If public intervention in risk management may be necessary

GOVERNMENT POLICY
AND WORLD TRADE
ORGANISATION
AGREEMENTS – CROP
INSURANCE REFORMS
AND MARKET-
ORIENTED
LEGISLATION

in an effective, minimally distorting, well-targeted and decoupled way, it should not undermine the development of private initiatives, become production-enhancing and send wrong signals to producers (as has recently been the case in some countries).

In this context, the new WTO round of agricultural trade negotiations (the "Doha Round") may provide a new regulatory framework and disciplines. As the impact of the URAA discipline on domestic support has been found to be rather limited – at least in comparison with the market access and export competition commitments – a new tightening of the rules governing domestic agricultural support as well as a further reduction in amber-box measures may be expected in the Doha Round.

An examination of the country proposals put forward so far (USA, EU and Cairns Group) as well as of the draft modality paper presented by the chairman of the Committee on Agriculture shows that this concerns in particular the definition of the boxes (including the categorisation of domestic policy instruments into the boxes and the maintenance of the blue box) and the rate of reduction of these instruments. As far as risk management tools are concerned, no major changes in the classification of these instruments (such as crop insurance, a safety net, counter-cyclical payment and disaster aid) have been proposed, with the exception of the *de minimis* provision that seems to have been used by some countries as a loophole in disciplining trade-distorting support. This situation may be seen in the light of the widespread use of insurance systems by major countries.

However, questions remain concerning the precise classification, notification (product- or non-product-specific) and quantification of support for some agricultural – crop and income – insurance programmes, as they sometimes differ across countries. Furthermore, the production neutrality of these policy instruments is becoming increasingly challenged. Available empirical evidence appears limited and would tend to suggest that the production and trade impact of these measures is small. However, theoretical analysis would suggest a more cautious approach on the grounds that risk management tools may encourage an increase in production through the reduction in income variability, changes in producers' risk aversion, increasing producers' wealth, reducing capital and investment constraints and raising expectations about future policy decisions.

17

Subsidies in Agricultural Risk Management

Arie Oskam

Wageningen University

J ust as for many other areas of agricultural policy, governments have provided substantial subsidies for agricultural risk management. Several reasons could be provided:

1. stabilising and increasing farm income;
2. preventing disaster payments by governments; and
3. reducing risk for agribusiness.

We distinguish *ex ante-* and *ex post* risk management. The crucial question – whether risk management subsidies, compared with other government expenditure for agriculture, benefit the society – has not been answered. It is also a difficult question, because so many aspects are involved. The main focus of this chapter is on a number of important consequences of subsidising agricultural risk management on the basis of the available literature.

Introduction

Subsidising agricultural risk management implies the explicit intervention of governments or other legal bodies to encourage risk management programmes by providing additional budget. Examples are the crop insurance programmes in the US and Canada. Many other items of risk management, such as crop choice, diversifying of activities, contracting, hedging and normal insurance, belong to the important risk management strategies. Because no subsidies are involved, they are not considered in this chapter. Only the indirect effects of subsidies on those activities play a role.

First, we distinguish the *ex ante-* and *ex post* subsidy strategy. Within an *ex ante* subsidy strategy, farm programmes explicitly define the conditions that hold for subsidising risk management strategies (see, for example, USDA, 2002). Both farmers and insurance companies or other intermediates know the basic conditions for using such strategies. As an example, one can think of signing up to a crop insurance scheme whereby a certain amount is paid when average county crop yield is below a percentage of the long-term average yield. Within the *ex post* subsidy strategy, the government provides subsidies for realised risks, which are perceived to be larger than what can be carried by groups of farmers as part of their entrepreneurial responsibility. This might be with extreme rainfalls, droughts, hurricanes, specific diseases of animals or plants, etc. It has often been signalled that the differences between *ex ante* and *ex post* subsidy strategies are not large if:

1. governments adjust programmes because of special circumstances; or
2. if there is the trust that under special circumstances the government will define an *ex post* subsidy scheme (Skees, 1999; Meuwissen, *et al*, 1999).

Subsidies in agricultural risk management should be considered against the background of a large set of agricultural policy instruments, where agricultural price policy and direct income support play a dominant role (OECD, 2002).

Level and importance of subsidies

Subsidy amounts for agricultural risk management are low in comparison with support in agricultural price policy and direct income payments. Still, it is difficult to find good overviews. The total amount of subsidy in the US was US$19 billion during the period 1981–99 (Chite, 1999), which equals less than 1% of the net value added (NVA) in agriculture. This excludes the typical disaster payments included in price policy. After 1994, these subsidies increased to circa 2% of NVA (Gardner, 2002).[1] Subsidies in the US were highly concentrated in the crop sector. Countries such as Italy and Spain had a score of circa 2% and 1% respectively during the period 1988–97. For Italy, the share of disaster aid was 70%, for Spain only 20% (Sáez Gómez, 2002).

Table 1. Financial performance of multiperil crop risk insurance programmes

Country	Period	I/P	A/P	R = (I + A)/P
Brazil	75–81	4.29	0.28	4.57
Canada	59–88	1.19	1.64	2.83
Costa Rica	70–89	2.26	0.54	2.80
Japan	47–77	1.48	1.17	2.60
	85–89	0.99	3.57	4.56
Mexico	80–89	3.18	0.47	3.65
USA	80–89	1.87	0.55	2.42
	1999	2.71	0.55	3.68

Source: Skees (2000, p. 10), Hueth and Furtan (1994, p. 58); mainly based on Hazell (1992).

The well-known book of Hueth and Furtan (1994) provides a very good but slightly dated overview of subsidies in crop insurance. Part of this book is based on studies of Hazell *et al* (1986) and Hazell (1992). More recent overviews are provided by Skees (2000). Often data are provided as long-term ratios between indemnities paid to the farmers (I), and administrative costs (A), divided by premiums paid by the farmers (P). The ratio R=(I+A)/P should be smaller than 1 under normal market conditions. The data (see Table 1), however, show R-values above 2.4, which implies that farmers received subsidies (directly or via administrative support) equal to at least 140% of the premiums paid.[2]

Reasons for providing subsidies

The reasons for providing subsidies for agricultural risk management are quite diverse. Often the large variation in yields, prices or revenues of farmers plays an important role in the background and is nearly always used in texts proposing government-subsidised insurance schemes and disaster payments. If farmers can take more risk because of an insurance scheme, they can specialise more and realise, on average, a higher income. This also illustrates that insurance schemes and disaster payments are complementary. If insurance schemes are insufficiently developed, governments feel earlier the pressure to (partly) subsidise disasters. Farmers may include the opportunity to force the government in compensating for disasters and this:

1. reduces their premiums; and
2. provides help in situations where they have real problems.

The relation between disaster payments and insurance schemes is intensively discussed in the literature. Gardner, Just and Calvin (see Chapters 2 and 8 of Hueth and

Furtan, 1994) are not convinced of this relation. Others (see eg, Skees, 1999) support the opposite view.

The third reason for subsidising agricultural risk management is often related to agribusiness. That can be due to insurance companies, who nearly always ask for subsidies. A whole bunch of insurance products were developed under favourable conditions (Barnett, 2003). Such requests come also from banks providing loans to agriculture (Hueth and Furtan, 1994, p. 3). But also upstream and downstream industries, which are interested in the continuity of agricultural production, ply for subsidising risk management programmes.

Many of these characteristics are reflected in the Federal Crop Insurance Programme for the US. This is a subsidised insurance programme providing farmers with a means to manage the risk of crop losses resulting from natural disasters. Starting with the Federal Crop Insurance Reform Act of 1994, coverage is classified as "catastrophic" (CAT) or "additional". CAT coverage guarantees 50% of a farmer's average yield, at 55% of the expected price, for a nominal processing fee. This can be considered as the disaster part of crop insurance, which is provided at very low costs and therefore by implication subsidised. Farmers can buy additional insurance but here they pay a higher share of the premium (USDA, 2002; Babcock et al, 2002).

The approach of the European Union has been oriented more in the direction of disaster payments in case of natural disasters (flooding, drought, frost, etc). Such losses are mainly handled at the national level and the European Union legislation provides conditions for providing compensation for crop loss. Losses resulting from adverse weather conditions may receive compensation up to 100%, if the level of damage reaches 30% of normal production. For less favoured areas this limit is 30% (Saez Gomez, 2002). The rules seem to be rather generous, but weather fluctuations and natural disasters are less severe in the European Union than in the US.

The European Union considers animal or plant diseases as "exceptional occurrences" and not "natural disasters". Subsidies for combating animal and plant diseases may be provided only as part of disease prevention, control or eradication programmes. Subsidies may be granted for up to 100% of such measures, if Community legislation does not specify that such costs have to be borne by producers (Saez Gomez, 2002).

Of course, it would go much too far to provide a more detailed overview of reasons for subsidising agricultural risk management at the country level.

The analysis of the effects

The basic assumption with respect to risk management is that farmers are risk-averse. When they are risk-averse, they are willing to give up some income to protect themselves from uncertain future events that may cost them a lot of income. Others can bare this risk on the basis of the risk premium. The basic idea in a private market (without government subsidies) is that individual entrepreneurs who are risk-averse may seek a type of insurance that leads to reducing risks while the net expected revenue remains good.

Subsidising such steps, however, may cause several unintended consequences. One of the most cynical observations is, "Attempts to force people to reduce risk simply cause people to take on more and different risks until their risk level returns to the pre-policy intervention level" (Skees, 1999). This may hold for enforcing risk reductions by legislation, but also for subsidies. *Ex ante* subsidising risk management will induce more risky behaviour.

With respect to risk management in agriculture, the following types of effect are given in the literature.

1. Inducing farmers to plant crops and keep animals at more risky places. Most of the government subsidies go to areas and farmers who bare more risk (Hueth and Furtan, 1994; Skees, 1999).
2. Adverse selection, which implies that any subsidised risk management programme attracts the farmers who run more than average risk. They are more interested in such

programmes unless insurance companies can exactly determine the risk they bear by providing them with insurance. Subsidised insurance and putting pressure on high sign-up rates, however, diminish the interest of insurance companies in preventing adverse selection (Hueth and Furtan, 1994, Ch. 9; Just *et al*, 1999; Skees, 1999)

3. Moral hazard, which induces more risky behaviour if crops or animals are insured (Hueth and Furtan, Ch. 9; Vercammen and Van Kooten, 1994; Coble, *et al*, 1997; Skees, 1999).

4. Preventing the development of "normal insurance products" and other instruments of risk management such as future markets and unsubsidised reinsurance opportunities (Skees, 1999; Barnett, 2003).[3]

5. Encouraging farmers to use more input, because the output is partly secured and this brings rational farmers to higher input levels of, eg, nitrate and pesticides. This causes negative external effects (Hueth and Furtan, 1994, Ch. 12).

6. To keep less efficient farmers in business. In fact, many subsidised risk management programmes operate at the costs of the better farmers, who receive lower prices for their products "at the end of the day" (Hueth and Furtan, 1994, Ch. 9; Skees, 1999).

But there are also positive effects of subsidising agricultural risk management. We mention the following:

1. Inducing farmers to seek more specialisation, which may encourage efficiency at farm level but also for upstream and downstream industries.

2. Keeping starting farmers in business after "bad luck". Otherwise, such farms might be discontinued.

3. It may lead to a reduction of even less efficient farm programmes. This has been the reason for putting more emphasis on the crop insurance in the US before introducing the FAIR Act of 1996 or by studying insurance by the European Union as part of a more market-oriented policy approach.

The third reason has nowadays a profound place in the different ideas about possibly subsidising agricultural risk management. With more market-oriented prices and more price fluctuation, insurance schemes received more attention; but, in the USA, Canada and the European Union, this happened without studying the effectiveness and efficiency of insurance programmes versus price support. For the US, there holds that both the insurance programmes and countercyclical price support received more budget (USA, 2002). The EU limited itself mostly to studying the problem, what to do under conditions of reduced price support and more income support (Meuwissen *et al*, 1999; European Commission, 2001). The increased price volatility in open markets, however, might not be that big (see eg, Roche and McQuinn, 2003). Moreover, other opportunities of risk management (future markets, private insurance, etc) are increasing and direct income payments have a stabilising influence on farm income.

Discussion and conclusions

Numerous articles have been written about agricultural risk management. The smaller area of agricultural crop and disaster risk and insurance covers also many articles and books. Several of those articles argue that government-involved risk management programmes run into serious difficulties of adverse selection, moral hazard and systemic risks, which makes it very difficult to operation such programmes on the basis of normal commercial risk management firms (insurance companies). If governments are supportive to agricultural risk management, this nearly by definition implies that subsidies should be provided. Such subsidies, however, have serious negative side effects, as mentioned in this chapter.

It is not yet clear whether the *ex ante* (see eg, the US) or *ex post* (see eg, the European Union) method of subsidising agricultural risk management works better to achieve the goals of risk management programmes.[4] Both methods are subject to substantial influence of pressure groups. However, one of the differences is that incorporating the risk management programmes that have been developed in the successive US farm acts builds up strong pressure groups, which depends on the continuation of such programmes, while the approach of the EU is more concentrated on subsidising catastrophic risks in incidental cases (BSE, foot-and-mouth disease, classical swine fever, extreme weather conditions etc).

What has not been addressed in the literature is a comparison of price support management, direct income payments and agricultural risk management as three options for supporting the agricultural sector. All three have the tendency to influence behaviour and to fade away from the agricultural sector (Dewbre *et al*, 2001), but a clear comparison among different policy instruments with respect to effectiveness and efficiency to realise particular goals is lacking. This is a pity, because we observe that governments follow different paths with respect to subsidising agricultural risk management and economists should be interested to see which paths should be preferred under different conditions.

Of course, it could be argued (as Gardner and Skees did) that subsidising agricultural risk management as it has been done in the US is "a waste of money". The programmes change cropping patterns in the wrong direction and influence individual behaviour such that, at the end of the day, actual risk is not reduced. Still, the final effects on the different supportive measures have never been compared in a convincing way and this makes it difficult to provide clear statements of whether such subsidies are effective and efficient. The literature, however, provides a lot of information on market-oriented risk management methods (which are by definition efficient and effective within the existing conditions) and about improving contract design and insurance mechanisms that would reduce adverse selection, moral hazard and crowding out of insurance schemes by getting the government involved at crucial moments.

1 *Similar developments hold for Canada (see eg, Hueth and Furtan, 1994, Ch. 3; Agriculture and Agri-Food Canada (2002).*

2 *Although quick readers may think that the "formal requirement" of I/P < 1.08 for the more recent crop insurance in the US, this does not hold as shown by Skees (1999), Gardner (2002) and Barnett (2003). Including also disaster payments, the US$1 billion premiums paid by the farmers still raise an expected level of indemnities of US$4 billion, while administrative costs account also for US$1 billion. This suggests R = 5.*

3 *Many reinsurance issues come up with the existence of so-called "systemic risk", which implies that the clients of insurance companies bear the same types of risk, leading to similar claims in the same period.*

4 *The differences may also be caused by the orientation on crops and animals in the US and the EU respectively.*

BIBLIOGRAPHY

Agricultural and Agri-Food Canada, 2002, Federal-Provincial Crop Insurance Programme, URL: http://www.agr.gc.ca/ policy/epad/english/pubs/adhoc/98009r/sec1.htm (16 July 2003).

Babcock, B. A., C. E. Hart, and D. J. Hayes, 2002, "Crop Insurance Rates and the Laws of Probability", CARD Working Paper 02-WP 298 (Iowa State University).

Barnett, B. J., 2003, "The federal crop insurance programme: Opportunities and challenges", Agricultural Outlook Forum, URL:http://www.agecon.uga.edu/~bbarnett/Agricultural%20Outlook%20Forum%20 2003%20 Manuscript.pdf (16 July 2002).

Chite, R. M., 1999, "Federal Crop Insurance: Reform Issues in the 106th Congress", URL: http://www. agriculturelaw. com/links/cropins/crsbrief.htm (16 July 2003).

Coble, K. H., T. O. Knight, R. D. Pope, and J. R. Williams, 1997, "An Expected-Indemnity Approach to the Measurement of Moral Hazard in Crop Insurance", *American Journal of Agricultural Economics*, February, pp. 216-26.

Dewbre, J., J. Anton, and W. Thompson, 2001, "The Transfer Efficiency and Trade Effects of Direct Payments", *American Journal of Agricultural Economics* 83(5), pp. 1204–14.

European Commission, 2001, "Risk management tools for EU Agriculture with a special focus on insurance", working document, DG Agriculture. URL: http://www.europa.eu. int/comm/agriculture/ index_es.htm (16 July, 2003).

Hazell, Peter B. R., 1992, "The Appropriate Role of Agricultural Insurance in Developing Countries", *Journal of International Development* 4, pp. 567–81.

Hazell, P., C. Pomerada, and A. Valdes, 1986, *Crop Insurance for Agricultural Development: Issues and Experience* (Baltimore: Johns Hopkins University Press).

Hueth, D. L., and W. H. Furtan, 1994, *Economics of Agricultural Crop Insurance: Theory and Evidence* (Boston MA: Kluwer Academic Publishers).

Just, R. E., L. Calvin, and J. Quiggin, 1999, "Adverse Selection in Crop Insurance." *American Journal of Agricultural Economics* 81, November, pp. 835–49.

Gardner, 2002, "Farm Policy Goals as Related to Crop Insurance", URL: http://www.arec.umd.edu/ Policycenter/ Crop-Insurance-and-Farm-Policy-Conference/presentations/gardner.pdf (10 July 2003).

Meuwissen, M. P. M., R. B. M. Huirne, and J. B. Hardaker, 1999, "Income insurance in European Agriculture. European Economy", *Report and Studies* No. 2 (Brussels).

OECD, 2002, "Agricultural Policies in OECD Countries: Monitoring and Outlook 2002" (Paris: OECD).

Roche, M . J., and K. McQuinn, 2003, "Grain price volatility in a small open economy", *European Review of Agricultural Economics* 30(1), pp. 77–98.

Sáez Gómez, D. R., 2002, "Agricultural insurance seen from the European Commission". International Conference: "Agricultural insurance and income security", Madrid 13 and 14 May 2002.

Skees, J. R., 1999, "Agricultural Risk Management or Income Enhancement?", *Regulation* 22(1), pp. 35–43.

Skees, J. R., 2000, "Agricultural insurance programmes: Challenges and lessons learned", Workshop on Income Risk Management (May), pp. 15–16 (Paris: OECD).

USDA, 2002, Farm Bill 2002, http://www.usda.gov/ farmbill/farmbill2003.htm (9 July 2003).

Vercammen, J., and G. C. Van Kooten, 1994, "Moral Hazard Cycles in Individual Crop Insurance", *American Journal of Agricultural Economics*, May, pp. 250–61.

Young, C. E., R. D. Schnepf, J. R. Skees, and W. W. Lin, 1999, "Production and price impacts of U.S. crop insurance subsidies: Some preliminary results", URL: http://www.ers. usda.gov/Briefing/FarmPolicy/ ffc_insurrance.pdf (16 July, 2003).

INDEX